GENESIS

World of Myths and Patriarchs

GENESIS

World of Myths and Patriarchs

ADA FEYERICK

Contributing Authors
CYRUS H. GORDON and NAHUM M. SARNA

With a Foreword by WILLIAM G. DEVER

An Academia Book

NEW YORK UNIVERSITY PRESS
New York and London

Editorial Consultant: Joseph J. Thorndike, Jr.

Picture Research: Jeanne-Francoise Roche, Paris

Irene Lewitt, Jerusalem

Designer: Philip Grushkin

Printed in China

NEW YORK UNIVERSITY PRESS
Washington Square
New York, N. Y. 10003

An Academia Book

Library of Congress Cataloging-in-Publication Data

Feyerick, Ada.
    Genesis : world of myths and patriarchs / by Ada Feyerick ;
contributing authors, Cyrus H. Gordon and Nahum M. Sarna ; with a
foreword by William G. Dever.
       p.   cm.
    "An Academia book."
    Includes bibliographical references and index.
    ISBN 0-8147-2668-2
    1. Bible. O.T. Genesis—Criticism, interpretation, etc.
2. Bible. O.T. Genesis—Antiquities.   I. Gordon, Cyrus Herzl,
1908- . II. Sarna, Nahum M.   III. Title.
BS1235.2.F47 1996
222'.11095—dc20   96-41809
                                        CIP

FRONTISPIECE:

The Patriarchal figure from Mari bringing an animal
offering, 3rd millennium B. C., reflects an age when man
began to explore the nature of his gods and his relationship
to them. Out of a remote nomadic tribe, a new monotheistic
ethic emerged which would reach into modern times.

To my husband
and
the memory of my parents

AF

CONTENTS

MAPS and CHARTS

CHRONOLOGY SOURCES, pp. 18-19

MESOPOTAMIA: [to 2900]: Robert Ehrich. *Chronologies in Old World Archaeology,* Chicago: University of Chicago, 1992.
[Chronology]: J.A. Brinkman, in A. Leo Oppenheim, *Ancient Mesopotamia.* Chicago: University of Chicago, 1977.
[Eannatum , Guti, Gudea, Kassites]: Joan Oates. *Babylon.* London: Thames & Hudson, 1979.

CANAAN: Amihai Mazar. *Archaeology of the Land of the Bible.* New York: Doubleday, 1990.
[Ebla dates]: Paolo Matthiae. *High, Middle, or Low?* Part 3. Gothenburg: Ästroms, 1987.
Alfonso Archi, Ebla epigrapher, personal correspondence.

EGYPT: [Prehistoric]: *Cambridge Ancient History.* Vol. 1-2. London: Cambridge University Press, 1971.
[Early Dynastic to 2nd Persian period]: J. von Beckerath. *Handbuch der ägyptischen Königsnamen.* Munich: Deutscher Kunstverlag, 1984. (Note: For ready reference, similar dating from the New Kingdom to the Late Period is recorded in the Brooklyn Museum's publication, *Ancient Egyptian Art,* © 1989, pp.xi-xii.)

PREFACE

IN THE BEGINNING were Mesopotamia, Canaan, and Egypt. Then came Genesis.

Genesis—World of Myths and Patriarchs is an in-depth look at the civilizations which formed the background of the first book of the Bible. It tells us what the authors of Genesis saw and what events, concerns, ideas, and forces moved them to write the story of their people's origins as they did. As they refined, and rejected, elements of that pagan world in order to create their own ethic, there arose the concept of one all-powerful God who brought the universe into being in an orderly progression—the root of monotheism.

Drawing upon the great archaeological discoveries in the Middle East over the past century, Genesis, a testament of faith, is seen as a product of its cultural milieu. In the ancient Near East, it was a time of human accomplishments, hopes, and disappointments. Rulers, some benevolent, often tyrannical, guided the lives of men and women who were expected to serve their gods with unquestioning devotion. Myths were created to explain man's relationship to these gods and to define his purpose on earth. "Myths," as used in the title, refers to early man's understanding of his world in the absence of scientific knowledge.

Two eminent scholars wrote the brief overviews of history and Bible which introduce the comprehensive illustrated sections of the book. Dr. Cyrus H. Gordon, one of the great synthesizers of Near Eastern civilizations and a master of ancient languages, described the cultures and contributions of Mesopotamia, Canaan, and Egypt and their impact on the Biblical authors. Dr. Gordon is professor emeritus at both Brandeis and at New York Universities. At the latter, he is the director of the Center for Ebla Research. Dr. Nahum M. Sarna, a renowned scholar of Genesis, wrote the three alternating Biblical chapters, relating the Genesis narratives to the ancient world. These encompass all of Genesis 1-50, from the early universal history, the Patriarchal lives of Abraham, Isaac, and Jacob, up to Joseph's death in Egypt. Dr. Sarna is professor emeritus at Brandeis and is general editor of the Jewish Publication Society's Torah Commentary.

The time span of the book is the 3rd to 1st millenniums B.C., the Early Bronze to Iron Ages, thereby giving Genesis a wide historic framework. Dr. Gordon notes that ideas last for thousands of years, and in studying any one period of Israelite history, "we cannot confine our investigation to the materials of that period." Aiding in that study and selectively chosen within the book are historical, cultural, and literary elements from ancient texts, as deciphered by scholars, written centuries before they appear as motifs within the Patriarchal lives. In the 2nd millennium B.C., for example, texts from Mari on the middle Euphrates River give insights into migrations of nomads and seminomadic Amorites, population groups who also inhabited the Patriarchal world. Social customs in the Nuzi documents from northern Iraq compare to those of the Patriarchs, while the feuding chiefs in Canaan, known from the Amarna letters found in Egypt, are reflected in the attack of Jacob's sons against the city of Shechem when they arrived from Haran.

Several editors, or redactors, are credited with composing the five books of the Pentateuch, beginning with Genesis, from both an oral and written tradition that extended in time from the United Monarchy of David and Solomon in the 10th century B.C. to the return of the Jews from Babylonian exile by the edict of Cyrus the Great of Persia in the 6th century B.C. These Biblical writers brought their unique historic emphasis and interpretation to their own generations. First compiled during the golden age of the Monarchy, Genesis was a reminder to the people that the religion of the Patriarchs was valid for their time and that they were the heirs to the Covenant that God made with Abraham, promising that his descendants would inherit the land and become great and numerous. It was the Prophets who later would urge the people to righteous behavior in order to be worthy of their heritage.

Remote from us in years, the world of Genesis mirrors our own in many ways. The rivalry of Arab and Jew is seen in the story of Ishmael and Isaac, the two sons of Abraham, who remains the Patriarch of both. The need for water in arid regions, today called "water politics," is as much a subject of current Arab-Israeli negotiations as when Abimelech of Gerar conceded to Abraham the right to dig a well at a place called Beersheba. The many tribes and sects of ancient Canaan foreshadow a modern Lebanon torn by feudal and factional warfare. Even surrogate motherhood as we know it was used by the Matriarchs, Sarah, Rachel, and Leah, who "loaned" their handmaids to their husbands to assure family continuity through the birth of sons. In the captions of the pictorial sections of the book, the names of Abram and Sarai are used as they are up to Genesis 17:5, 15, when God changed them to Abraham and Sarah, who would be the founders of many nations.

Two elements supplement the book. "Biblical Memory," both within the alternate Genesis chapters and in the center portfolio, contains color views of sites within the Fertile Crescent from Iraq to Egypt still venerated by people in the region. These were taken by internationally known photographers and show the vitality and longevity of the Genesis tradition as it is shared by the world's great religions. The "Discovery" pages in each chapter are brief texts written by those archaeologists who were among the first to search for evidence of ancient Near Eastern cultures (often with the Bible in mind). They remind us that in the scholarly world "there were giants in the earth in those days" and acknowledge with gratitude those who continue their efforts today to reveal our past and to expand our sense of continuity.

Various "schools" of opinion inevitably develop within academic disciplines. An attempt to recognize these has been made in several text footnotes. Other differences often include proper name spellings and historic dates. It is an ongoing debate as to whether the "low" Egyptian chronology used here, as opposed to "high" or "middle," will stand the test of time. But as one savant commented, "Between high and low there are only twenty-five years," less than the blink of an eye to those who deal in millenniums. The importance of differing opinions, however, was encouraged by the dean of archaeology, Sir W. M. Flinders Petrie, whose "Discovery" appears in Chapter V. Writing in his book, *Researches in Sinai*, E. P. Dutton, 1906, he warned that building only on one class of evidence is perilous to research. In history, archaeology, and religion, the converging of different lines of research was not only essential to detect unnoticed errors but "to avoid mere fantasies."

The choice of illustrations attempted to meet the standards of Joseph J. Thorndike, Jr., who was my editor at *Horizon Magazine* and my indispensable advisor from the book's inception. My thanks, also, to former magazine colleagues Gertrudis Feliu for her pictorial expertise and to Robert Emmet Ginna and Hilde Kagan for their editorial judgment. Drew University in Madison, New Jersey, extended every courtesy in the use of its superb library for my research.

My personal hope is that this book will increase our understanding of our ethical heritage and that in the troubled lands of the Middle East, the birthplace of Genesis and of monotheism, we shall recognize our shared origins rather than our differences.

ADA FEYERICK

FOREWORD

Genesis—World of Myths and Patriarchs is eloquently and sensitively written by two of the most distinguished senior scholars of our time who have interpreted the Bible in its ancient Near Eastern setting, Cyrus H. Gordon and Nahum M. Sarna. It is also lavishly illustrated with photographs, drawings, and maps that help to bring the long-lost world of the Bible vividly back to life.

Much of the book depends on archaeological discoveries made in the Middle East. As an archaeologist with thirty years of experience in that region, I want to comment on the contribution that archaeology can make to our understanding of the Bible.

Throughout its 150-year history, archaeology in the lands of the Bible has been plagued by the popular misconception that its primary role should be to "prove the Bible." By that, most have meant that archaeological discoveries prove that the personalities and events described in the Bible are factual, that things really happened as the Bible says, that these stories were not simply invented by later Jewish and Christian writers. And for a long time archaeology—especially in what is modern-day Israel—seemed to fulfill that promise. Scores of dramatic discoveries—now well known to millions of avid readers—have illuminated the era of the Patriarchs, the conquest and settlement of Canaan, the Israelite and Judaean monarchies, religion and cult in Canaan and Israel, and even, less often, the context of Greco-Roman Palestine in which Rabbinic Judaism and early Christianity were shaped.

In the larger Biblical world, similar archaeological discoveries resurrected long-lost peoples and cultures of the ancient Near East, only dimly hinted at in the Hebrew Bible but now seen in the full light of day: Egyptians, Assyrians, Babylonians, Hittites, Hurrians, Canaanites, Aramaeans, Moabites, Edomites, Phoenicians, Persians, and others. Not only their monuments were recovered but their lost literatures as well. At last, the historical stage upon which the events of the Bible had played themselves out across two millenniums was peopled with all its dramatis personae. By the 1950s, the enthusiasm of both the religious and secular public was captured by the best-seller of a German journalist, Werner Keller, in his book *Und die Bibel hat doch Recht*, roughly translated as "The Bible Was Right After All" (published in English as *The Bible as History*).

Today the former enterprise of "Biblical Archaeology," often an amateur affair with more than its share of scandals and misinterpretations, has matured into a professional, highly specialized, independent discipline, focusing on modern Israel, Jordan, and parts of Syria. Its purview includes the "Biblical World," of course, but it is much broader. The discipline also still interacts with Biblical studies, although it is no longer dominated by theological concerns. It embraces many other disciplines, such as geology, geomorphology, paleobotany and zoology, ecology, the history of technology, economics, sociology, physical and cultural anthropology, and innumerable scientific techniques of data gathering, analysis, and information processing.

All of this "new archaeology" can be intimidating, even for the would-be professional. For many lay people, the "romance"—the Indiana Jones sense of adventure—has given way to teamwork science that is complex, expensive, controversial, often jargon-laden, and, above all, raises more questions than answers about the Bible. Yet the fascination of the public continues unabated.

The unresolved question is this: What is the contribution that we can reasonably expect modern interdisciplinary archaeology to make to our understanding of the Bible? Specifically, can archaeology lend any historical character to a masterpiece of literature like the Book of Genesis, or are these simply "folk-tales?" And the more fundamental question, troubling for many, may be this: If Genesis is not "history," can we believe then in its religious message? Can it have any moral authority for us today?

We should begin to formulate our answers (and they are inevitably personal), by seeing clearly the differences between history and theology, between knowledge and belief. In particular, we must distinguish between the questions of What happened in the past? What did it mean? and What does/may it mean in the present?

What archaeology can contribute to this task is simply to comment on what may (or may not) have happened. Archaeology cannot validate either the interpretation given to events, supposed or real, either by the Biblical writers or by later religious commentators. To put it another way, archaeology may often answer such questions as what, where, when, or how, but it is poorly equipped to answer the question of why. In answering these important but preliminary inquiries, archaeology can, however, provide what I think is unique and makes this approach to the Bible so fruitful, so potentially revolutionary—*context*. Archaeology alone can reconstruct the actual circumstantial world in which the Bible came into being, the backdrop against which events described in the Bible finally "make sense." Archaeology gives to the Bible a "tangibility" that it might not otherwise have and thus helps to make it credible. Archaeology reminds us that the Bible is not a collection of fairy tales but is the profound story of the experiences of people in a real time and place and circumstance—people like us.

In summary, archaeology brings the Bible down to earth, but that can enhance, not diminish, its enduring religious and moral value. Archaeology cannot, however, create faith, but then neither can it destroy it. It is a helpful tool in bringing understanding. But since the real truth of the Bible is supra-historical, not simply historical, that truth may be grasped only by transcending simpleminded categories of "truth" and "myth," by risking one's life on the chance that the Biblical writers' intuition into the meaning of community and history may have been right.

The mystery, the real challenge of the Book of Genesis, does not lie in the question of whether Abraham was a historical figure whom archaeological investigation can "confirm," thus apparently compelling us to belief. Rather, the Bible depicts Abraham as a larger-than-life figure—the "father of the faithful"—because he dared to respond to God's call to uproot his family and migrate from Mesopotamia to a promised land where a new world would be in the making. Archaeology cannot map that "promised land," for it is in the human mind and spirit; but it can, at its best, offer some signposts along the way.

WILLIAM G. DEVER

Professor of Near Eastern Archaeology and Anthropology
University of Arizona, Tucson

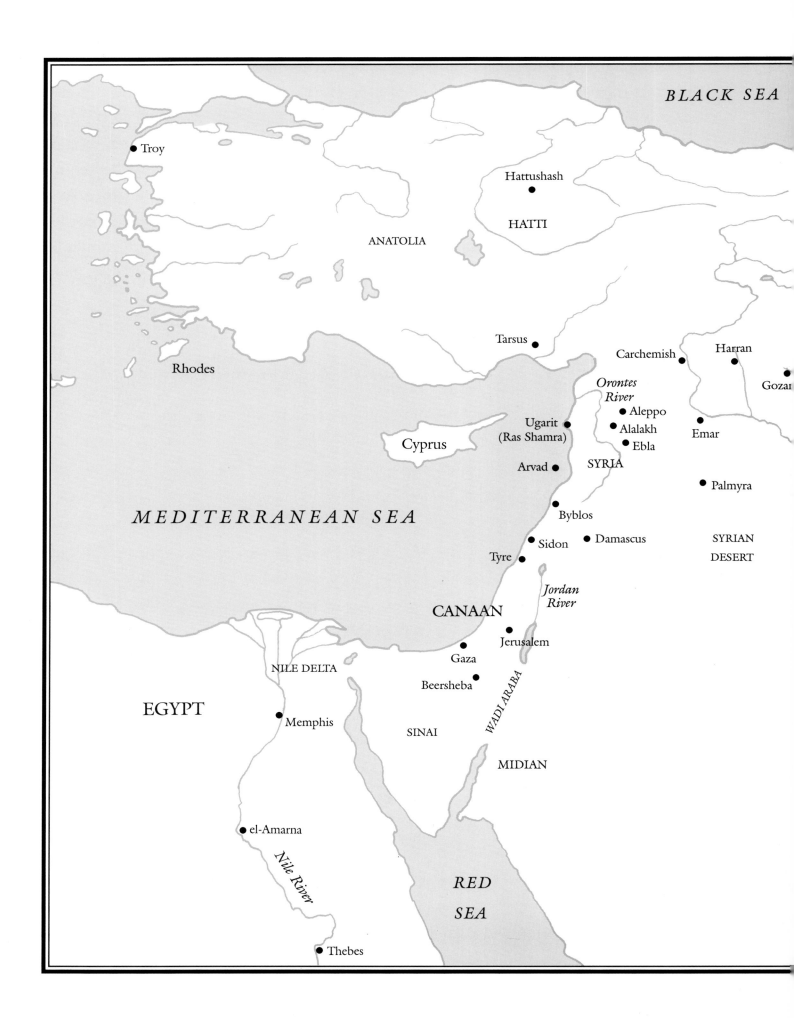

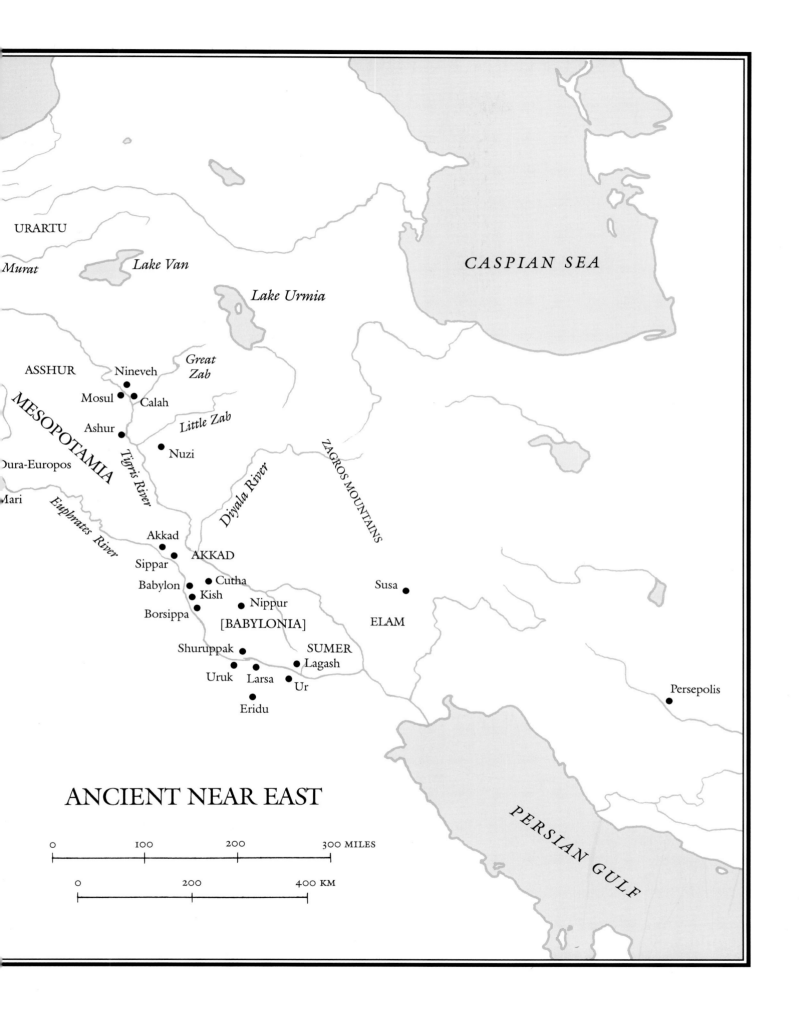

URARTU

Murat

Lake Van

Lake Urmia

CASPIAN SEA

ASSHUR   Nineveh

Great Zab

Mosul   Calah

MESOPOTAMIA

Ashur

Little Zab

Nuzi

Dura-Europos

Tigris River

Diyala River

ZAGROS MOUNTAINS

Mari

Euphrates River

Akkad

AKKAD

Sippar

Babylon   Cutha

Kish

Susa

Borsippa

[BABYLONIA]

ELAM

Nippur

SUMER

Shuruppak

Lagash

Uruk   Larsa

Ur

Eridu

Persepolis

ANCIENT NEAR EAST

PERSIAN GULF

```
0        100        200        300 MILES
|---------|----------|----------|

0            200            400 KM
|-------------|--------------|
```

SELECTED CHRONOLOGY

(All dates are B.C. and approximate. See p. 8 for Chronology Sources)

MESOPOTAMIA

UBAID I-IV   *5500–4000*

Religious architecture: Eridu
(Abu Shahrain), Temple of Enki

URUK
(mod. Warka, Bibl. Erech)   *4000–3100*

Earliest pictograph writing
for economic temple records;
potter's wheel invented;
White Temple, Anu ziggurat

[Tradition: Gilgamesh built city walls]

JAMDAT NASR   *3100–2900*

Tablets written in Sumerian; cylinder
seals; distinct polychrome pottery

EARLY DYNASTIC   *2900–2334*

Growth of city-states; kingship;
public buildings, canals constructed;
literature, decorative arts develop

Some major cities:

Shuruppak (Fara)
[Tradition: site of Sumerian
Flood story, hero Ziusudra]

Kish

Nippur

Mari (Tell Hariri)

Ur (Tell Muqayyar)
Royal tombs   *2600*
[Tradition: Patriarchal city]

Lagash (al-Hiba)
Eannatum conquers Umma   *2450*

Girsu (Telloh)

AKKAD (Semitic dynasty)   *2334–2154*

Foreign trade expands;
Akkadian lingua franca

Sargon I the Great   *2334–2279*

Naram-Sin   *2254–2218*

Guti invaders from Zagros
mountains establish dynasty   *2220*

Shu-Turul, last Akkad ruler   *2168–2154*

SUMERIAN REVIVAL

Gudea, *ensi* of Lagash   *2141–2122*

Utu-hegal of Uruk expels Guti   *2120*

King List compiled

CANAAN

NEOLITHIC   *8500–4300*

Economy based on agriculture
and herding; beginning of
pottery making

CHALCOLITHIC   *4300–3300*

Copper industry develops

Ghassulian culture (named for
Teleilat Ghassul, NE shore of
Dead Sea)

Settlements in semi-arid regions

EARLY BRONZE AGE I-III   *3300–2300*

Intensive urbanization: fortified
cities, public buildings, temples,
palaces, granaries, city-state system

Byblos, port for Egyptian sea
trade for cedar wood   *2800*

Ebla (Tell Mardikh),
N Syria, *Archives*   *2400 2350*

Palace G destroyed   *2330*
(probably by Sargon the Great)

Collapse of urban culture in
W Palestine; Egyptian military
raids in region.

EARLY BRONZE AGE IV /
MIDDLE BRONZE I*   *2300–2000*

Pastoral nomadism and agriculture
fill urban vacuum; occupation of
arid Negev highland, N and C Sinai

*Composite term, William G. Dever.

EGYPT

MESOLITHIC   *8000*

NEOLITHIC-CHALCOLITHIC   *4500*

NAQADA II, FAIYUM B, MA'ADI   *3500*

Settlements in Nile Valley; canal
irrigation systems develop

EARLY DYNASTIC PERIOD   *pre-3000–2670*

1st Dynasty   *3000–2820*

Menes unites the two lands;
capital in Memphis; temple of
Ptah; hieroglyphic writing

2nd Dynasty   *2820–2670*

OLD KINGDOM   *2670–2160*

3rd Dynasty   *2670–2600*

King Djoser, vizier Imhotep
built Step Pyramid, Saqqara;
mining expeditions to Sinai

4th Dynasty (Pyramid Age)   *2600–2475*
Snefru, founder
Dahshur pyramids
Cheops (Khufu)
Great Pyramid of Giza
Chephren (Khafre)
2nd Giza pyramid; sphinx
Mycerinus (Menkaure)
3rd Giza pyramid

5th Dynasty   *2475–2345*
Isesi, 8th king
vizier Ptahhotep
Unas, last king
Pyramid Texts in tomb

6th Dynasty   *2345–2195*
Pepi I, third king   *2332–2290*

7th Dynasty (evolving)

8th Dynasty   *2195–2160*

FIRST INTERMEDIATE PERIOD   *2160–1994*

9th-10th Dynasties   *2160–2040*
11th Dynasty   *2160–1994*
Mentuhotep of Thebes
reunites the two lands

[NB. Some sources place the 7th-8th Dynasties
in the First Intermediate Period, and the final
years of the 11th Dynasty, from Mentuhotep's
reunification, in the Middle Kingdom.]

MESOPOTAMIA / ANATOLIA / ASSYRIA		CANAAN		EGYPT	
THIRD DYNASTY OF UR	*2112–2004*	MIDDLE BRONZE II	*2000–1550*	MIDDLE KINGDOM	*1994–1781*
Ur-Nammu, founder	*2112–2095*	[Tradition: Patriarchal Age]		12th Dynasty	
First-known *Law Code*; ziggurat constructed		MBIIA	*2000–1800/1750*	Execration Texts indicate Egyptian influence in Canaan Sinai mining expeditions expanded; Asiatics imported as domestic labor; rise of Egyptian middle class; short story form develops	
Ibbi-Sin, last king	*2028–2004*	Bronze replaces copper for tools and weapons			
Ur falls to Amorites from W, Elamites from E	*2004*	Amorite chiefs rule city-states, as seen in Egyptian Execration Texts			
		Byblos: royal tombs; Temple of the Obelisks		Amenemhet I	*1994–1964*
FIRST ISIN DYNASTY	*2017–1794*			Sesostris I	*1974–1929*
King List finalized	*1950*			Amenemhet II	*1932–1898*
Lipit-Ishtar *Law Code*	*1934–1924*			Sesostris II	*1900–1881*
				Sesostris III	*1881–1842*
				Amenemhet III	*1842–1794*
LARSA DYNASTY	*2025–1763*			Amenemhet IV	*1798 (?)–1785*
				Sobknefru	*1785–1781*
FIRST BABYLONIAN DYNASTY (Amorite rule)	*1894–1595*	MBIIB-C	*1800–1550*		
Assyrian influence, trading colonies in Kanish (Kultepe)		Further Amorite expansion and rule in Mesopotamia		SECOND INTERMEDIATE PERIOD	*1781–1550*
Mari prominent; *Archives*	*1810–1760*	Canaanite heqau-khasut, "foreign rulers," settle in Delta and found 15th Egyptian Dynasty		13th Dynasty	*1781–1650*
Hammurapi, sixth ruler, king of Babylonia; *Law Code*; destroyed Mari palace of Zimri-Lim	*1792–1750* *1759*	Hurrians in N Syria		14th Dynasty Hyksos settle in NE Delta	*1710–1650 (?)*
Babylonian Dynasty ended by Hittite Mursilis	*1595*			15th Dynasty (Hyksos)	*1650–1540*
				16th Dynasty	*1650–1550*
KASSITE PERIOD	*1570–1157*	LATE BRONZE AGE	*1550–1200*	17th Dynasty (Theban)	*1650–1550*
Invaders from Zagros rule four centuries		LBIA	*1550–1470*	NEW KINGDOM	*1550–1075 (alt. 1070)*
		Defeated Hyksos besieged in Sharuhen by Egyptians		18th Dynasty	*1550–1291*
		LBIB	*1470–1400*	Ahmose I	*1550–1525*
MITANNI EMPIRE	*1500–1350*	Thutmose III consolidates rule in Canaan		Hyksos expelled	*1540*
Hurrian population transmits Babylonian culture		LBIIA	*1400–1300*	Proto-Sinaitic script	*1500*
Nuzi (Yorghan Tepe); *Tablets*	*1460*	Ugarit (Ras Shamra), alphabetic cuneiform introduced; *Archives*		Hatshepsut	*1475 (?)–1458*
Hittite Suppiluliumas expands to N Mesopotamia and Syria	*1380–1340*	Canaanite chiefs in diplomatic correspondence with pharaohs		Thutmose III vizier Rekhmire; victory at Megiddo	*1479–1425* *1457*
Mitanni empire falls		LBIIB	*1300–1200*	Amenhotep III vizier Ramose	*1387–1350*
		[Traditions: Exodus of Israelites from Egypt; conquest of Canaan]		Amenhotep IV (Akhenaten) Amarna Age; *Letters*	*1350–1333*
SEA PEOPLES MIGRATE	*1200*	IRON AGE	*1200–586*	Horemheb	*1319–1291*
Hittite power ended; Egypt and Assyria retreat; Kassite rule ended by Assyrians and Elamites	*1157*	IAIA-IB Judges	*1200–1000*	19th Dynasty	*1291–1185*
		Ugarit destroyed by Sea Peoples; Philistines settle on coast of Canaan	*1185*	Ramses I	*1291–1289*
				Seti I	*1289–1278*
		United Monarchy Saul, first king	*1020*	Ramses II	*1279–1212*
SECOND ISIN DYNASTY	*1157–1026*			Merneptah	*1212–1202*
Aramaeans gain prominence	*1100*	IAIIA David; Solomon	*1000–925*	20th Dynasty	*1185–1075*
		IAIIB Divided Monarchy	*925*	Ramses III	*1184–1153*
NEO-ASSYRIAN PERIOD	*885–609*	Northern Kingdom/Israel fell to Assyrians	*720*	THIRD INTERMEDIATE PERIOD	*1075–653*
Sargon II	*721–705*			21st Dynasty	*1075–945*
Ashurbanipal	*668–627*	Southern Kingdom/Judah		22nd Dynasty	*945–718*
				Shoshenq I (Bibl. Shishak), invades Palestine	*923*
NEO-BABYLONIAN PERIOD	*625–539*	Josiah	*639–609*	23rd–25th Dynasties	*820–650*
Nebuchadnezzar II	*604–562*	Babylonians conquer; Temple destroyed, Jews exiled	*586*	Necho I	*672–664*
ACHAEMENID PERIOD	*538–331*			LATE PERIOD	*664–332*
Cyrus the Great	*538–530*	Edict of Cyrus the Great Jews return to Jerusalem.	*538*	26th Dynasty	*664–535*
				Necho II	*610–595*
				-to-	
				2nd Persian period	*342–332*

GODS OF THE ANCIENT NEAR EAST*

MESOPOTAMIA		CANAAN	EGYPT
SUMERIAN	*AKKADIAN*	EL (*Elohim, Yahweh*), Hebrew God	AMON [Thebes] (*ram*), air, wind, "hidden one"
AN [Uruk], sky, head of divine assembly	ANU	EL, father of gods and mankind	AMON-RE (Amon combined with solar aspect of Re)
KI (*Ninmah,Nintu,Ninhursag*) [Adab], earth goddess		ATHIRAT (*Asherah, Elat*), El's wife, mother-nurse of the gods, sea	RE [Heliopolis], sun, father of gods
**INANNA, An's consort, love, war, rain, queen of heaven	**ISHTAR [Uruk, Nineveh]	ATHTART (*Ashtaroth, Astarte*), goddess of love, war	***RE-HARAKHTE (Re combined with Horus)
			ATUM, creator, setting sun
		ANAT, wife-sister of Baal, divine nurse, warrior	ANHUR (*Onuris*) [Thinis], power of the sun
			ATEN, sun disk of Akhenaten
			OSIRIS [Abydos] death, resurrection, dead king
ENLIL [Nippur], air, storm son of An and Ki	ENLIL		ISIS, wife of Osiris, magic, domestic arts
	MARDUK [Babylon]		HORUS [Edfu] (*falcon*), son of Osiris and Isis, sky, living king
NINURTA, Enlil's son, warrior, spring storms	NINURTA	BAAL (*Hadad*), storms	***RE-HARAKHTE (Horus combined with solar aspect of Re)
NINGIRSU [Lagash] ENTEN, winter; EMESH, summer	ADAD, storms	DAGON, grain, vegetation, father of Baal	HARPOKRATES, infant Horus
			FOUR SONS OF HORUS, guardians of Canopic jars in underworld, and cardinal points
ENKI [Eridu], sweet waters, wisdom, crafts, magic	EA	KOTHAR-AND-KHASIS, crafts	
ISIMUD, Enki's minister	USMU		PTAH [Memphis], formed the world, crafts
			KHNUM [Elephantine] (*ram*), molder of man, guarded source of Nile
	APSU, watery deep		IMHOTEP, deified vizier of Djoser, healing, medicine
	TIAMAT, sea monster goddess, chaos	YAMM, sea	
			MIN, rain, fertility, sexual powers
NANNA [Ur], Enlil's son, moon	SIN [Ur, Harran]	YARIKH, moon; NIKKAL, his wife	THOTH [Hermopolis](*ibis, baboon*), wisdom, moon, magic, writing, learning
NINGAL, his wife			

**[Inanna/Ishtar in different myths]:

INANNA, Nanna's daughter	ISHTAR	BAALAT, Lady of Byblos	HATHOR [Dendera] (*cow*), sky goddess, love, music, turquoise, sycamore
DUMUZI, her shepherd husband	TAMMUZ	SHACHAR, dawn; SHALIM, dusk	
UTU [Larsa, Sippar], sun, law, justice, Nanna's son	SHAMASH	SHAPASH, sun goddess	MAAT, goddess of truth, order, justice
NERGAL [Cutha], underworld, plague, war	NERGAL ERESHKIGAL	RESHEF, plague, lightning	RESHEF, war, thunder
ERESHKIGAL, his wife		HORON, underworld, death, healing	
NINGIZZIDA [Lagash], personal god of Gudea	NINNI-ZAZA [Mari]	MOT, death	SETH (*Sutekh*) [Avaris], brother-murderer of Osiris, evil, disorder, desert, storm, frontiers
GILGAMESH [Uruk], deified king	AMURRU (Amorites)	MEKAL [Beth-shean], plague	
NINSUN, his mother		BAAL HARAN (Aramaeans)	
		KHA-TAW [Negau], forests	*As mentioned in the book

I

MESOPOTAMIA
Land of Myths

CYRUS H. GORDON

THE NEAR EAST is the cradle of Western civilization. But the part which contributed more features than any other area, and at an earlier date, is Mesopotamia. After a long development during which the arts of agriculture and the domestication of animals were developed in and around Mesopotamia, there came a period of about a thousand years, the Early Bronze Age, from 3000 to 2000 B.C., during which the art of writing catapulted humanity from prehistory into the full light of history.

The most dynamic people in Mesopotamia to take part in this process were the Sumerians. Their origins constitute a many-sided problem. When they arrived, early in the 4th millennium B.C., they found a native population settled there. That is why so many geographical and even divine names in Sumerian Mesopotamia have no Sumerian etymology. The Sumerian language is agglutinative like Hungarian and tonal like the Far Eastern tongues. These people who were so creative were forgotten in subsequent history, even to the point that the very name of Sumer has left hardly a trace. Its only survival that has reached us through familiar literature is the name Shinar that designates Babylonia, found in the Old Testament, starting with Genesis. The phonetic differences between "Sumer" and "Shinar" are more apparent than real, for the two terms can be equated phonetically.

The reason for settling in Sumer is clear. It has a plethora of a precious need in the Near East—water—which is necessary for sustaining large numbers of people and domesticated animals. Although there was plenty of water in the Tigris and Euphrates Rivers, this water had to be brought to the dry soil of Mesopotamia between the two rivers. The engineering art of irrigation developed in Mesopotamia, as it was the duty of the ruler to see that the land produced enough for the needs of the people. A network of canals, which provided shipping lanes for the region, turned the dry land into a garden spot famous throughout the world. It was this fertility which made possible the feeding of a large population, a necessary component of an organized society. The plain of Sumer is called in Sumerian *edin*, and the very word has reached us through the early part of Genesis. Eden, or the Garden of Eden, is the same term, and that is where civilization was formed and the beginning of mankind is placed according to Biblical tradition.

The Sumerians were the foremost contributors to the development of civilization in early Mesopotamia. They developed urban architecture and introduced the ziggurat ("step pyramid"). Their most characteristic small artifacts were the seal cylinder, and by 3000 B.C., the clay tablet for writing Sumerian, the world's first-known literary language. It should be noted that Genesis is interested in civilized, not primitive, man. The narrative moves swiftly from Adam and Eve to their sons who represent herding (Abel), and agriculture (Cain). The first city is built and named after Cain's son Enoch, representing urban civilization.

Along with the Sumerians, there were Semites working with them, but they were mainly on the borrowing rather than on the giving end during this early period. The Semites can only be defined linguistically. They were, and are, the speakers of rather closely related, inflected languages with a distinctive vocabulary. They share words like *ab* (father), *umm* (mother), *akh* (brother), the numerals, pronouns, nouns designating parts of the body, etc. Some Semitic words are embedded in Sumerian from the start. The Semites were spread in antiquity over the Near East and Northwest Africa. Scholarly writers usually trace them either to Arabia, the Fertile Crescent, or to Northeast Africa. The Semites in Mesopotamia absorbed Sumerian civilization, including the art of writing, and thereby equipped their more numerous population to succeed their dwindling Sumerian predecessors.

Sumerian city life went hand in hand with organized government and the stratification of the populace according to specialized occupations. The cosmic gods of Mesopotamia also had specialized tasks in the running of the universe and in the daily lives of mankind. Each human art and craft had a divine prototype. Utu, who was called Shamash in the Akkadian language, was the sun and was concerned with justice. Enki, or Ea, as he is generally but inexactly called in Akkadian, the water god, was interested in life, specifically in man's life, whereas Nergal and his wife, Ereshkigal, dealt with sickness and death. In general, the gods were capricious and dangerous. How else could one account for natural disasters, war, famine, sickness, and death in a world ruled by the gods? It was against such systems that the Hebrews eventually reacted and gradually arrived at a world view that a good God governed the world and would see that history would have a happy ending—the Golden Age to come.

In theory, the head of each city-state was the local deity, such as Ningirsu at Lagash or Nergal at Cutha. The human ruler was the "executive officer" of the local god, his deputy on earth, who governed the people in accordance with the divine commands of the god. It was the ruler's responsibility to defend the borders of his state from the occasional incursions of neighboring rivals as well as the aggressive hordes from the eastern mountains in Iran. The defeat of a city in war meant to the people that their patron god had failed them and was in eclipse, at least temporarily.

Shortly after the middle of the 3rd millennium B.C., there emerged the first great Semitic ruler in the Near East. His name is Sargon, and he founded a dynasty in the city of Akkad, which gave its name also to the lands which he conquered. Akkad was a country as well as a capital city. Through his conquests in thirty-four battles, which are recorded, Sargon succeeded in uniting Sumer and Akkad in the first known world empire. He proclaimed himself ruler of the "four quarters of the world."

In Mesopotamia in the old land of Sumer and Akkad, which is the southern part, later to be known as Babylonia, there are no minerals or stone, although archaeological evidence shows that early contacts were made with sources of minerals in Asia and southeastern Europe. Accordingly, clay and earth had to be used for the basic necessities—clay for writing tablets, and mud-brick for building blocks. The particular civilization which is called *Babil* for the Tower, or ziggurat, of Babel, is in that area. As described in Genesis 11, one language united many different people so that they could cooperate together. This one language, in all probability, by the time of the Biblical account, was the Babylonian language, the lingua franca that enabled people of different origins to share in important enterprises. They were able to construct ziggurats or, to use the terminology of the English Bible, towers, such as the Tower of Babel. The text tells us that baked brick was used, and the baking had made it hard as stone.

The sciences that have come down to us, including the hard sciences of astronomy and mathematics, originated in Babylonia. We still use the same terminology for the heavenly bodies as the Sumerians and Akkadians, albeit in translation. The star, actually the planet that they called Inanna in Sumerian and Ishtar in Babylonian, was translated into Greek as Aphrodite, the same goddess of love and war, especially of love and fertility, and into Latin as Venus. We still call that planet Venus today. The most prominent heavenly bodies, the sun and the moon, were worshiped as major gods. Genesis attributed the creation of the heavenly bodies to God, but the text carefully avoids their names "Sun" and "Moon" and instead calls them respectively the Greater and Lesser Luminary so as not to attribute two prominent pagan deities to God. In arithmetic and mathematics there developed the sexagesimal system where 60 was the main round number. In science, such as in keeping time and in dealing with the angles of mathematics dividing the circle into its degrees, we still use the sexagesimal system of the ancient Sumerians and Akkadians and not merely our own decimal system, which is built into the Indo-European language that we speak. Because of this Sumero-Akkadian heritage, the hour is divided into 60 minutes and the minute into 60 seconds. Astronomers and other scientists divide the circle into 360 degrees, as 360 was a large number of the same sexagesimal system.

Mesopotamian culture had major offshoots in the West. In Syria, by the middle of the second half of the 3rd millennium B.C., there flourished a city called Ebla, some thirty miles south of Aleppo. The Italian expedition at Ebla during the 1970s found archives numbering around fifteen thousand tablets. The library at Ebla is more extensive than any Early Bronze Age archive found so far in the homeland of Mesopotamia or, for that matter, anywhere in the world.

At Ebla in this period there was a cuneiform academy with an ongoing curriculum for training scribes. These scribes and their teachers were in many cases exchanged. A mathematics professor at Ebla, whom we know by name, was imported from the Babylonian city of Kish, and a group of students from Mari on the middle Euphrates came to Ebla for a kind of "semester abroad." Part of the archives of Ebla are bilinguals—Sumerian ideograms being defined in the written Semitic language used at Ebla. This was a border language, so that it has East Semitic, or Akkadian elements, as well as Northwest Semitic elements related to Hebrew, Ugaritic, and Aramaic.

The picture we get of the Cuneiform World is that of a sophisticated order. It was already, and had been for centuries before, multi-lingual. The bilinguals at Ebla show that the training in philology was comparative. Textbooks of various subjects found in Ebla are sometimes merely local editions of textbooks found at other sites in Mesopotamia, indicating that the academy in Ebla belonged to a university system spread over a wide area. The great centers were actually hundreds of miles apart. We should never speak of the Early Bronze Age in the Near East as a primitive or prehistoric period. As we know from Ebla, the Near East, including Syria-Palestine, was highly civilized before as well as during the periods reflected in Genesis.

A second wave of immigrants into Mesopotamia were the Northwest Semites known as the Amorites. The migration of the Hebrew tribes is sometimes considered as part of this movement. Eventually, in a swift pincer attack, the Amorites, and the Elamites from southwest Iran brought an end to the Third Dynasty of Ur, c. 2004 B.C., whose kings had made the Sumerian city-state a center of commerce, industry, and culture. The refinements of the Mesopotamian cities attracted the Amorites who established their dynasty in Babylon and exalted its local deity, Marduk, as their god.

In the 18th century B.C., a Semitic ruler named Hammurapi succeeded to the throne during the First Dynasty of Babylon. Hammurapi was able to enlarge his kingdom through conquest and establish an empire, not only the one which he administered directly but also a far-flung economic empire. A number of Babylonian seal cylinders found in ancient Crete are largely of the Hammurapi dynasty. His influence as lawgiver, conqueror and ruler, and his methods, spread to a great extent by his traders in many directions, including westward, affected Syria, Palestine, the whole eastern Mediterranean, and the Aegean.

From the flourishing Amorite city of Mari, which Hammurapi destroyed in a treacherous attack, c. 1759 B.C., royal correspondence has been unearthed which describes the interaction of seminomadic pastoralists with the city residents. A troublesome tribe was the Banuyamina, who would not readily obey the established government be it for a census count or restrictions of their movements to pasture their flocks. Their name is cognate with "Benjamin," the impetuous youngest son of Jacob, who was described in the Patriarch's deathbed blessing as a wolf who devoured his prey and divided the spoils by night. In a letter from the royal archives, the Banu-yamina complain, "There are no pasturelands and we are making for the upper land," a move which was punishable in Mari by imprisonment. While there is no direct contact between Mari and the Hebrews, the Mari tablets have shed light on many aspects of Biblical institutions, including covenants, oracles through prophets, and rituals.

Not only has our writing come down to us from the Cuneiform World but also specific elements of our literature which began with the Sumerians and continued with the Akkadians and the Babylonians and then came to us through the Bible. Part of the *Epic of Gilgamesh* is the flood story, the deluge. There is also a Sumerian version, but the Babylonian version is embedded in Tablet XI of the Epic. The Flood described in Genesis is in large measure derived literarily and culturally from this Mesopotamian original.

There were other towns that have yielded cuneiform tablets of the greatest interest for Biblical as well as general studies. One of them in northeast Mesopotamia was the town of Nuzi. The parallel customs between Nuzi and those of the Old Testament are many. For example, a father with a number of sons made a will in which all of the household gods that were necessary for the family religion were bequeathed to the chief heir. The other sons were to come to the home of the chief heir for religious celebrations and ceremonies and were enjoined not to make other gods on pain of losing their inheritance. This prohibition is obviously to keep the family together. Thus the eventual Mosaic commandment against making and worshiping graven images had a practical purpose—to keep the people together and not to let them split up through loyalties to different gods. This adds another dimension to the forbidding of idolatry that was not understood previously. Getting rid of other gods is graphically described in Genesis 35:4, where Jacob buries pagan idols under an oak at Shechem.

Mesopotamian influence extended all the way through Palestine, even southern Palestine, into Egypt. In the late 15th and first half of the 14th centuries B.C., the diplomatic medium of the whole Near East was Babylonian cuneiform. The pharaohs Amenhotep III and his son Amenhotep IV (Akhenaten) corresponded in that language with the monarchs of Mesopotamia, Syria, Palestine, and the whole east Mediterranean world. At el-Amarna in Middle Egypt, over four hundred Babylonian tablets have been found. From Mesopotamia to the Nile, there was one Mesopotamian system of writing and also a language for which this writing was used that bound the whole Near East together from Anatolia to Egypt and to Mesopotamia. At the coastal Syrian town of Ugarit, Mesopotamian writing and literature and internationalism also flourished. It was there on clay tablets and in cuneiform writing that our ABC made its first appearance, arranged in the same order that we learn and teach it today.

By the 11th century B.C., the Aramaeans from northern Mesopotamia came to prominence. These Semitic people had intermingled with the Hurrians and Indo-European Hittites. The Aramaic language displaced Akkadian as the lingua franca of Western Asia. The Hebrews claimed kinship with the Aramaeans who occupied Harran (Biblical Haran), the city to which Abraham sent his eldest servant, presumably Eliezer, to find a wife for Isaac, and where Jacob labored in the house of his uncle, Laban, for Rachel. Genesis clearly recalls the mixed origins of the Hebrews who intermarried with the existing population.

From the time of Hammurapi on, while we call all of Mesopotamian civilization Akkadian, the area of Mesopotamia was divided into the Babylonian south and the Assyrian north. Assyria, the great conqueror of the lands of the Fertile Crescent from the 10th to the 7th centuries B.C., figures prominently in the historic books of the Old Testament. It was the Assyrians who destroyed the Northern Kingdom of Israel in 720 B.C.

Babylonia after the Assyrian period, the end of the 7th century B.C., became the dominant power. Under a great king, Nebuchadnezzar, the Babylonians conquered the Southern Kingdom of Judah, taking the Judaeans into exile in two main movements. The early movement was in 597 B.C. when Jehoiachin, a young king of Judah who had reigned only a short while, was exiled to Babylonia and was taken care of and supported by the king of Babylon.

The destruction of Jerusalem by Nebuchadnezzar in 586 B.C. brought another group of exiles to Babylonia. Like all conquests, it was not to endure. In 539 B.C., Cyrus the Great of Persia had conquered the city of Babylon. In 538 B.C., he issued an edict in the Babylonian language, permitting subject peoples to return to their original shrines and to enjoy autonomy. One of the people who were beneficiaries of this policy were the Judaeans. Cyrus the Great was the architect of the return to Zion. The last verse in the Hebrew Old Testament, the ending of the books of Chronicles, had to do with the edict of Cyrus authorizing the return. This final ray of hope was placed by the scribes and teachers who arranged the books of the Bible at the very end so as to inspire future generations for all time.

From the time of the account of Eden in Genesis to the last verse of the Hebrew Old Testament, we feel the impact of Mesopotamia on the Old Testament.

THE NATURE OF THE LAND

The once great city of Ur in southern Mesopotamia, nurtured by the Euphrates, today lies in a lifeless, sun-baked plain, a victim of invasions, the elements, and the changing course of the river.

A monument to its ancient glory is the ziggurat (*center*), the temple of the moon god. In Judaic tradition, it was in Ur of the Chaldees that Abram's family originated.

THE NATURE OF THE GODS

If the gods of nature were truly served and exalted by man, they would provide him with sweet water and sun to nourish the pastures, and plant and animal life for sustenance. Fear of famine would be dispelled. Man and nature in harmony are seen in a hunt scene on an Akkadian cylinder seal (*above*), 3rd millennium B.C. The idea of such a Paradise originated in Sumer. In the myth, *Enki and Ninhursag*, it was called the pure land of Dilmun, the garden of the gods, where sickness and old age were unknown. The generative forces of nature were embodied in Inanna, the goddess of fertility and procreation, and her husband, the shepherd Dumuzi. Their Sacred Marriage was reenacted during the annual New Year's festival, when the king, as Dumuzi, married a surrogate Inanna in order to ensure the earth's renewal. A shepherd (*below*), probably Dumuzi, feeds the herds of Inanna, whose emblems of tall reed bundles are behind them, on a cylinder seal from Uruk, late 4th millennium B.C. On an alabaster vase from Uruk, *facing page*, Inanna receives an offering.

The Universe as a State

Erech, the handiwork of the gods . . .
Its lofty dwelling place established by An . . .
— *Gilgamesh and Agga*, Sumerian poem

By the authority of An, the head of the divine
assembly, the fate of men and gods was decided.
An, believed to be represented on a cylinder seal
from Mari, 3rd millennium B.C. (*right*), shared his
dominion with the goddess Inanna, who brought
divine laws to their city of Uruk (modern Warka,
and the Biblical Erech). The high-terraced White
Temple (*below*), was raised as a symbolic link
between heaven and earth. The most famous king
of Uruk was the legendary Gilgamesh, born of the
goddess Ninsun. According to the Sumerian King
List (*facing page*), Gilgamesh reigned 126 years.
Tablet I of the *Epic of Gilgamesh* in Akkadian describes the sturdy walls of the city which he built:

Behold its wall, whose cornice is of copper;
Examine the bastion, which none can rival;
Touch the threshold
    which is from hoary antiquity.

Who was king? Who was not king?
— Sumerian King List

Unsettled political fortunes of kings and cities were accepted by the Sumerians as the will of the gods. These were reflected in the King List (*left*), a combination of history and legend compiled during a burst of national pride following the defeat of the Gutian armies in the east by Utu-hegal of Uruk, c. 2120 B.C. The list was expanded over a 170-year period ending with the Isin Dynasty. As noted on the excerpt below, divine "kingship was lowered from heaven" [1], not only to the legendary, such as Dumuzi [15] and Gilgamesh, but to the humble alike. Kish boasted of a female "king," Ku(g)-Baba, who was a barmaid, or "woman wine seller." Sargon (Sharrukin) the Great of Akkad was a mere "date grower." With mythological fancy, kings reigned for thousands of years [4, 5, 12, 15, 38]. It was only after the flood swept over the earth [39, 40], that the length of their rule took on human proportions.

EXCERPTS FROM THE KING LIST,
COLUMN I

1. When kingship was lowered from heaven.
2. kingship was in Eridu.
3. (In) Eridu A-lulim (became) king
4. and reigned 28,800 years.
5. Alalgar reigned 36,000 years.
8. I drop (the topic) Eridu.
9. its kingship to Bad-tibira
10. was carried.
11. (In) Bad-tibira En-men-lu-Anna
12. reigned 43,200 years.
15. divine Dumu-zi, a shepherd, reigned 36,000 years.
19. its kingship to Larak was carried.
25. its kingship to Sippar was carried.
31. its kingship to Shuruppak was carried.
36. Five cities were they.
37 Eight kings
38. reigned their 241,200 years.
39. The Flood swept thereover.
40. After the Flood swept thereover,
41. when kingship was lowered from heaven
42. kingship was in Kish.

Divine Favor

When Enki rose, the fishes rose and adored him.
He stood, a marvel unto the Apsu (Deep). . .
— *Enki and Eridu*, Sumerian myth

In a world of insecurity and doubt, Enki, the god of
wisdom and sweet waters, was a friend to man. His gifts
of the arts and sciences provided the creative means to
carry out the decisions of the divine assembly, while the
canals which he supervised brought fertility to the land.
Enki sits in his chamber of the watery deep before his
double-faced minister, Isimud, on an Akkadian cylinder
seal (*above*). Enki's divine gifts to mankind of animal
husbandry, music, and metallurgy were human skills
attributed in Genesis to Cain's descendants. Enki's city
was Eridu, modern Abu Shahrain, the southernmost
Sumerian city and the first to be mentioned in the King
List. Cain also founded the first city and named it after
his son Enoch. In Eridu, a series of superimposed
temples (*left*), dedicated to Enki, spans a period from the
Ubaid, 5th millennium B.C., to the Third Dynasty of
Ur, two millenniums later, confirming that the people
continued to worship on the same site the god on whom
its agricultural prosperity depended.

Divine Vengeance

Enlil, because his beloved Ekur had been attacked,
what destruction he wrought.

— *The Curse of Agade*, Sumerian narrative

Enlil, the power in the storm, was the force behind
the verdicts of the divine assembly, who led the gods
in war. As the son of An, he decreed the fates, often
with a vengeance. "The word commanded by An
(and) Enlil, who can oppose it!" states a Sumerian
lamentation. His city was Nippur (*above*), whose
modern desolation recalls the attack by Naram-Sin
of Akkad on Enlil's temple, Ekur, which evoked the
god's curse on him. At the height of his power,
Naram-Sin, grandson of Sargon the Great, is shown
conquering the Lullubians on a stele from Susa,
23rd century B.C. (*right*). With his axe and spear, he
leads his soldiers up a mountain as the enemy is
trampled underfoot. But Naram-Sin soon was
defeated after striking out at Nippur. As told in the
historic narrative, quoted above, Enlil brought down
the Gutian armies on Akkad—"Like locusts they
covered the earth." The Hebrews were to seek their
destiny far from the wars and gods of Mesopotamia.

ROYAL
OBLIGATIONS

IN WAR

It was the duty of the king in Mesopotamia to defend his
land against enemy attacks, including organizing, training,
and leading his armies into battle. Eannatum of Lagash,
c. 2450 B.C., marches his phalanx over the prostrate bodies
of the men of Umma who had violated his borders, as seen
on the Stele of the Vultures (*above*). In the lower register,
Eannatum rides in a war chariot holding a spear. A Biblical
parallel to this royal duty is recounted in Gen.14 when Abram,
as tribal leader, armed his 318 servants in order to pursue
the four invading kings who had kidnapped his nephew Lot.

IN PEACE

The first task of the ruler was to satisfy his patron god by
building and beautifying his temple. Gudea of Lagash,
c. 2141-2122 B.C. , holds an architectural plan on his lap, on
his headless statue (*right*), reflecting an ancient text which
describes how the god Ningirsu came to Gudea in a dream
commanding him to build his shrine Eninnu. The finest
woods, metals, and stones were gathered to construct it.
When God appeared in dreams to Abram and later to
Jacob, it was not for temple building but to establish his
Covenant and to promise the land as their inheritance.

THE FATE OF HUMANKIND

Farmers grew the food which the gods ate.

The will of the people was never free as they labored in the service of the gods while they performed their cosmic duties. Some human chores are shown on two terra-cotta votive plaques of the early 2nd millennium B.C., *above*, from Ishchali (Neribtum), and *center*, from Warka (Uruk); and on a vase, *below*, from Telloh (Girsu), of the late 3rd millennium B.C. In Genesis, although Adam was expected to tend the Garden of Eden, he was the passive recipient of God's care, having the fruit of every tree—save one—for food. When Adam and Eve disobeyed God's command not to eat of the tree of knowledge, they became responsible for their own actions, knowing "good and bad." The age of innocence had passed.

Artisans beautified the pagan temples.

Musicians played in cultic ceremonies.

MIGRATIONS AND INVASIONS—
Catalysts for Change

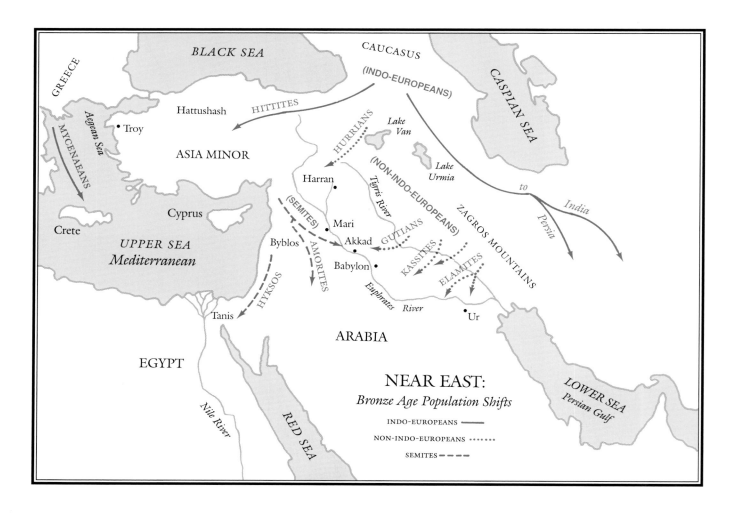

BLACK SEA

CAUCASUS

(INDO-EUROPEANS)

CASPIAN SEA

GREECE

Aegean Sea

Hattushash

HITTITES

• Troy

MYCENAEANS

ASIA MINOR

HURRIANS

Lake Van

(NON-INDO-EUROPEANS)

Harran •

Lake Urmia

to

India

Persia

Cyprus

Crete

Tigris River

ZAGROS MOUNTAINS

UPPER SEA
Mediterranean

Byblos

(SEMITES)

AMORITES

• Mari

Akkad •

GUTIANS

• Babylon

KASSITES

Euphrates River

ELAMITES

HYKSOS

• Ur

Tanis •

ARABIA

EGYPT

NEAR EAST:
Bronze Age Population Shifts

INDO-EUROPEANS ————

NON-INDO-EUROPEANS ·······

SEMITES – – – –

Nile River

RED SEA

LOWER SEA
Persian Gulf

Periodic migrations often grew to invasions as people sought living space and arable land within Mesopotamia's sphere. Infiltrators and conquerors became heirs to its writing, language, art, science, law, and religion. In the 3rd millennium B.C., these inheritors included the Gutians from the Zagros range who invaded Akkad, and the Semitic Amorites from the west and Elamites from the east who ended the Sumerian Third Dynasty of Ur. In the 2nd millennium B.C., also influenced were the Indo-European Hittites who raided Babylonia from Anatolia, the eastern Kassites who succeeded them, and the Hurrians from Lake Van. Such movements are reflected in Genesis 11:2 as the people who migrated from the east and who settled in Shinar, referring to Babylonia in southern Mesopotamia.

In the eastern Mediterranean world, invasions and counter-invasions transformed its social structure during half a millennium. The Hyksos from Canaan who overran the Nile Delta in the 17th century B.C. were, in turn, driven back by the Egyptians a hundred years later. The fall of Mycenae in the Aegean area, late 13th century B.C., set off waves of Sea Peoples, including the Philistines, whose incursions ended Egypt's economic domination of the Canaanite city-states, c. 1150 B.C. Seminomadic pastoralists, much like the Patriarchs, began to settle in Canaan's hill country and adopt grain-growing agriculture for their livelihood. Some scholars suggest that these were the earliest, or "proto" Israelites, a nucleus of the future nation.

Migration of Writing

Cuneiform writing originated in Sumer in the late 4th millennium B.C. as scribes began to impress economic temple records on clay tablets. The script was transmitted northward along caravan routes and waterways in a wide economic network by merchants and traders even before invaders entered the region. On the middle Euphrates, the archives of Mari name cities within its commercial orbit (*map below, right*), including Harran, the Patriarchal area where Abram sojourned, and others as far west as Ugarit on the Mediterranean. The Hebrews used writing to preserve their traditions of faith and national history but did not develop a distinct art form (*following page*), since their prohibition against portraying their God curtailed the basic expression of religious themes.

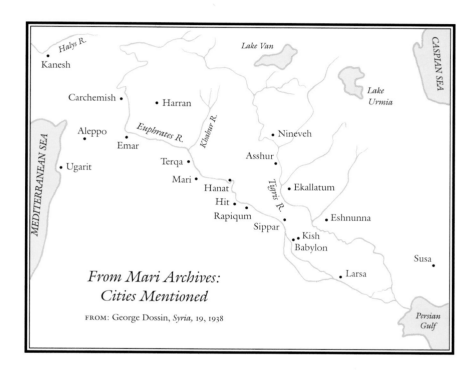

From Mari Archives: Cities Mentioned

FROM: George Dossin, *Syria*, 19, 1938

MARI [Tell Hariri]: In this strategic city, the Northwest Semitic Amorites adapted Sumerian cuneiform to the Akkadian language, as seen from the tablet (*above*), one of thousands found in the palace archives, c. 2000-1750 B.C. The texts vividly describe the interaction of nomads and cities and various Patriarchal customs such as treaties sworn to in the name of the God of one's father.

CARCHEMISH [Jerablus]: The Hittites also borrowed cuneiform writing for their Indo-European language. Hieroglyphic, or pictographic, writing, shown on a basalt slab (*right*), 9th century B.C., from this thriving city on the northern Euphrates, was used simultaneously with but later replaced cuneiform. The Hittites of Genesis, the children of Heth, formed an active enclave in Hebron.

Migration of Art

MESOPOTAMIA to EGYPT: Fantastic beasts captured the imagination of artists in the early 3rd millennium B.C. On a Mesopotamian cylinder seal (*above*), two such animals with elongated, intertwined necks also were depicted on the Egyptian Narmer palette (*right*).

EGYPT to SYRIA: The crown of Upper and Lower Egypt, as worn by Ramses II (*above, left*), was adopted by all rulers after Menes united the land in the First Dynasty, c. 3000 B.C. A seated man wears such a high double crown on a Syrian cylinder seal (*above, right*), c. 1750-1600 B.C.

MESOPOTAMIA to CRETE: Fashion, as it will, also traveled. The tiered dress of the goddess (*above*), presenting a worshiper to Ur-Nammu of Ur on this cylinder seal, c. 2050 B.C., was adapted more daringly for the bare-breasted Minoan snake goddess from Knossos (*right*), c. 1600 B.C.

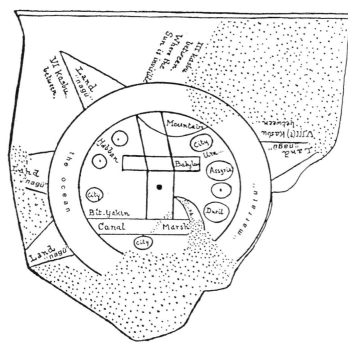

The Babylonians' knowledge of mathematics is evident in the use of the rectangle and triangle, and the circle which they divided into 360 degrees, as seen on this only known world map of the 7th-6th centuries B.C., inscribed on a clay tablet (*above, left; drawing, right*), possibly from Sippar or Borsippa. Babylon, imagined as the center of the earth, is named in the rectangle straddling the major artery of the Euphrates River, stretching from the Turkish mountains in the north to the southern Mesopotamian marshes.

The ocean (*marratu*), within the concentric circles, surrounds the land mass, while distant, unspecified areas (*nagû*), appear as triangles emanating from the outer circle. Movements of planets also were recorded, along with fluctuations in river levels and the weather. To the Jews exiled to Babylon in 586 B.C., these scientific observations merely proved the greatness of their God who, in his infinite wisdom, created and ordered the universe and who one day would bring them back to restore Jerusalem.

The Beginning of Law

The first law code governing the actions of men is attributed to Ur-Nammu, 2112-2095 B.C., the founder of the Third Dynasty of Ur, who established the code "by the might of Nanna," the moon god, lord of Ur, "and in accordance with the true word of Utu," the sun god of justice. Thus did Ur-Nammu "establish equity in the land, (and) he banished malediction, violence and strife." Although current research does not specifically identify the figures on the above "Stele of Ur-Nammu," the original discoverers of this contempory stele from Ur described the scene as the lawgiver and builder, Ur-Nammu, receiving the architects' tools of coiled rope and measuring rod from Nanna, the seated god (*right*) who ordered the king to construct his temple. On the lower register, Ur-Nammu (*center*), carrying tools on his shoulders, follows the god while a clean-shaven priest helps to support the royal load. The atmosphere of law giving is reflected after the Flood when divine laws confirmed the sanctity of human life. Capital punishment was the penalty for murder: "Whoso sheddeth man's blood, by man shall his blood be shed; for in the image of God made he man," Gen. 9:6.

Building on older legal codes, Hammurapi of Babylon compiled a body of laws regulating the life of his empire in the 18th century B.C. These were inscribed in the Akkadian language on this eight-foot diorite stele (*right*), below the depiction of Hammurapi standing before the enthroned sun god, Shamash, the Sumerian Utu, lord of light and righteousness. Both the Hammurapi Code and the documents from the Hurrian city of Nuzi (*below*), 15th-14th centuries B.C., are reflected in the Patriarchal lives. According to these laws, Sarah acted illegally when she drove out the concubine Hagar and her son Ishmael. Since Abraham had acknowledged him as his offspring, Ishmael was entitled to an equal share of the paternal inheritance. Only after God revealed that the Hebrew lineage was meant to descend through Isaac did Abraham accept Sarah's harsh decision.

The Evolution of the Gods

Godhead awesome as the faraway heavens, as the broad sea.
— *To the Moon God*, Sumero-Akkadian hymn.

Strong-willed Sumerian gods of nature and the universe were worshiped under their Semitic names by the Akkadians in the mid-3rd millennium B.C. These remote divinities often battled amongst themselves while determining mankind's fate, as the spirit moved them. On the Akkadian cylinder seal of Adda the scribe (*above*), members of the divine family are seen with their emblems. Their original Sumerian names are in brackets:

Shamash [Utu], the sun god of justice (*center*), rises from the cosmic mountain with rays emanating from his shoulders. He holds the saw with which he cuts decisions and opens the gates of heaven when he arises in the East. Greeting him is his sister Ishtar [Inanna], the winged goddess of love and war. Hers was the power immanent in the rain, the date, and the storehouse. Her fertility attribute is shown in the plants growing from the mountain and her shoulders. Ninurta (*left*), was the warrior god of the spring thunderstorm and floods. His bow signifies lightning, and his lion, the roar of thunder. Ea [Enki] (*right*), the god of sweet waters, is shown with fish swimming upwards in two streams flowing from his shoulders. He holds a bird, while beneath his raised foot rests a bull associated with the sun. Ea's double-faced minister, Usmu [Isimud], stands in his usual place behind him.

Although the Mesopotamian conceptions of Creation and the great Flood are reflected in Gen. 1-11, the Hebrew God was above nature, which he created according to his divine plan. People were considered to be creatures of free will, capable of intelligence and reason.

44

—TO THE PERSONAL GOD

> Without the (personal) god, man eats no bread.
> — *Man and His God*, Sumerian poem.

As Hammurapi brought order into society by establishing laws and strengthening the monarchy, a new kind of personal god evolved who looked after his worshipers, as a shepherd tends his flock, and who interceded on their behalf with the great cosmic gods. The Northwest Semitic Amorites, from whom Hammurapi was descended, worshiped Amurru, who is identified as a personal god holding a shepherd's crook, his foot resting on a gazelle, on a First Babylonian Dynasty cylinder seal, 1800-1600 B.C. (*above*). In the Prelude to his Law Code, Hammurapi referred to himself as "the shepherd of the people . . . who makes law prevail." The Creation Epic, *Enuma Elish*, recounts that when Babylon became the capital of Mesopotamia, its god Marduk was elevated to permanent kingship of the universe by the divine assembly. The gods expected him to be exalted, yet caring, as they joined in to revere him, "May he shepherd the black-headed ones (the human race) . . . to the end of days . ." This paternalism of a personal god is inherent in Genesis. After the Flood, God confirmed that order in nature, not chaos, was his divine will. His covenant with Noah and his sons assured that all living creatures never again would be destroyed. Divine grace was extended from the individual to a whole people. And the rainbow was its token.

MARI (Tell Hariri)

André Parrot (*below, left*), directed the French Archaeological Mission to Mari on the Euphrates Valley trade route between Mesopotamia and Syria during twenty expeditions between 1933 to 1974. Parrot's team uncovered a vast two-and-a-half-acre palace (*below*), the city's administrative center, and royal archives attesting to frequent tribal migrations northward, recalling the trek of Abram's family from Ur to Haran, possibly due to unstable political alliances of the city-states. The following excerpt is from Parrot's book *Mari*, Editions Ides et Calendes, Neuchatel, 1953.

"Ex Oriente Lux"—light came to us from the East. Together with Egypt, Mesopotamia was the oldest source of knowledge, and in Mesopotamia, Mari held a position of great distinction.

A world unto itself; countless civilizations emerging from the soil and arising from the grave. From about 3000 B.C. until the Christian era, we were able to rediscover the life of a city, follow not only its achievements and its victories, but also its reverses. Time and again, war had left unmistakable traces; fire, ruins and plunder. Often, too often, we found pieces of sculpture barbarously mutilated, and buildings still bearing traces of the flames which had destroyed them.

Assembled documents illustrate two specific phases in the unfolding of Mesopotamian civilization: the first part of the 3rd millennium B.C., and the beginning of the 2nd millennium B.C. Everything of beauty and grandeur created by Mari, can be attributed to these two epochs.

The aftermath is a tale of decline. Towards 1750 B.C., Mari suffered the most brutal destruction that could be inflicted on a vanquished capital. After having overthrown all his nearest neighbors, Hammurapi, king of Babylon, with a ruthless determination to dominate, finally attacked the only man capable of withstanding him, and of barring his way to the Mediterranean: Zimri-Lim, king of Mari.

Never before had this city attained such heights. It had reached the zenith of prosperity and power. From his mighty palace, the monarch controlled vast tracts of the Near East, and held within his hands the destinies of many nations. Following a merciless struggle, Mari was to perish and be replaced by Babylon. After this eclipse, the city only recovered a small portion of its former animation with the arrival of an Assyrian garrison, established there to watch over the caravan route which united the two seas of the "rising sun" and the "setting sun": the Persian Gulf and the Mediterranean. With the departure of the Assyrians, it became scarcely more than a village, to linger on a while, and finally become extinct. Like many another prosperous and famous city, Mari, in the words of the Scriptures, "descended into hell."

The men of Mari of the 3rd and 2nd millenniums were portrayed with their hands folded in prayer, an attitude which did not, however, prevent them from making war. Their eyes were turned towards heaven, but their bare feet were firmly planted on the earth. Reality and spirituality, dual forces from which life springs, and the rulers of Mari, set out to harness force to facilitate existence. In the palace, a stronghold difficult to capture, but as subsequent events were to prove, not impregnable, the sovereigns surrounded themselves with statues and paintings. Goddesses encircled them, with hands uplifted in blessing. Zimri-Lim posed for his portrait in this attitude, standing before Ishtar, the goddess of war, but also the goddess of love.* Love and War. In truth, Paradise exists only in the shadow of swords, but even swords are sometimes powerless to defend this Paradise.

*see pages 58-9

Shibum, the land surveyor.
Temple of Ninni-zaza, Mari.

MYTH AND MANKIND—*Literary Tradition*

Show thou to me the plant of birth:
[Remove my burden and] produce for me a name!
— *The Myth of Etana*, Neo-Assyrian version

The longing for a son and the rivalry of brothers were themes from Mesopotamian myths and epics which were echoed in Genesis. In *The Myth of Etana*, this legendary, childless shepherd-king of Kish was carried to heaven on the back of an eagle to obtain the plant which would assure the birth of an heir. On an Akkadian cylinder seal, 2nd half of the 3rd millennium B.C., herdsmen and animals gaze in wonder as Etana rises skyward (*above, right*). In the Patriarchal narratives, it was God's will that sons were born to barren wives. In the *Epic of Gilgamesh,* the wise Utnapishtim noted that the terms of a family inheritance could cause fraternal discord. The two brothers on the enlarged cylinder seal of Kalki, mid-3rd millennium B.C. (*detail, right*), suggest the rivals, Esau, the "cunning hunter, " with his bow, followed by Jacob, "a plain man dwelling in tents."

Do brothers divide shares forever?
Does hatred persist forever in [the land]?
— *Epic of Gilgamesh*, Tablet X,
Babylonian version

II

THE MISTS OF TIME
Genesis I-II

———

NAHUM M. SARNA

"I N THE BEGINNING . . ."—the majestic first words of Genesis—set the stage for the divine creation of the world. The first book of the Bible emerged as one of the earliest records of an ancient people in search of life's meaning.

Although there were profound differences between the various civilizations of the ancient Near East, the entire region, nevertheless, did constitute a cultural continuum. On the banks of the Euphrates River in Mesopotamia, man was preoccupied with how the world was created or who ordered nature and mankind. He believed that it was the province of a pantheon of gods, each one performing individual assignments in the running of the cosmos. If the gods so willed, rain would fall, sun would shine, and crops would grow to sustain life. If the gods did not, all would suffer. The people of Israel shared in the common culture of the ancient Near East but also stood apart from it. It is this separateness that is its distinctive characteristic.

As the Hebrews embarked on their quest for their own moral and religious vision, the narratives of Genesis 1–11 were written as a universal history in which one omnipotent God interacted with human beings as creatures of free will in a covenant relationship. In order to develop their beliefs, the Hebrews borrowed some Mesopotamian themes but adapted them to the unique conception of their one God.

On the one hand, therefore, the texts of Genesis 1–11 exhibit numerous external points of contact with extant literary sources from neighboring cultures. On the other hand, in their conception of God, of human beings, and of the relationships between God and humankind, as well as in their understanding of human destiny, the ancient Hebrews largely rejected prevailing notions and produced their own independent, often revolutionary, approach.

The Biblical Creation account presents a graduated, six-day succession of divine fiats that bring the world and its constitutent elements into being. It is a narrative distinguished by its austerity, by its uncompromising monotheism, and by the complete absence of myths that attempt to account for the origin of God (theogony) or that tell of resistance to the reduction of chaos to order (theomachy). These myths, such as the Babylonian Creation Epic, *Enuma Elish*, which begins in familiar cadence, "When on high the heavens had not been named, firm ground below had not been called by name . . . ," are the hallmarks of all other Near Eastern creation stories. In Genesis God's self-existence is taken for granted. He does not inhere in nature, but nature is wholly his willful creation over which he exercises unchallenged and unlimited sovereignty.

An extraordinary aspect of the Biblical narrative is that God desisted from creativity on the seventh day. While the institution of the Sabbath is not mentioned, there can be no doubt that the intention is to provide the rationale for it. Indeed, in the Ten Commandments the Sabbath is explicitly grounded in the Creation story. The idea of a divinely mandated, weekly, fixed day of rest for all human beings, irrespective of social class, for the beasts of burden, and for nature itself, is wholly unparalleled in any other known culture.

The one God personally creates man and woman as the crowning act of cosmogony, the evolution of civilization. Moreover, human beings are said to be created in the image and likeness of God. In the ancient Near East, this phrase is used to distinguish the ruling monarch from his subjects. For instance, one cuneiform document reads, "The king, my lord, is the very image of [the god] Bel, " and another says, "The king, lord of the lands, is the image of [the god] Shamash." Similarly, in Egypt, Pharaoh Thutmose IV is described as "the likeness of [the god] Re."

In Genesis there has taken place a democratizing of this designation. It is applied to the entire human race, which is conceived to be a family in that all human beings are descended from a single pair of ancestors, Adam and Eve. This, in turn, conveys the fundamental idea of human equality, while the entire account of the appearance of human beings on earth connotes a unique relationship between them and God not shared by the animal world. Implicit in the narrative is the notion that human life is infinitely precious, and the Genesis text advances the basic teaching that human beings have been endowed by God with free will.

Several other radically new ideas emphasize the chasm between Israelite concepts and those of Israel's contemporaries. God implants in nature, in the animal world, and in humankind the capacity for reproduction. Sexuality, therefore, is no longer personified as a divinity as, for instance, is Ishtar, the Babylonian goddess of love, or Ashtaroth, the Canaanite goddess of fertility, love, and sex. Nor is it regarded as a magical force, but it is a divine gift. The effect of this is that the religion of Israel, in contrast to that of surrounding cultures, avoids all magical rites associated with enhancing human fertility, animal fecundity, and the productivity of the soil.

A seemingly strange feature of the Biblical Creation account is the repeated statement that God saw that what he had made "was good," and the verdict on the completion of the entire six-day work that it was "very good." Behind these judgments is a process of demythologizing. Near Eastern cultures saw evil as an independent, primordial power beyond the control of both men and gods which could only be appeased by cultic or magical means. Genesis, in effect, denies the existence of any such autonomous, malevolent forces not subject to divine will. Evil is introduced into a good world by human beings, the implication being that human beings can, by their own conduct, repair the evil they produce.

This theme of the origins of humanly wrought evil, with its concomitant principle of responsibility and accountability, is also the message of the Garden of Eden, the Cain and

Abel and Flood stories, and of the Tower of Babel as well. In the first of these, Adam and Eve exercise their freedom of will by violating God's command not to eat of the tree of knowledge. They thereby disrupt the harmony between humankind and its Maker. While the story has no parallel so far in ancient Near Eastern sources, a Sumerian myth about *Enki and Ninhursag* also tells of an idyllic site, Dilmun, in which there is neither sickness nor old age and in which perfect harmony prevails. However, unlike the Biblical tale, it has no ethical, instructional function. Further, the "tree of life" is a well-known motif, but in the Bible it is not the focus of the Eden story. Instead, it is the "tree of knowledge" that occupies the center of the stage, and this has no counterpart in Near Eastern mythology. Morality and the human potential for understanding—not immortality—were the concerns of the Biblical authors.

Once again, a shift away from accepted notions is evident in the role of the serpent. Throughout the region, the serpent was treated as a mysterious creature believed to be divine or, at least, semi-divine. It was the subject of mythological tales and the object of worship. Here in Genesis it is deliberately described as being merely "one of the wild beasts that the Lord God had made," even if the mythic element of a talking serpent is retained. Its supposed divinity is thereby undercut.

The process of demythologizing is carried on in the account of developments outside of Eden. Divine creation in seven days is paralleled by human creativity in the course of seven generations after Adam. The arts of civilization are produced: the city, animal husbandry, musical instruments, and metalworking. All these advances in material culture are ascribed to human beings, whereas outside of Israel, it is gods or demi-gods who are credited with their origin.

At the same time as civilization progresses, the Bible depicts a process of moral degeneration: anger and irrationality that end in homicide (Cain's murder of Abel), cosmic disorder (the consorting of the daughters of men with divine beings), polygamy (Lamech's marriage to two wives, Adah and Zillah), and the exhibition of vengefulness (Lamech's boast of murdering a man and a child). All this prepares the way for the story of the Flood, which occurs in the tenth generation after Creation. Human evil has reached such a degree of intensity and universality that God's Creation has become thoroughly disordered. Divine intervention is called for.

The Genesis account of the Flood displays so many points of contact with the flood stories that have come down to us in several versions from Mesopotamia that a common origin must be presumed. The flat alluvial plain of lower Mesopotamia between the Euphrates and Tigris Rivers provides the natural provenance for such traditions. The Sumerian version with its hero, Ziusudra, the Babylonian Gilgamesh epic, and the late account of Berossus in the 3rd pre-Christian century, all narrate the event. The singularity of the Biblical version lies in its pervasive moral atmosphere. The Flood is decreed as a punishment for human corruption and as a purging process, and not as a whim of a god or gods or because the sleep of these deities is disturbed by men's tumult, as we read in another version, the Old Babylonian *Atrahasis Epic*. The hero, Noah, is delivered on account of his integrity alone; a single family is made to survive so that the concept of humankind as one family may be preserved. Noah thereby becomes a second Adam, his offspring having been ordered to repeople the earth. He is not set apart from humanity by being granted divinity, as occurs with Utnapishtim, the hero of the Gilgamesh version. Then, after the Flood, a new world order is proclaimed. Humanity is to be governed by certain basic rules and institutions designed to promote universal norms of civilized conduct. Finally, only in the Biblical version does God make a covenant with humankind pledging that a deluge on a cosmic scale would never recur.

The universal history of the Book of Genesis closes with the story of the building of the Tower of Babel in Chapter 11. While the narrative has no parallel in Near Eastern texts, it is permeated with authentic knowledge of Babylonian building techniques and royal inscriptional clichés. Behind the story is certainly the phenomenon of the ziggurat, the multi-storied tower that supposedly connected heaven and earth and that most likely substituted for a natural mountain, which usually served this purpose. The famous ziggurat of Babylon was, in fact, named Etemenanki, "The House of the Foundation of Heaven and Earth." Kiln-fired bricks were unknown in Canaan but were extensively used in Babylon; bitumen similarly was distinctively characteristic of that country's construction methods. Phrases such as "its top in the sky," "to make a name for oneself," appear repeatedly on Akkadian building inscriptions.

The essence of the story is an explanation for the diversity of languages among human beings who are conceived as belonging to a single family. Another function is to contravert Babylonian myth which assigned the origin of the ziggurat to the work of the gods at creation. In *Enuma Elish*, the gods molded bricks for the temple of Babylon for one whole year. The Genesis story makes it a postdiluvian, human enterprise, a product of human arrogance.

As the primeval history of mankind ends, the sacred history of Genesis begins with Abraham who will be a blessing to those nations which God scattered after man's failed attempt to build the ill-fated Tower of Babel.

CREATION

In the beginning God created the heaven and the earth. — Gen. 1:1

> After Heaven had been moved away from earth,
> After earth had been separated from heaven,
> After the name of man had been fixed,
> After (the heaven-god) An carried off the heaven,
> After (the air-god) Enlil carried off the earth . . .
> — *Gilgamesh, Enkidu, and the Nether World,* Sumerian poem

With the simple majesty of God's word, as told in Genesis, the heaven and earth were created. The light was divided from the darkness on the first day, as suggested by the photograph of a modern solar eclipse (*facing page*). In the comparative Sumerian view of the universe, quoted above, the male heaven, An, originally was united with the female earth, Ki. The cylinder seal (*above*), from Tell Asmar, early 3rd millennium BC, has been interpreted as the physical union of heaven and earth in human forms before they were separated. Another explanation of the seal reflects the Mesopotamian New Year's marriage ritual in which the conjugal union of a god and goddess, actually performed by the king and a surrogate bride, assured the fertility of the earth for the coming year. The figure at the foot of the nuptial bed (*left*), might be a priest who officiated at the Sacred Marriage.

Order Out of Chaos

God created the world in a calm and orderly six-day progression, whereas in the Babylonian epic, *Enuma Elish* (compared *below, right,* in three seal impressions), creation was preceded by conflict between the forces of light, led by Marduk, god of Babylon, and the forces of darkness, who rallied to the sea monster goddess, Tiamat. From the blood of Kingu, ally of the vanquished Tiamat, man was created to serve the gods and to free them from their labors. In Genesis God exalted both man and woman by giving them dominion over all other living creatures. They also would receive the gift of rest from daily toil, as intended in the seventh day, the Sabbath, which God blessed and sanctified after completing his Creation.

And the spirit of God moved upon
    the face of the waters,
       — Gen. 1:2

All the gods went over to her
    [Tiamat]. . .They took up the
    fight, fuming, and raging . . .
       — *Enuma Elish*, Tablet III

Gods battling. Akkadian seal.

And God said, Let there be a firm-
    ament in the midst of the waters.
       —Gen. 1:6

He [Marduk] split her [Tiamat]
    open like a mussel into two (parts);
Half of her he set in place and formed
    the sky (therewith) as a roof.
       — *Enuma Elish*, Tablet IV

Marduk vanquishes Tiamat. Babylonian seal.

So God created man in his own
    image. . . male and female
    created he them.
       — Gen. 1:27

They bound him [Kingu] and held
    him before Ea; . . .With his blood
    they created mankind; He [Ea]
    imposed the services of the gods
    (upon them) and set the gods free.
       — *Enuma Elish*, Tablet VI

Deity (*left*) slits victim's throat. Akkadian seal.

The Divine Gift of Water

Before God created man, a flow arose and watered the ground. Plants and herbs now could grow to provide sustenance in the Garden of Eden. Man's only obligation was to cultivate and tend it as God wished. These waters of creation, which were divinely directed, did not have innate magic force, as the Mesopotamians believed. On the detail from the top of the reverse side of Ur-Nammu's stele, the king (*above, right*), and a flying angel (*left*), wearing a horned miter, pour libations over a sacred tree below (not seen). Ur-Nammu might dig his many canals, but only such life-giving waters divinely provided could fill them, making Ur an earthly Eden. In the Sumerian paradise myth, *Enki and Ninhursag*, the gods of Sumer were in charge of irrigation and cultivation. At the command of Enki, the water god, the pure, clean land of Dilmun was filled with fresh water from the earth to make it a worthy dwelling for the gods with trees and fruit in abundance.

(*Overleaf*): A view of Paradise has been imagined from the scene of the "Investiture of Zimri-Lim," king of Mari. On a wall painting copy from his palace, 18th century B.C., the king receives his ring and staff of office from the goddess Ishtar (*center*). The fertility goddesses, in the frame *below*, hold jars from which flow four streams, suggesting the divisions of the river which watered the Garden of Eden—Pishon, Gihon, the Tigris, and Euphrates. Climbing a date-palm in which a bird nests in its top branches (*far right*), two men seek the sweet fruit, as it was in Eden where God put "every tree that is pleasant to the sight, and good for food." The winged creatures flanking the flowering trees recall the cherubim who barred the access to Eden after Adam and Eve were expelled for tasting the forbidden fruit of the tree of knowledge. In *Enki and Ninhursag*, the mother-goddess pronounced the curse of death on Enki when he ate the eight plants she had nurtured so carefully.

The Way of the Gods

When Adam and Eve were forbidden to eat of the "tree of knowledge of good and evil," it reflected the Mesopotamian concept that wisdom as well as immortality were jealously guarded prerogatives of the gods which they rarely bestowed on man. The source of evil in Eden was man's disobedience. In Mesopotamia evil was a negative, supernatural force inherent in the universe. A familiar ancient motif was the tree of life in a civilization where man feared death and sought vainly for immortality. Such a tree rises from a stylized mountain on an Akkadian cylinder seal, *above*, between rampant bulls held by a bull man, *left*, and a nude hero, *right*. Ancient man believed that the wily serpent with its ability to shed its skin knew the secret of rejuvenation, recalling events in the *Epic of Gilgamesh,* opposite page. A snake motif adorns a bowl from Khafaje (*below*), 3rd millennium B.C.

The Human Condition

Man's lost opportunity to become immortal was an ancient theme. In Genesis, since man had acquired knowledge against God's will, he was expelled from Eden before he could eat of the tree of life and so live forever. Reflecting the *Epic of Gilamesh*, the man in the center of the boat (*above, right*), on a seal impression drawing, 3rd millennium B.C., might be Gilgamesh holding the plant of new life called "Man Becomes Young in Old Age," which he found at the bottom of the sea. But the Epic tells, a snake stole the plant while Gilgamesh bathed in the water. Also in the boat might be Utnapishtim, wearing the crown of divinity, the only man to whom the gods granted immortality after he survived the flood, and the boatman, Urshanabi, holding the rudder. The Akkadian seal (*below*), with elements from Eden, actually fertility gods, has been dubbed the "Temptation Seal."

. . . the tree of life also in the midst of the garden,

The Garden of Eden

and the tree of knowledge of good and evil.
— Gen. 2:9

The nourishing fruit of the date palm, here standing tall in Iraq's southern marshes, *opposite,* renders it "the tree of life" to many Middle Easterners. Local tradition places the Garden of Eden in Al Qurna where the Tigris and Euphrates merge into the Shatt-al-Arab. The town fathers fenced off a tree, *above,* recalling the Biblical Eden, with a sign that reads:

> On this holy spot where Tigris
>
> meet Euphrates this holy tree
>
> of our Father Adam grew
>
> symbolising the
>
> Garden of Eden on
>
> earth. Abraham prayed
>
> here two thousand years B.C.

CAIN and ABEL

And Abel was a keeper of sheep,   but   Cain was a tiller of the ground. —Gen. 4:2

In a growing spirit of evil, the first murder occurred as man became increasingly alienated from his God. Cain's jealousy of his brother Abel, ending in fratricide, was a crime against God's moral law, since man was created in his image. The underlying rivalry of the nomadic shepherd Abel, who daily sought fertile pastures for his flocks, with the settled farmer Cain is an accurate reflection of ancient society when agriculture had replaced food gathering as a way of life. The professions of the brothers are shown *above*: as a shepherd, on a clay plaque, *left*, and as a farmer, actually an acolyte, on a cylinder seal, *right*, both 3rd millennium B.C.. In the Sumerian myth, *The Dispute Between Summer and Winter*, the farmer Enten (Winter), quarreled with his brother, the shepherd Emesh (Summer), as they brought offerings to the air god, Enlil, after completing their duties to increase the earth's bounty. But unlike Cain and Abel, the brothers settled their argument "in brotherhood and companionship," as Enten was chosen "farmer of the gods."

And the Lord had respect unto Abel and to his offering:
But unto Cain and to his offering he had not respect.

— Gen. 4:4-5

Daily offerings were brought to the gods to insure the prosperity of the crops or to atone for sins. The man in the net skirt, sometimes identified as the shepherd Dumuzi (*second from left*), and his servant, *following*, bring animals, fruits, and fish to the shrine of Inanna, symbolized by the gatepost with streamers (*far right*), on a late 4th millennium B.C. cylinder seal.

In the Hebrew ethic, offerings to God were acceptable only if presented with sincere devotion. Although no reason is given for God's refusal of Cain's offering, the importance of each individual's relationship to his God is established. A self-serving offering is evident from an alabaster statue from Telloh, 21st century B.C., dedicated by Gudea's son Ur-Ningirsu of Lagash, to his god Ningizzida. On the base (*right*), Semitic tributaries bring gifts. An inscription reads, "I am he who loves his god that he may prolong my life."

Evil Inclination

. . . sin coucheth at the door; and unto thee is its
desire, but thou mayest rule over it.   — Gen. 4:7

Fierce demons inhabited houses, the air, and the human body, according
to the Babylonians, who depicted such a creature on a terra cotta (*above*),
7th-6th centuries B.C. Such superstitions were retained by the Hebrews
who described sin as the demon at the door if Cain "doest not well." A
Babylonian incantation similarly refers to "an evil demon couching like an
ass, that lurketh in wait for the man." When God condemned Cain to be a
fugitive, he cried that it was more than he could bear. Besides the hazards
of brigandage on the open road, man feared the wicked spirits which
roamed the deserts, "scorching the wanderer like the day, and filling him
with bitterness." But whereas Babylonian priest-magicians exorcised
demons from the body with chants, spells, and amulets, the Hebrew
concept of individual responsibility obligated Cain to overcome his own
evil instincts and desires.

Divine Compassion

And the Lord set a mark upon Cain, lest any
finding him should kill him. — Gen. 4:15

The Babylonians believed that when a man sinned his god abandoned
him, allowing demons to enter his body. Although Cain was a
murderer, God did not desert him but protected him with his sign as
he wandered. Spilling Abel's blood on the ground caused it to be
cursed and all growth stopped, as in the Ugaritic *Tale of Aqhat* (*tablet
above*), 15th-14th centuries B.C., when the goddess Anat had young
Prince Aqhat slain in order to have his strong bow: ". . . through his
death . . ., the [fr]uits of summer are withered, the ear [in] its husk . . . .
Blasted are the buds." In Aqhat's tale, his sister Paghat swore, "I'll slay
the slayer of my brother, [Destroy] the [de]stroyer of my [si]bling."
Cain's divine protection was a Biblical indictment against such blood
feuds in which a family or tribe member sought to avenge the death of
a kinsman. Cain then settled in Nod "east of Eden."

Art and Morality

JABAL: the father of such as dwell in tents, and have cattle.
— Gen. 4:20

JUBAL: the father all such as handle the lyre and pipe.
— Gen. 4:21

TUBAL-CAIN: the forger of every cutting instrument of copper and iron.
— Gen. 4:22

The sons of Lamech, as named above, who were descendants of Cain, were credited with the arts and skills of civilization. In Sumerian myth, these were given to mankind by Enki, god of water, wisdom, and craftsmen. Bearded men from Asia transport such artifacts to Egypt, on a detail of a wall painting copy from the tomb of Khnumhotep (*above*), in Beni Hasan, Middle Egypt, 19th century B.C. These include a bow and throw stick (*left*), a lyre (*center*), and a bellows for metalworking (*right*), carried on donkey back. Despite these refinements, Cain's legacy of vengeance prevailed. Lamech invoked his name after killing a foe—"If Cain shall be avenged sevenfold, truly Lamech seventy and sevenfold," Gen. 4:24—in a form of taunt, an ancient poetic device used by an adversary usually before combat. The gold dagger and sheath, *right*, from a royal tomb of Ur, 3rd millennium B.C., show the high artistry of the weapons with which men now could kill each other in personal conflict and in war.

Abel's Tomb

In the rocky hills west of Damascus, a small white-domed shrine is held in special reverence by the Druse sect as the tomb of Abel, murdered in the fields by his jealous brother Cain.

Mount Ararat

The site in northeastern Turkey where the ark traditionally landed is called "the mountain of Noah" by its neighbors. It looms here over the Khor Virap church inside Armenia.

THE PATH OF THE FLOOD

In the Tigris and Euphrates Valleys where river flooding was common, a myth arose of a universal flood which destroyed mankind. The oldest version was written in Sumerian and found in Nippur on the lower third of a clay tablet, obverse (*above*), c. 1700 B.C. An expanded version of this "Deluge Tablet" later was written in Akkadian and was included as Tablet XI in the Babylonian *Epic of Gilgamesh*. While retaining the basic literary elements, the Biblical Flood became a moral parable. God finally accepts that "man's heart is evil from his youth" but, nevertheless, establishes his first covenant, assuring mankind that the cycles of the seasons and life on earth will continue, Gen. 8:22.

A fragment of the *Epic of Gilgamesh*, c. 1400 B.C., discovered in Megiddo, confirms that the flood tradition had reached Canaan. The change of the ark's resting place from Mount Nisir, east of the Tigris, to Mount Ararat (*facing page*), in the Bible, suggests that the Hurrians who were an important component both in the Ararat area and in Canaan were the literary transmitters.

The Reuses of Myth

God's decision to destroy the world of Noah was based on man's corruption and wickedness. The Sumerian and later Akkadian accounts give no such moral reason for the impending Flood.

> And God said unto Noah: "The end of all flesh
> is come before me; for the earth is filled with
> violence through them; and, behold, I will
> destroy them with the earth." — Gen. 6:13

> . . . a flood [will sweep] over the cult-centers;
> To destroy the seed of mankind. . . ,
> Is the decision, the word of the assembly [of the gods].
> — *Deluge Tablet*, Sumerian

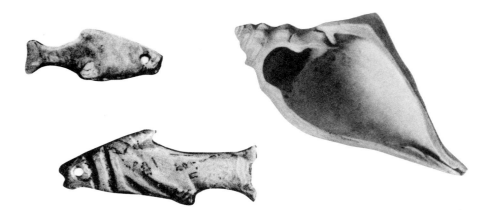

"Ziusudra, the king . . . humbly obedient," the god-fearing hero who survived the flood in the Sumerian version, might have resembled the clean-shaven Sumerian carrying a gazelle (*above*). The seal impression was found in Ziusudra's home city of Shuruppak, modern Fara (*left*), in the Fara II level, 29th-27th centuries B.C. The shell and fish artifacts from the site recall Shuruppak, named on the Sumerian King List as the fifth and last city to be founded before the flood. A two-foot alluvial layer uncovered in the city confirms that an actual inundation occurred, as it did at different times in Ur, Kish, and Nineveh. Such local flooding probably inspired the myth of one universal flood.

Noah's divine orders on loading the animals aboard the ark were specific. Utnapishtim, a hero of the *Epic of Gilgamesh*, received only vague directions.

> And of every living thing of all flesh, two of every sort shalt thou bring into the ark, to keep them alive with thee; they shall be male and female.
>
> — Gen. 6:19

> Aboard the ship take thou the seed of all living things.
>
> — *Epic of Gilgamesh*, Tablet XI
> Old Babylonian version

A roaring bull (*above*), possibly held by Gilgamesh, preceded by a pottery sheep and, traditionally, two traveling companions, all from Shuruppak, evoke a picture of the animals which Utnapishtim and Noah led onto their respective vessels. Contrary to divine orders, Utnapishtim took silver and gold with him. Noah boarded only what God had instructed. Although dubbed "the ark" by its excavators, a crafted boat (*right*), found in the Fara III level, 21st-20th centuries B.C., bears no resemblance to the Epic's seven-story cube or the Biblical three-story rectangular ark. A boatman navigated Utnapishtim's craft through a storm of six days and six nights. Noah's ark was guided through the Flood of forty days by the hand of God.

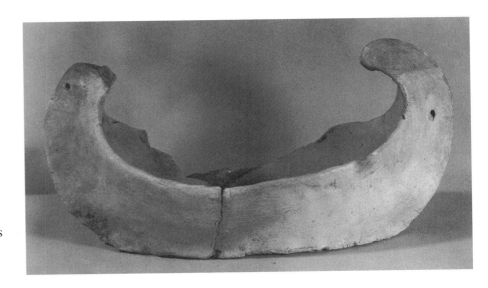

Be fruitful, and multiply, and replenish the earth.
—Gen. 9:1

Henceforth Utnapishtim and his wife shall be like unto us gods.
—*Epic of Gilgamesh*, Tablet XI

Detail, "Investiture of Zimri-Lim," Mari royal palace, 18th century B.C.

The Flood Remembered

[Comparative quotes of the Flood story in Genesis and the Babylonian *Epic of Gilgamesh*, Tablet XI, opposite page, and right, show the monotheistic intention of the Bible.]

(*Opposite page*): The dove which returned to Noah's ark with an olive leaf, indicating that the Flood waters had receded, became the symbol of peace between God and man. The righteous Noah, divinely chosen as the preserver of life, remained mortal, whereas Utnapishtim and, in the earlier Sumerian version, his counterpart, Ziusudra, who were saved by Enki from Enlil's intended annihilation of the human race, were rewarded with immortality and placed in a far-off land. With the same blessing which God gave to Adam, Noah and his sons were to populate the earth. But restrictions now were added. Man must abide by certain moral laws to respect the sanctity of life, for "in the image of God made He man," Gen. 9:6

THE TOKENS

As God chose the rainbow as the sign of his covenant with Noah, so the goddess Ishtar swore on her lapis necklace, such as those from Shuruppak of the Fara II period (*above, right*), to remember the Flood. In Genesis God promised never again to destroy the earth. After the Mesopotamian deluge, Enlil gave no such assurance. When Noah planted a vineyard, the curse on the ground caused by Adam and Eve's disobedience in Eden now ended. The earth once again would yield. Tradition attributes the invention of the plow to Noah. In Sumerian myth Enlil created the hoe. Nature's generative power is evident on an Akkadian cylinder seal from Tell Asmar (*right*), on which a vegetation god plows a heavenly field among symbols of the sun god.

And the bow shall be in the cloud;
And I will look upon it,
    that I may remember
    the everlasting covenant between God
    and every living creature of all flesh
    that is upon the earth.
        — Gen. 9:16

Ye gods here, as surely as this lapis
Upon my neck I shall not forget,
I shall be mindful of these days,
    forgetting (them) never,
        — *Epic of Gilgamesh*, Tablet XI

And Noah began to be a husbandman,
and he planted a vineyard. — Gen. 9:20

Cursed Be Canaan!

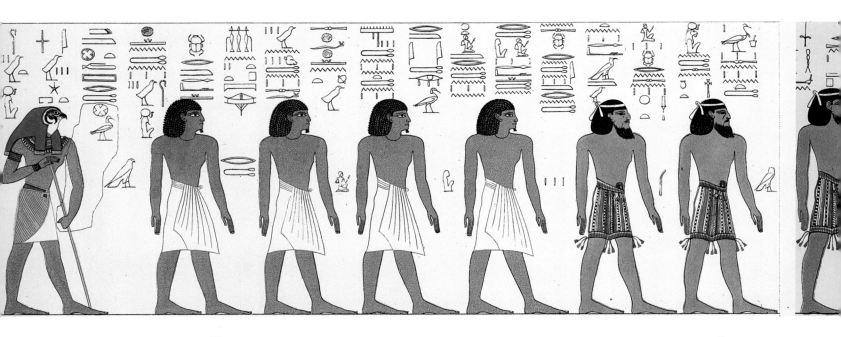

EGYPTIANS   CANAANITES

Noah's sons, Shem, Ham, and Japheth, and their descendants were the eponymous, or name-giving, ancestors of nations known to the Hebrews at that time. The four sons of Ham resemble the four ethnic groups in a procession (*above*), on a wall painting from the tomb of Seti I, c. 1289 B.C. They include, *left to right*: *Mizraim*, ruddy-skinned Egyptians; *Canaan*, bearded Canaanites; and, *facing page*, *Cush*, swarthy Nubians; and *Put*, richly-robed Libyans. The inferior status of Canaan as a "servant" to his brothers relates to the incident in which the disrespectful Ham saw his father drunk and naked but did not cover him, Gen. 9:22. Since God already had blessed Ham and his brothers after the Flood, Noah cursed Ham's son Canaan in his stead, the Biblical explanation for the origin of slavery and a warning to Israel to reject Canaan's pagan religious customs. After cursing Canaan, Noah blessed his oldest son, Shem, the progenitor of the Semites and the ancestor of Eber from whom Abraham would descend. The stage now was set and the genealogy established for the history of the Patriarchs to unfold.

After the Flood, the Hebrews believed that the nations of the world were related through Noah and his sons. In ethical terms, all men were brothers. The Table of Nations, *opposite*, "every one after his tongue, after their families, in their nations," Gen. 10:5, was based not only on geography and ethnicity but also on political and economic considerations. The sons of Japheth were the Indo-Europeans who settled throughout Asia Minor, the Aegean, parts of Europe, and eastward in Persia and India. Ham's sons, the Hamites, encompassed Africa and Arabia and lands familiar to the Patriarchs—Egypt, Canaan, and Shinar in southern Mesopotamia, the site of the Tower of Babel, and possibly included with the Hamites because of its trade contacts with the west. Shem's sons, the Semites, were from areas near Mesopotamia where the Hebrews traditionally originated: Elam, the Elamites northeast of the Persian Gulf; Asshur, the Assyrians; Arpachshad, the Chaldaeans; and Aram, the Aramaeans, called by Abraham "my country" and "my kindred."

NUBIANS   LIBYANS

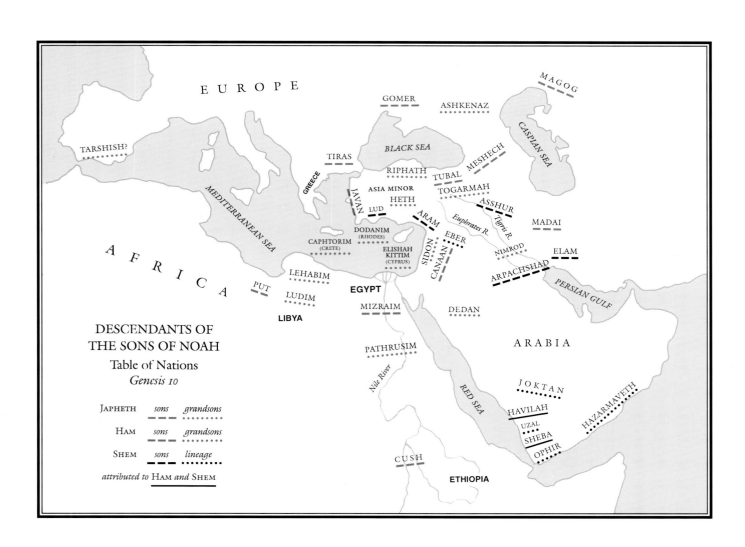

DESCENDANTS OF
THE SONS OF NOAH

Table of Nations
Genesis 10

JAPHETH	*sons*	*grandsons*
HAM	*sons*	*grandsons*
SHEM	*sons*	*lineage*

attributed to HAM *and* SHEM

THE TOWER OF BABEL

And the whole earth
  was of one language
  and of one speech.
    — Gen. 11:1

The whole universe,
  the people in unison,
  to Enlil in one
  tongue gave praise.
    — *Enmerkar and
      the Lord of Aratta*
    Sumerian poem

A prevalent belief in the ancient world was that once there had been one universal language, as quoted above. This boon to humanity in Genesis was annulled by God who confused all speech after men decided to build a city and a tower in direct defiance of the divine command after the Flood that they should "fill the earth," rather than settle in one place. The Biblical theme of man against God differed from the Sumerian god against god in the epic poem of Enmerkar (cuneiform fragment, *above*), a king of Uruk, 4th millennium BC. As men praised Enlil "in one tongue," it was the jealous water god, Enki, who disrupted the world with wars and conflict. On an Akkadian cylinder seal (*below*), gods battling, *center*, and hauling mortar up ladders to construct a building, *left-right*, recall the Babylonian Creation Epic when Marduk defeated the forces of chaos. His reward was the temple Esagila, the "house which lifts its head."

Come, let us build us a city, and a tower, with its top in heaven.   — Gen. 11:4

So the Lord scattered them
abroad from thence upon
the face of all the earth.
— Gen. 11:8

O Nanna,
Ur has been destroyed,
its people have been dispersed.
— *Lamentation Over the
Destruction of Ur*, 5th Song,
Sumerian poem

Because men defied God's will, they were scattered, quoted above, left, and their language confused. Thus Genesis explains the reason for polyglot humanity. The lament of the goddess Ningal, wife of Nanna, the moon god of Ur, as quoted above, right, from the cuneiform fragment, *center*, records another dispersion caused by the Elamite invaders who sacked Ur and then carried Nanna's statue to their city of Anshan.

With the story of the Tower of Babel, the universal history of Genesis 1-11 ends. Although the people were dispersed, they were not excluded from God's purpose. The focus narrows to one man, the Patriarch Abraham. As his migration begins a new destiny for his people, so the "peace" side of the royal Standard of Ur, 25th century B.C. (*below*), shows Sumerians transporting goods during a time of hope for the city.

So Abram departed, as the Lord had spoken unto him. — Gen. 12:4

UR (Tell Muqqayar)

Work on the site of Ur in southern Iraq, one of the great religious centers of ancient Sumer, began in 1922 under the direction of the English archaeologist, Sir Leonard Woolley (*right*), seen unearthing a limestone female statue from a wayside chapel in the city. Woolley led the Joint Expedition of the British Museum and the Museum of the University of Pennsylvania to Mesopotamia for twelve years, during which time he discovered the royal cemetery with its treasures and cleared the great ziggurrat (*opposite page*). His vivid sense of history and of the Bible is evident in his article reprinted in *The Great Archeologists*, ed. Edward Bacon, Illustrated London News and Martin Secker & Warburg Ltd., ©1976.

A Second "Tower of Babel":
The "House of the Mountain" at Ur
October 25, 1924

The Ziggurat of Babylon has been made famous to us by the Biblical story of the Tower of Babel and the confusion of tongues; and it was only one of many, for every great city of ancient Babylonia possessed a similar staged tower, and today the ruins of these are the most conspicuous features of the flat Euphrates Valley. But though they were so numerous, and though the chief of them had attained such renown, we knew very little about the form and appearance of these gigantic piles. So during last season in Mesopotamia, the Joint Expedition had for its main object the clearing of the Ziggurat of Ur, and for months a gang of about two hundred Arabs was busy carrying off the thousands of tons of broken brick and sand that concealed what was left of the ancient building. When we started there was only a mound higher and steeper than the other mounds that mark the site of the city; now there stands up four-square a huge mass of brickwork which may claim to be the most imposing monument in the land.

The normal ziggurat was a rectangular tower built in stages by superimposing a smaller cube upon a larger, so as to give something of the effect of a stepped pyramid; steps or a sloped ramp, led to the summit; and on the flat top of the upmost stage there stood a little shrine dedicated to the patron god of that particular city. At Ur this patron was the Moon God, Nannar, and his temple crowned a rather irregular building whose stages numbered three at one side and four at the other.

The original tower, as we know from inscriptions, was put up by Ur-Engur [*now called Ur-Nammu*], who was King of Ur about 2300 B.C., some three-hundred years before Abraham lived here; and the greater part, and the best preserved, of what survives today is the work of this early ruler . . . .

The whole structure, except for the shrine on the top, is solid throughout. The core is of mud-brick, the outer walls are kiln-burnt bricks laid in pitch (the "slime" of the writer in Genesis). These walls are provided with rows of "weeper holes" to allow any moisture in the core to drain away—otherwise the mud-brick would swell and

burst the retaining walls—and are relieved with the shallow panels characteristic of Sumerian architecture. The lower stages were painted black, the top stage was of brick fired a deep red, and the shrine was of bricks covered with a bright blue vitreous glaze. . . .

. . . the lower stage alone (Ur-Engur's work) is a solid mass of brickwork nearly 200 feet long by 150 feet broad and about 50 feet high. . .

. . . one may well ask whatever induced people to go to all this labor? The explanation seems to be this. The Sumerians, who are the authors of the ziggurats, came into Mesopotamia from somewhere in the northeast, a mountainous country where, like all mountain folk, they had worshiped mountain gods and had built their temples on the hilltops. When they moved down to the rich newly-formed plains of the river country, they must have been terribly upset to find that there was no hill whereon a temple could be built—and what was the use of a temple on level ground? God would never be at home in a house on the flat. So they set piously to work and built artificial mountains of brick where God might have his seat as of old on the holy hills. Primarily the ziggurat is a hill, yet no ordinary hill, but the throne of God, which is Heaven; so it takes a formal shape, is built up in those ascending stages which compose the upper and the lower heavens, and even its coloring reflects the celestial spheres; yet it remains a hill, as the name "House of the Mountain" clearly shows. And if, as certain inscriptions seem to imply, trees were planted round it, and even set in tubs on its terraces, the man-made ziggurat could not fail to recall to the Sumerians the highlands where once his fathers lived and the true nature of the gods he worshiped, bidding him lift up his eyes to the hills from which came his help.

The Ladders: On Earth, In Heaven

On the stele of Ur-Nammu, [currently under restoration], the ladder (*below, left*), was used by the builders of the ziggurat which the moon god, Nanna, commanded Ur-Nammu to construct (*see p. 42*). The ziggurat's stepped form was intended as such a ladder, or stairway, leading to the god's shrine at the highest level. This Sumerian view of the king before his god recalls Jacob's dream of a ladder reaching to the sky with angels ascending and descending and God standing above it. As the ziggurat linked heaven and earth, so the name Babel, site of the ill-fated Tower, reflects the folk etymology of Babylon as derived from two Akkadian words, *bab-ilum*, "the gate of the god."

III

CANAAN

Land Between Empires

—

CYRUS H. GORDON

CANAAN, AND SPECIFICALLY PALESTINE, is uniquely situated geographically. It is the only land bridge between the world's two largest continents, Asia and Africa, and, with Egypt, the only country with ports on both the Mediterranean and on the Red Sea. Canaan, then, is a crossroads between the two great continents and also a sea lane extending to the Indian Ocean. This made Palestine a great trading center, and it was trade more than anything else which determined the importance of that country. It is interesting to note that the word *kena*ani* in Hebrew means two things. It is both a proper noun meaning a person from the land of Canaan, defined as Syria-Palestine (including Lebanon), or a common noun meaning "merchant."

There were many contributors to the structure of civilization in Canaan: Semitic Amorites and Aramaeans, Indo-European Hittites from Anatolia, Aegean folk, and numerous others. This rich combination of cultural forces preconditioned Palestine to be the center of a high civilization. The Ebla tablets, as previously mentioned, show how cosmopolitan Syria-Palestine already was in the Early Bronze Age.

Egypt exerted a continuous influence on Canaan. Byblos was an Egyptian center since the Early Bronze Age. From this coastal city north of modern Beirut, Egypt secured the cedars of Lebanon, since the Nile Valley produced almost no timber for architecture and ship building. Egyptian texts, from the story of Sinuhe (pp. 95, 169), to the adventures of Wenamon (p.87), vividly describe Egyptian contacts with Syria-Palestine throughout the 2nd and 1st millenniums B.C.

By the Late Bronze Age, the tablets of Ugarit, 1400-1200 B.C., on the north coast of Syria, reflect a brilliant international civilization with close ties to Mesopotamia, Anatolia, Egypt, and the Aegean. From a series of expeditions begun by the French in Ugarit in 1929 have come clay tablets in cuneiform writing on which our alphabet made its first known appearance, arranged in essentially the same order as the Hebrews, the Greeks, the Romans, and we ourselves transmit it from generation to generation. Student scribes were using vocabularies in which each word was written in Sumerian, Akkadian, Hurrian, and the native Ugaritic dialect of Northwest Semitic. It is such an international background that produced a heightened awareness of the oneness of mankind and of the one deity acknowledged by the Hebrews as ultimately responsible for the entire universe. When Abraham and Isaac make covenants with the Philistines in Genesis, it is the one God of the whole universe who is invoked.

The question of Hebrew origins is complex. A federation of kindred Northwest Semitic tribes, schematized as the "twelve tribes of Israel," conquered the land of Canaan by the early

12th century B.C. and accepted each other as forming one people sharing a common past and future.* They confronted and absorbed a number of earlier inhabitants, the Semitic Canaanites and Amorites, non-Semitic Hurrians and Hittites, and still others. From the Ugaritic documents of the first half of the 13th century B.C., we know, for instance, that the ambitious Hittite kings sent merchants through Canaan in order to look after commercial interests. It was from the Hittites in Hebron that Abraham purchased the Cave of Machpelah to bury his dead.

The conquering Hebrews occupied whatever parts of the country they could, notably the sparsely populated hill country of Judah, developing this available land agriculturally. For quite some time they could not occupy the coastal strip controlled by the Philistines and other Sea Peoples, nor the great walled cities held by the Canaanites.

That the Hebrews borrowed much from the people in Canaan is clear from the tablets unearthed at Ugarit. The language of the Hebrews, which we call "Hebrew," was not the original language of Abraham. His native language would have been Aramaic (as it was spoken throughout the region, including the land of his kinsmen in Padan-aram, and in Canaan with the coming of the Aramaeans in the 11th century B.C.). The Hebrews adopted the language of Canaan. In the Bible, the Hebrew language is never called "Hebrew," although it can be called "the speech of Canaan" or "Judaean." The Hebrews also borrowed the ABC, the alphabet which is first attested at Ugarit. The Amarna letters found in Akhetaten, the capital of Akhenaten, the heretic pharaoh, are also of special interest to Hebraists for the history of the Hebrew language. Very often the scribes render words into the language of Canaan, which, for all intents and purposes, is the same as Biblical Hebrew recorded as it was pronounced around 1400 B.C.

The literary forms, including poetic structures of the Old Testament, are anticipated in Ugaritic, while the literary documents themselves foreshadow the themes and ethical content of the Patriarchal narratives. There are two epic texts, one having to do with a king called Kret, whose name reflects his connections with the island of Crete. Part of the story of Kret is that his dynasty is threatened with extinction. With the blessing of the gods, he and his destined bride produce the next generation so that the dynasty can go on. This feature of the importance of family continuity is very prominent in the Patriarchal narratives of Genesis, where the birth of the heir is crucial and, against all odds, is made possible through the intervention of God. Abraham, the ancestor of King David, must sire his legitimate successor

---

*Ed. note: In addition to a military conquest, current theories of Israelite origins in Canaan during Iron Age I include a peaceful infiltration into the central hill country (p.38), or an internal peasant revolt against oppressive urban overlords.

through his noble bride, Sarah. Hagar, whom the barren Sarah had given to Abraham to be the surrogate for her, had borne Ishmael. However, as we know from the tablets of Nuzi, east of the middle Tigris, a handmaid's child had to give way as chief heir to the real child of the noble wife if the latter eventually bore a son to her husband.

The other epic is that of a hero named Dan'el. The name has the same meaning as Daniel, but is spelled Dan'el, meaning "the god El is judge." Dan'el fathered a son named Aqhat. But Dan'el, a wise and virtuous king, loses his son through the malevolence of the goddess Anat. Although the text is not preserved completely, there is reason to think that after being killed by Anat, Aqhat was restored to life.

In that epic, Dan'el performs his duty as a ruler by showing kindness to the under-dog, specifically to the widow and the orphan. In the ancient Near East, including Ugarit, defending the weaker in any conflict between the weaker and stronger is the duty of kings. What the Hebrews did was to make this royal obligation the duty of the common man. According to the Prophets of the Old Testament, it is not only the king who is to defend the widow, orphan, and victim in any conflict of interest, but all of us. Social justice, which is what God demands of us according to Scripture, is the duty of every single individual. Such a beautiful, even if unattainable, ideal is something the Hebrews took over from the Canaanites and other neighbors and extended from the ruling class to the entire community.

The gods worshiped by the Ugaritians included El, the head of the pantheon. El is also a common name of the God of Israel, although he sometimes has other names, like Elohim or Yahweh. In addition to the God of Israel, numerous other gods are mentioned, and, indeed, they were worshiped in Ugarit. These deities appear in the Old Testament as those one should not worship. Among them are Baal, Asherah, who was the consort of El, and even Reshef, the god of death and evil. These are not part of the official Old Testament religion. Howev-er, they are vestiges of the pagan past and are often invoked for literary effect, just as in West-ern Christian literature the gods of the Greeks and the Romans may be mentioned and invoked as part of our literary past.

At Ugarit, there was a developed fertility cult because the productivity of the land was uncertain. Blights caused by locust plagues, and especially by droughts, could have a devas-tating effect on the welfare of the whole society. Accordingly, there were rites bringing about the fertility of the land. Part of these rites included letting the soil lie fallow every seventh year. The rites of the fertility cult were to a great extent taken over by the Hebrews upon entering the land of Canaan. They also succumbed to "abominations," such as idol worship, spouses committing adultery, or daughters given to harlotry. The reaction against them per-meates Scripture, especially in the Prophets, such as Hosea and Ezekiel.

To be sure, the Hebrew reactions against the Canaanites were strong. For one thing, the Hebrews rejected the exaggerated materialism of Canaanite commercial society. Such conditions are reflected in Canaan during the 11th century B.C., the period of the Judges, in the story of the Egyptian Wenamon, who was sent on a mission to Lebanon in order to get timber for reconstructing the sacred boat of Amon-Re. After demanding the respect of the princes in Lebanon where the cedar trees grew, Wenamon makes the statement that all of this belongs to his god, Amon-Re, king of the gods. The prince of Byblos there tells him that he realizes that Amon-Re is the master of the universe who founded all lands and agrees to give Wenamon, his representative, the wood, provided he has the cash: "If you pay me for doing it, I will do it." Nothing was going to be extended on credit. Whatever reputation Amon-Re had, it was not prized as highly as gold or silver. The tale also indicates not only the decline of Egyptian prestige but an element of lawlessness, as Wenamon was robbed aboard his ship in the Palestinian seaport of Dor.

The dictatorship of the king also was opposed by the Hebrews. We find such absolute rule in Ugarit where the kings gave and took away at will without any court of appeal. People in Canaanite city-states were not consulted when a new king was to be chosen from a royal line. The Hebrews, on the other hand, established their ideal of a balance of power in society in which priests, Prophets, wise men, elders, land owners, and, indeed, the general citizenry all had their input. When Solomon died, the ten tribes of northern Israel rejected his son Rehoboam because he refused to offer the people a less oppressive regime.

Human sacrifice was anathema to the Hebrews, especially the sacrifice of the first-born, which continued among the Canaanites in their colonies, such as Carthage, into late Roman times in order to propitiate their deities and induce them to grant abundant progeny. Abraham's sacrifice of a ram instead of Isaac reflects the Hebrew break with such human sacrifice.

It would be a mistake to imagine that the Hebrew abolition of these abuses, including the sacrificing of innocent babies, was sudden. The Prophets had plenty to complain about—and they did complain. Two kings of Judah, Ahaz and Manasseh, sacrificed their children ritually. But the reaction started very early. Through a long polemic and battle against Canaanite excesses, the Hebrews eventually purified their religion and social usages.

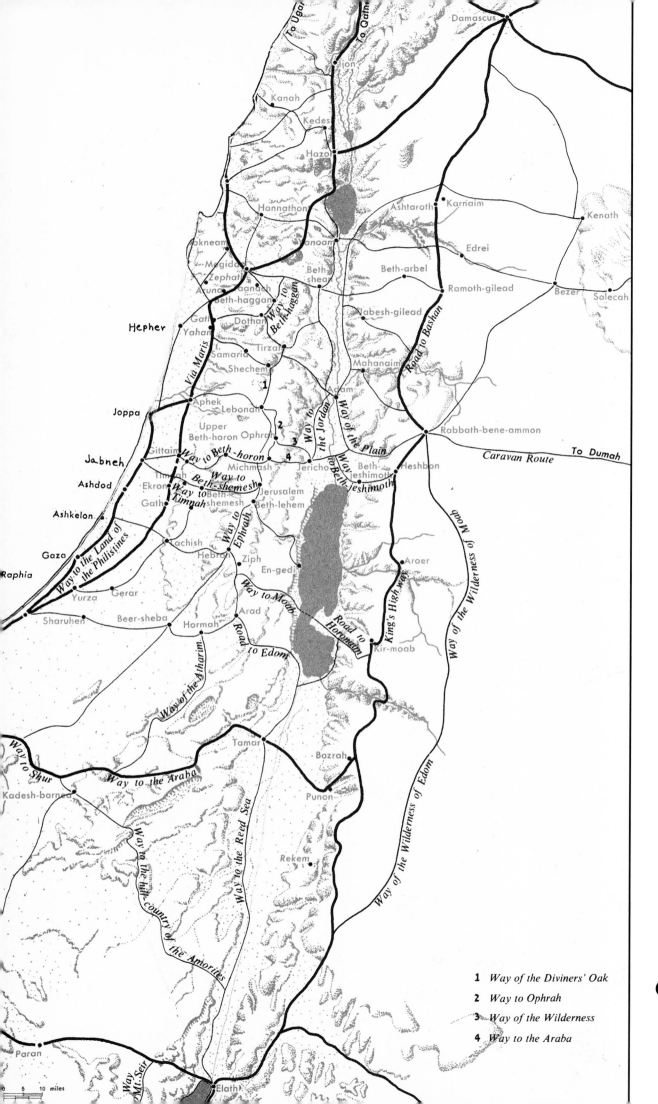

To Ugar
To Qatn
Damascus

ion

Kanah

Kedes

Hazor

Ashtaroth   Karnaim   Kenath
Hannathon

kneam   Edrei
Megiddo   Beth-arbel
Zephat   Beth-   Bezer   Salecah
Aruna aanah   shean   Ramoth-gilead
Beth-haggan   Way to   Jabesh-gilead
Beth-haggan

Hepher   Gath   Road to Bashan
Yaham   Dothan
Tirzah   Mahanaim

Samaria
Shechem

1

Aphek   Lebonah
Joppa   Upper
Beth-horon Ophrah   Rabbath-bene-ammon
2   To Dumah
3   Caravan Route
Gittaim Way to Beth-horon   4
Jabneh   Michmash   Beth-   Heshbon
Way to   Jericho jeshimoth
Ashdod   Ekron Way to Beth-shemesh   Way to Beth-jeshimoth
Gath   Beth-   Jerusalem
Ashkelon   Timnah shemesh   Beth-lehem

Lachish
Gaza   Way to the Land of   Hebron
Raphia   the Philistines   Ziph
En-gedi   Aroer
Way to Moab

Yurza   Gerar   Arad
Sharuhen   Beer-sheba   Hormah
Road to Edom   Kir-moab

Tamar   Bozrah

Way to Shur   Punon
Kadesh-barnea   Way to the Araba

Rekem

Paran

Elath

0   5   10 miles

1   Way of the Diviners' Oak

2   Way to Ophrah

3   Way of the Wilderness

4   Way to the Araba

CANAAN

PREFACE
The Antiquity of Written Tradition

From two areas of Syria, called "the least excavated region of the ancient Near East," have come the coveted archaeological prize—written records. The archives of Ebla (Tell Mardikh), found in the royal palace (*above*), and dating from the second half of the 24th century B.C., were written in a languge now called Eblaite. They confirm the existence of a written tradition in the region a thousand years earlier than previously thought. The name "Canaan" in the archives is the oldest written designation of that land yet found. Both the tablets from Ebla, and from Ugarit (Ras Shamra), *following page*, where a thirty-sign alphabetic script was developed a millennium later, reveal highly organized Semitic city-states in political and commercial contact with their powerful neighbors. The names of such gods as El and Baal and the epic theme of the divine promise of a son to a barren wife later appear in the Bible, which was composed from an oral and written tradition in the 1st millennium B.C.

UGARIT

The Ingathering of Noah's Descendants:

Mizraim (Egypt), son of Ham.

A sphinx sent by Amenemhet III of the 12th Dynasty, 1842-1794 B.C., found at the entrance to the temple of Baal, indicates the favor shown to Ugarit by the pharaohs of the Middle Kingdom who sought commercial markets and security beyond their northern frontier. The Biblical journey to Egypt first was taken by Abram and later by the sons of Jacob in times of famine. It was Hagar the Egyptian who bore Abram his first son.

Javan (Ionia), son of Japheth.

In Ugarit near the north Syrian coast, a French archaeological team unearthed remains of a cosmopolitan city, where ancient nations met to trade and seek diplomatic advantage.

Aegean civilization reached the Levant through energetic sea traders from mainland Greece and the islands. This fragment (*left*), of a Cypro-Mycenaean krater, 14th-13th centuries B.C., showing two warriors with swords, was found in Ugarit's nearby port of Minet el-Beida. These sea routes were followed by the invading Sea Peoples of Aegean origin, identified in Gen. 26:15 as the hostile Philistines who stopped up Isaac's wells in Gerar.

— to the Fourth Generation

It was against such a backdrop of Ugarit's ethnic diversity, reminiscent of Noah's family and the many languages of Babel, that the lives of the Patriarchs evolved in Canaan.

Heth (Hatti), son of Canaan, grandson of Ham.

The commercial interests of the Hittite kings in the north were represented abroad by merchants traveling under their protection. On a seal impression (*above*), Ini-Teshup, king of Carchemish (*center, right,*), faces the weather god who is standing on a bull. Damages are claimed against Ugarit for a Hittite merchant slain in the city. It was from Ephron the Hittite that Abraham purchased the field of Machpelah in Hebron for a burial ground.

Nimrod (Babylonia), son of Cush, grandson of Ham.

Traditional Babylonian presentation scenes were used on the dynastic seals of Ugarit's kings, confirming the important cultural influence of Mesopotamia. King Niqmad II, 14th century B.C., used this seal (*right*), dating four hundred years prior to his reign, as proof of the antiquity of his dynasty and right to kingship. Due to their close clan ties to Mesopotamia, the Patriarchs took wives from Haran rather than from alien Canaan.

THE GREAT GOD EL

God and king interacting for the common good was a theme of the Ugaritic epics, indicating a moral atmosphere conducive to the evolving Hebrew ethic in Canaan. The wise El, head of the Canaanite pantheon, counseled the king in war and peace through the medium of dreams. In turn, the king rendered justice to the widow and orphan and, as the "son of El," performed priestly rituals. This closeness of man to the divine is suggested on a stele, *above*, 14th century B.C., from Ras Shamra, site of ancient Ugarit, as the enthroned El (*right*), receives an offering from a dignitary, possibly the king of Ugarit. In his role as merciful creator, the name of El was assimilated by the Patriarchs with the ancestral God of their fathers.

> Your decree, El, is wise, your wisdom is everlasting.
> A life of good fortune is your decree.
>
> — *The Palace of Baal*

Although the name and attributes of El in the Ugaritic epics also reflect in Genesis, the two differ in their concept of godhead. The Ugaritic El not only interacted with mortals but with the gods whom he created. In Genesis, the one God of Creation is Elohim, a plural of El, connoting totality. Although God's relationship with humankind was personal and caring, he transcended all living creatures, which were created by his will.

In the Ugaritic epic, quoted above, despite El's exalted position as head of the divine assembly whose word was final, his strong-willed daughter, Anat, threatened him mercilessly if he did not grant her beloved Baal a house like the other gods which would assure his place in the pantheon:

> I shall [surely] drag him
>   like a lamb to the ground,
> [I shall make] his gray hairs
>   [run] with blood,
> the gray hairs of his beard
>   [with gore] . . .

Such disrespect to the great El contrasts with the awe and devotion of Abraham to Elohim who commanded him to sacrifice his son Isaac in the land of Moriah. In the Akedah, or "binding" of Isaac, Gen. 22:1–18, because Abraham did not withhold his son, God promised that his descendants would be as numerous as the stars and that they would triumph over their foes.

A remnant of Canaanite mythology in Genesis is seen in the name of El Elyon (God Most High), whom the priest-king, Melchizedek of Jerusalem, acknowledged as the creator of heaven and earth, Gen. 14:19. In extra-Biblical sources, El and Elyon are two different Canaanite gods. Their combined names in Genesis disassociate them from pagan tradition while reinforcing the idea of one cosmic creator. It was only in the worship of an ancestral deity (the God of the Fathers), that both traditions were similar. In the Ugaritic story of Aqhat, the worthy Dan'el pleaded to the gods for a son who would "stand as a steward of his father's god." In the Patriarchal narratives, the tribal God is respectively called "the God of Abraham," "the Fear of Isaac," and "the Mighty One of Jacob."

A familiar mythological theme is that of the competition between the gods. El's prominence in the Ugaritic texts often seems eclipsed by the vigorous Baal, the Rider of the Clouds, upon whose favor the welfare of farmers, sea traders, and fishermen depended. The Hebrew concept of one all-powerful God eliminated such divine rivalry. When God revealed to Moses that his name was Yahweh, although he was known to the Patriarchs as El Shaddai (God Almighty), Exodus 6:3, the monotheistic continuity intended by the Biblical writers was confirmed. The names by which God was called might differ in different times, but it was the same God, all-knowing and unchallenged, bestowing his beneficence from father to son.

"IT WAS A GOOD LAND . . ."

As a land bridge between the civilizations of the ancient Near East, Canaan was a melting pot of clans and cultures. The well-watered Bekaa Valley (*left*), between the Lebanon and Anti-Lebanon Mountains, was described as such a crossroads in an Egyptian manuscript of the Middle Kingdom by Sinuhe, a royal official who found refuge there during a time of political unrest. "It was a good land," he claimed, and in familiar Biblical terms added, "Plentiful was its honey. . . and milk prepared in every way." Sinuhe lived among Amorite tribesmen, frequently offered hospitality to messengers from Egypt, and advised his adopted tribe how to deal with the troublesome heqau-khasut, the "rulers of foreign lands." This is the earliest reference to the presence in Canaan of the Hyksos who conquered Egypt in the 17th century B.C. and ruled for one hundred years during the 2nd Intermediate Period. Genesis 15:19-21 confirms the diversity of people in the region. Besides the Canaanite and Amorite, Abraham lived among the Kenite, Kenizzite, Kadmonite, Hittite, Perizzite, Rephaim, Girgashite, and Jebusite.

A View
of the Amorites

The weapon is his companion,
who eats uncooked meat,
who knows no submission,
who has no house in his lifetime,
who does not bury his dead
companion.

A Sumerian hymn derides as crude the Amorites, or "westerners", who were part of the great migrations which occurred in the lands of the Fertile Crescent at the end of the 3rd millennium B.C. A battle scene of that date from Mari on the middle Euphrates (*left*), reflects the unrest which the Amorites provoked in the settled cities. A spear carrier, *foreground*, stands behind a curved reed screen. An archer following him aims high at a naked, fallen enemy. Against this background of migration, the journey of Abram from Haran in upper Mesopotamia southwest to Canaan often is placed. As a major cause of the fall of the Third Dynasty of Ur, the Amorites extended their influence from the Mediterranean Sea to the Persian Gulf. They founded the First Babylonian Dynasty by the 19th century B.C., gradually changing the concept of the city-state to that of a broad territorial rule. Trade relations were expanded, and in international politics, swiftly shifting alliances were commonplace. The Amorites populated northern Syria and the central hill country of Canaan. In Genesis they are identified in turn as Abram's allies in his foray against the four kings of the east, Gen.14, and later remembered by Jacob on his deathbed as his enemies, Gen. 48:22, when he first returned to Canaan with his family. It was the "iniquity of the Amorites," Gen. 15:16, which justified the divine legacy of Canaan to the Hebrews.

(*Facing page*) Remains of Amorite dwellings, such as this Middle Bronze Age house and circular courtyard in central Sinai, indicate migrations much further south than the Biblical borders of "Gerar unto Gaza," Gen. 10:19.

BEGINNING OF
INTERNATIONAL TRADE

The massive walls of Byblos, modern Jubayl on the Lebanese coast, were built around the residential area, c. 2800 B.C., to protect it from nomadic incursions. In keeping with the ancient tradition that the gods established cities, Philo of Byblos, 2nd century A.D., citing an earlier Phoenician source, wrote that the god El encircled his habitation with walls, thus founding Byblos. The Egyptians developed a flourishing sea trade with Byblos by the 3rd millennium B.C., as they imported the coveted cedar wood for their temples and tombs. These inhospitable walled cities would have been avoided by the nomadic Hebrews who sought the sparsely populated central hill country to the south where they could graze their flocks in peace and remain culturally separate from the Canaanites.

The Sea Routes

Phoenician merchant ships were important agents by which the products and cultures of the Levant were spread abroad. On a single mast ship with a square sail, sailors prepare to unload cargo and storage jars at the city quay, as shown on a Theban tomb painting of the 18th Dynasty. In exchange for Lebanese cedars, Egypt sent papyrus to Byblos which then was exported to Greece. The word "Bible" derives from the Greek *bublos*, named after Byblos, referring to the papyrus scroll.

Peaceful commercial relations often were followed by militant ambitions. The cedars which were exported from Byblos to Egypt later were demanded as tribute by Seti I, 1289-1278 B.C., after he established an eastern empire in Asia. On a wall relief from the great hypostyle hall in the temple of Amon at Karnak, two chiefs of the Lebanon pay homage to Seti while others behind them haul down a leafy tree. The timber is specified for the "great river barge" and "big flagstaves of Amon."

The Land Routes

Where is Raphia. . . How many leagues march is it to Gaza?
— Papyrus Anastasi I, 13th century B.C.

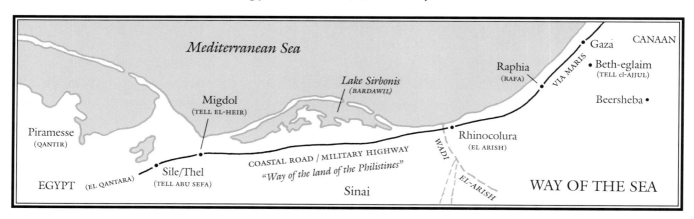

The 140-mile corridor in the northern Sinai between El Qantara in Egypt and Gaza in Canaan linked the destinies of the two countries. It was the Biblical Way of the Land of the Philistines. The Romans called it the Via Maris, or Way of the Sea. Following the Canaanite coast northward a few miles inland, the road divided at Megiddo overlooking the Valley of Jezreel, where two eastern branches continued their separate ways toward Damascus and on to Mesopotamia. Canaan's location between Egypt and Mesopotamia made it a strategic objective in the military campaigns of these great powers. In the early 13th century B.C., Seti I expanded a line of fortresses with cisterns along the Sinai road in an attempt to recover the Egyptian empire in Asia. These are lettered on a drawing of a relief from the northern wall of the great hypostyle hall in the temple of Amon at Karnak (*below*), which shows Seti returning from a successful foray against marauding Semites, here called "Shasu." With his captives in tow, Seti approaches the fortress of Thel (Sile) [B], synonymous with the "Ways-of-Horus," built on both sides of a crocodile-infested canal [A], named *ta-denit*, the "dividing waters," which separated Egypt from the desert. Station [C] is unnamed. Other fortresses [D to H], vary in size, some with palm groves and others with garden ponds. Jubilant Egyptians on the far side of the canal prepare to greet Seti who has triumphed "by the might of his father, Amon."

(*Following page*): Merchant caravans, royal messengers, and armies made their way in both directions along the Sinai road, where shifting sands today encroach on scrub, fig, and palm trees. In times of famine, the Patriarchs would have followed its track to the Nile Delta for sustenance.

Spheres of Influence

The extent of Egypt's presence in western Asia is inferred from the cursive hieratic inscription on a clay figurine of a bound prisoner found in Saqqara, 19th century B.C. In these so-called Execration Texts are Semitic names of chiefs and their city-states from the southern coast of Palestine to central Syria. The artifact is believed to have been buried by the Egyptians in a symbolic act of controlling or destroying their enemies, real or potential, beyond their borders. A reflection of such political reality is seen in Genesis 14 when the four powerful eastern overlords faced a rebellion of five vassal kings from the Valley of Siddim in the area of the Dead Sea.

(*opposite*): The cities mentioned in the Execration Texts were connected by the well-worn roads of Canaan. Ashkelon, on the route later called the Via Maris, was linked inland to Hazor by an eastern branch which ran through Megiddo and up along the west shore of the Sea of Galilee. On the north-south road in the central hill country were Jerusalem and Shechem, cities familiar to the Patriarchs.

Along the Via Maris

Ashkelon: southern seaport.

Hazor: gateway to Damascus.

On the North-South Road

Jerusalem: Jebusite city.

Shechem: Canaanite religious center.

Cross-Cultures of Art

Canaanite craftsmen combined the art motifs of Mesopotamia and Egypt
to produce such masterworks as this gold foil dagger sheath and handle,
found in the Temple of the Obelisks in Byblos, 19th-18th centuries B.C.
The local artisan expanded the traditional Mesopotamian hunt theme of a
lion attacking a stag to include two kneeling figures accompanied by an
unusual coterie of a baboon, dog, and fish, approaching the mounted
king (*left*). The handle features Reshef, the pest god, wearing an Egyptian-
style tunic and collar, and the high Phoenician cap called the *lebbadé*.

Cross-Cultures of Religion

The sea lanes of the Mediterranean formed a bridge between the civilizations of Egypt and Byblos. On a drawing of a cylinder seal (*above*), of the 3rd millennium B.C., found in the temple of the goddess Baalat in Byblos, the use of simplified hieroglyphs was an attempt to imitate Egyptian customs and phrases. The ruler for whom the seal was made is here "given life eternally" and is "beloved by" three deities:

> Baalat, Lady of Byblos (seated, *upper right corner*), wearing the solar disk and horned headdress of the Egyptian goddess Hathor. The tilted hieroglyph probably was due to a spacing problem of the artist.

> The foreign sun-(god), whom the Egyptians knew as Re, represented by the sun sign beneath Baalat's chair, and

> Kha'taw, god of Negau, a forested area near Byblos, (*signs in upper left corner*).

A millennium later, Zakar-Baal, a prince of Byblos, admitted to the visiting Egyptian Wenamon that Egypt had taught his country all it knew of craftsmanship and learning.

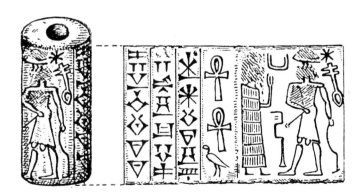

Along the caravan routes from Mesopotamia to Egypt, men brought their gods and symbols with them. Such a cultural mix is seen on a drawing of a rolled out cylinder seal, 18th century B.C., from Taanach on the trade and military highway in Canaan's Jezreel Valley. In the cuneiform text, Atanah-ili, son of Habsi, proclaims himself the servant of Nergal, the Babylonian pest god. Two Egyptian *ankhs*, the life symbol, and a bird bringing a good wish decorate the seal's center. To their right, a priestly figure in a long Babylonian robe, with hand raised, faces a god in Egyptian dress, holding a rod and ritual sickle. The Canaanite equivalent of Nergal was Reshef, whose cult was among those brought to Egypt by Asiatic prisoners after the successful campaigns of the 18th Dynasty pharaohs in the east.

The warrior kings of Canaan maintained their independence by skillful diplomatic maneuvering between the Egyptians and Hittites—and the use of force when necessary. Such conflict was mirrored in Ugaritic mythology by the battle of the storm god, Baal, with the sea god, Yamm, for divine kingship. From Ugarit come two scenes confirming the warlike aspects of both the king and Baal, patron god of the city. On an ivory bed panel (*opposite page*), from the royal palace, the king draws his sword on a fallen enemy who pleads for mercy. This ivory of the 14th century B.C. could represent Ugarit's King Niqmad II and one of the three invading rulers from the north whom he repulsed with the help of a Hittite army. A limestone stele (*right*), of the early 2nd millennium B.C., found in the sanctuary of the temple of Baal, shows the bellicose storm god wielding a mace over his head while protecting the small figure of the king before him. Baal's fertility attributes are the bull horns on his helmet and the branching thunderbolt, which he holds in his left hand. An image of God as a divine warrior is implied in Gen. 15:1 after Abram defeated the four kings of the east. In words symbolic of battle, God promised the Patriarch, "I am thy shield, thy reward shall be exceedingly great."

THE IMPORTANCE OF SONS

Divinely Promised Progeny — from — the Ugaritic Epics

(*Opposite page*): The basic aim of the family in Canaan was to provide sons who would assist their fathers in worldly pursuits and honor their memories beyond the grave. Sons were particularly desired by hereditary kings who wished them to continue the ruling succession. In an intimate domestic scene from the ivory bed panel of Ugarit's palace, the king embraces his wife, whose rounded abdomen is thought to confirm their hopes for an heir to the throne. A pervading theme of the Ugaritic epics is the divine promise of progeny to kings whose royal line was in danger of extinction. In Genesis this theme is reflected in God's promise to grant Abraham a son to be miraculously conceived by the barren Sarah well beyond childbearing age, Gen. 17:16.

To Kret

After the seven sons of Kret died in a series of misfortunes, the god El came to him in a dream. The wise El, believed to be represented on a stone statuette (*left*), from Ugarit, 14th-13th centuries B.C., advised Kret to raise an army, march to King Pabil of Udm, and demand his daughter, the fair Huray, in marriage. Kret confirmed El's promise:

> . . .because El in my dream has granted, the father of mankind in my vision, the birth of a family to Kret and a boy to the servant of El.

To Dan'el

Baal intervened with El on behalf of Dan'el who had no son. El thereupon gave him specific instructions:

> . . . his couch let him mount [ ];
>   as he kisses his wife
>   as he embraces her let
>   her become pregnant
> [ ] let her be with child; . . .
> so that he may have a son [in (his)
>   house],
> [offspring] within his palace. . .

THE IMPORTANCE OF
THE EARTH'S FERTILITY

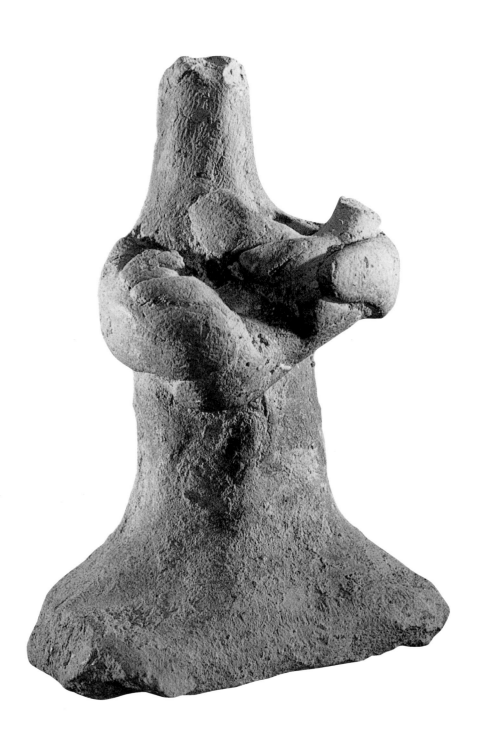

In the pagan, agricultural society of Canaan, the people's obsession with human and animal procreation gave rise to fertility cults and intricate rituals related to the seasonal cycles of the year. A pottery sculpture of a mother goddess and child (*left*), of the Early Canaanite period, from Beth-yerah, a developed agricultural area south of Tiberias, was an amulet, or votive offering, expressing the anxiety of its owner confronting the mysteries of life and birth. To the farmer, the productivity of the earth on which his subsistance depended came from life-giving waters. Divinities were worshiped who inhabited springs, wells, and high places where the clouds stored the rain dispensed by the storm god, Baal. Most fortunate would have been these two farmers standing with their oxen, on this terracotta figurine (*facing page*), 2nd millennium B.C., from Byblos, where plentiful rainfall off the northern coast made the hinterland fertile. The "strange gods" buried by Jacob in Shechem when he returned to Canaan, Gen. 35:4, were probably similar to the fertility idols which proliferated in the ancient world. But it was by divine fiat, and not with benefit of idols, that Jacob, now called Israel, would be fruitful, multiply, and be the father of nations.

UGARIT (Ras Shamra)

A flourishing commercial crossroads between Mesopotamia and the Mediterranean and Aegean civilizations, Ugarit, off the north Syrian coast, was excavated by Claude F.A. Schaeffer, the director of the French Archaeological Expedition to Ras Shamra, from 1931-1939, and 1949-1969. Schaeffer (*right*), examines a cache of bronze tools and weapons found under the dwelling of the high priest. Also in the priest's library and in the archives of the palace, literary texts on clay tablets from the 14th century B.C. were found written in the earliest alphabetic script in Ugaritic, a Semitic language akin to Hebrew. The contents and significance of the tablets as a witness to Canaan's religion are discussed, below, in Schaeffer's book, *The Cuneiform Texts of Ras Shamra-Ugarit*, originally delivered as the Schweich Lectures of the British Academy in 1936, and published by Oxford University Press, London, 1939.

"The Religious Texts of Ras Shamra: Their Bearing on Old Testament Studies"

Ras Shamra-Ugarit, by reason of its position, is certainly one of the richest sites and most productive of historical information ever excavated. It was during the reign of King Nigmed, [mid-2nd millennium B.C.], that a college of learned priests existed, where the poetical works and myths of the ancient Canaanites or proto-Phoenicians were recorded on clay tablets to be preserved in the library. These hitherto unknown texts of Ugarit shed a vivid light on the origin of the Phoenicians, their myths and their ancestral legends. More than that, what we dared not hope for, we now have external evidence of the value of some of the Patriarchal legends of the Israelites.

The modern school of Biblical criticism has admitted that the Canaanites were ignorant of the art of writing previous to the end of the 2nd millennium B.C. From this it appeared that very little reliance could be placed on their Patriarchal stories. It was supposed that these were handed down by oral tradition and in consequence largely altered and robbed of historical value.

The religious texts found at Ras Shamra compel us radically to alter this opinion. They prove conclusively that the Canaanites were familiar with writing from the middle of the 2nd millennium B.C. Moreover, these documents show that from the 14th century B.C. the Canaanites possessed a literary tradition even then far from its origin.

To us, influenced until now by the judgment of the Prophets of Israel, Canaanite civilization has appeared as backward and enveloped in a thick fog of barbarism. The fame of their depravity seemed well established. One remembers the vices attributed to the inhabitants of Sodom and Gomorrah, which justified the destruction of their cities by fire of Jehovah.

The tone of moral indignation which pervades the judgment of Israelites is obviously tinged by the desire to injure their adversary at all costs. With the same interests at stake these accusations are as biased as were the criticisms leveled at the pagan world by certain Christian historians. As it is, the Ras Shamra texts reveal

RAS SHAMRA: An airview of the tell after the 7th season, 1935.
Left (1), the temple of Baal. Center (2) the library. Right (3), the temple of Dagon, the god of the city.

a literature of a high moral tone tempered with order and justice.

One must also acknowledge that the Canaanites were not lacking in that religious feeling so splendidly developed among the Israelites. The piety of certain people in the Ras Shamra texts is equal to that of Abraham. The traditions, culture, and religion of the Israelites are bound up inextricably with the early Canaanites. The compilers of the Old Testament were fully aware of this, hence their obsession to break with such a past and to conceal their indebtedness to it.

At the head of the Canaanite pantheon, was the god El. His supremacy is a clear indication of a monotheistic tendency in the Canaanite religion. In the story (*Baal and Mot*), Latpon, a kind of divine herald, announces the death of Baal and Aliyan.* He then pronounces the ritual mourning, rigorously laid down in the rules of the Hebrew *Qinah*, such as we hear spoken by Jacob, when his sons tell him of the death of Joseph. And like the Patriarch, he ends his dirge with this decision: "I will go down into the

earth." The same text states that as a sign of mourning the Ras Shamra gods sprinkled dust on their heads, precisely as in the Bible.

In short, the analogies, cited here and many perforce omitted, between the Ras Shamra religious legends and the narratives of the Israelite Patriarchs are so striking that one can no longer doubt the antiquity of the latter.

The danger is the tendency to distort the texts in the hope of finding the required meaning. The fragmentary state of many of the tablets and the difficulties of translating a language that is often obscure, utilizing a dialect of limited resources, raise obstacles that are sometimes insurmountable in translation. Those who want to use the Ras Shamra texts to confirm what they call "the verbal truth of the Bible," must proceed with the greatest caution and absolute sincerity.

There was great literary activity in Palestine and Syria many centuries before the Israelite monarchy. The products of this activity were, in fact, the sources drawn on by the Biblical writers and by the Prophets. Our Bible stories today go back to this remote past. The revelation of this fact, resulting from the excavations at Ras Shamra, is acknowledged to be one of the most important discoveries ever made in Biblical research.

---

*Ed. note: More recent translations of Cyrus Gordon, J. C. L. Gibson, and H. L. Ginsberg identify Latpon and Aliyan not as two gods but as honorific titles: *Ltpn*, meaning "gentle, kindly," for El, as in Kindly El Benign, and *Aliyn*, meaning "mightiest," for Baal, as in Mightiest, or Puissant, Baal.

REMNANTS OF THE PANTHEON

I would call on the gracious gods . . .who established a city on high . . .
—Shachar and Shalim and the Gracious Gods

An echo of gods and goddesses lost in time can be heard in the names of modern cities and sites within what were once the borders of ancient Canaan. On a stone stele from Egypt (*left*), the seated warrior goddess Anat wields her weapons, facing Anathoth (*opposite page*), modern Anata, a city north of Jerusalem which bears her name, in which women were consecrated to her service. The name of the city was a Canaanite plural signifying the total manifestation of the deity, such as "Ashtaroth" for Astarte. A city combining "Beth" with a god's name meant the "house," or cult site of that god. The nature of a deity often is reflected in a city's location. Names with Baal usually refer to a high place, recalling that Baal was a mountain god whose home was on Mount Saphon, north of Ugarit. Elat, an alternate name for the goddess Athirat, or Asherah of the Sea, whose symbol was the *asherah*, a wooden post or tree trunk, might reflect the southern port city in Israel at the head of the gulf which leads into the Red Sea. The following city names bear witness to the once vibrant pantheon of Canaan, as documented in Ugaritic literature. Alternate names are in brackets, and common spelling variations in parenthesis. (For the descriptions and attributes of the gods, see the God's Chart, page 20.)

EL (Il)	Bethel (Beitan), 10 mi. N of Jerusalem.
ELAT(H) [Athirat(h), Asherah]	Elath, head of Gulf of Elath/Aqaba. Name also might be derived from *eilah* (*elah*), the ancient terebinth tree.
BAAL [Hadad]	Baal-hermon, S peak of Mount Hermon above Dan, N limit of Israelite settlement.
ANAT(H)	Anathoth (Anata, Ras el-Kharrubeh), 3 mi. NE of Jerusalem.
ATHTART (Astarte)	Ashtaroth (Tell Ashtarah), 21 mi. E of Sea of Galilee, anc. Bashan area, S Syria. [Gen. 14:5. Ashtaroth-karnaim, "Astarte of the two horns"]
DAGON (Dagan)	Beth-dagon. SE of Tel Aviv.
HORON	Beth-horon (Beit Ur el-Fauqa, Beit Ur et-Taḥta), 11 mi. NW of Jerusalem.
RESHEF (Resheph, Rashap)	Reshef, Herzliya suburb, N of Tel Aviv.
SHALIM (Shalam, Shalem)	Jerusalem [Gen. 14:18, city of Melchizedek] from: Yarah-Shalem, "Shalem has founded."
SHAPASH (Shapsh)	Beth-shemesh (Ain Shems, or Tell er-Rumeileh), 16 mi. SW of Jerusalem.
YARIKH (Yarih)	Jericho (Tell es-Sultan), 5 mi. N of the Dead Sea; Beth-yerah, SW of Sea of Galilee.

Fields sacred to Anat, as quoted in the Ugaritic myth, above, recall the sites in Canaan sanctified by the Patriarchs to their God. Between Ai (et-Tell), and nearby Bethel in the central hill country, Abram built an altar. The stepped landscape of Ai (*above*), resembles a ladder, such as that of Jacob's dream which reached to heaven. After God appeared to him, Jacob anointed the stone on which he slept and changed the city's Canaanite name, Luz, to Bethel, God's house.

IV

THE PATRIARCHS

Genesis 12-36

———

NAHUM M. SARNA

THE ORIGINS OF A PEOPLE is the theme of the Biblical narratives which begins with Genesis 12. It is a richly woven, theological history told through the lives of the three Patriarchs, Abraham, Isaac, and Jacob. The people of Israel thus traced their roots to venerable forebears who experienced every human emotion within a family context as events ultimately leading to nationhood were guided by their one, omnipotent God.

The contours of history in this "Patriarchal Period" are quite blurred. Our only direct source of information is the Hebrew Bible, and here the story is sketchy and highly selective. The modern scholarly bibliography on the subject is impressively extensive, but the fact remains that over one hundred years of scientific historical research have succeeded only in illuminating the cultural setting of the narratives about the Patriarchs but not in adding to our store of solid knowledge about the personalities themselves. One thing is certain—the advent of Abraham is presented as a turning point in history. Just as ten generations intervened between Adam and the climactic Flood, so another ten elapsed until the arrival of Abraham on the scene.

As a whole, the Patriarchal narratives possess a distinctive flavor unparalleled in the rest of the Bible. They reflect a pattern of living and several socio-legal institutions that are peculiar to the period but often attested in Near Eastern documents. Abraham, Isaac, and Jacob are semi-nomads who live in tents, not houses; their means of travel is the donkey; their primary vocation is the raising of sheep and cattle, although Isaac occasionally tills the soil. Constantly on the move, they stick to the fringes of the urban areas. They avoid the more populous northern part of Canaan, the coastal plain, and the Jordan Valley and largely restrict the range of their wanderings to the sparsely populated central hilly region of the land and to the Negev, the southern or southeastern territory, especially the area of Beersheba.

The antiquity of the Genesis traditions is confirmed by several Patriarchal practices that directly contradict the social mores and norms of a later age, as formulated in the Pentateuchal legislation of Exodus, Leviticus, and Deuteronomy. These include marriages to one's half-sister, such as that of Abraham and Sarah, and simultaneously to two sisters, as occurred with Jacob to Leah and Rachel. Also the Patriarchs sometimes disregarded primogeniture, or the rights of the first-born, in favor of a younger son, as with Abraham's choice of Isaac over the older Ishmael or Jacob's primary blessing given to Joseph's younger son, Ephraim, rather than to Manasseh. Deuteronomic law (Deut.21:17) insisted that "the right of the first-born is his." Other practices which later were condemned were intermarriages, such as the union of Jacob's sons Simeon and Judah to Canaanite women and of Joseph to the daughter of an Egyptian priest; and the inclusion of the father-in-law and not just the brothers of the late childless husband in the obligation of a levirate marriage to a widow, as told in the story of Judah and his daughter-in-law, Tamar. Deuteronomy limited the levirate obligation to brothers. In addition, the Canaanite customs of planting trees next to an altar, as Abraham did in Beersheba when he worshiped God after making a treaty with Abimelech over water rights, or erecting stone pillars, as Jacob did at Bethel and Gilead, were later to be swept away by specific legislation. In the continuing process of demythologizing ancient pagan ideas, trees, stones, and water that were believed to be inhabited by spirits are depicted by the Biblical authors as natural objects with no inherent magic force of their own.

Two other unusual features of the Patriarchal narratives, which also are recorded in ancient archives, are the shared theme of the infertility of the wife and, in two instances, the resort to concubinage in order to insure posterity. Sarah's handmaid, Hagar, bore a son for her, as Bilhah did for Rachel. In the Nuzi documents from northern Mesopotamia, dating from the middle of the 2nd millennium B.C., such surrogacy is confirmed in contracts which stipulate that a childless wife must provide her husband with a slave woman to bear for her.

Surprisingly, Genesis records very little about the lives of the Patriarchs, considering their longevity and individuality. Each of the fathers is unique in his own right, and the few selected episodes that are recounted define aspects of the character and personality of each. They also embody certain basic Israelite beliefs, such as the concept of one universal, omnipotent though personal God, whose interaction with humanity is based on principles of morality and not on caprice, as was the case with pagan gods. A fundamental Israelite institution—circumcision—also finds its origin in this period. While it was widely practised in the Near East, it was generally a rite of passage or pre-nuptial ritual. Exceptionally, it was transformed in Israel into a physical sign of the Covenant with God and was shifted to the eighth day after birth.

The biography of Abraham (Abram) opens with his presence at Biblical Haran at the age of seventy-five years. His family had migrated there from "Ur of the Chaldaeans." The city of Harran was an important trading center. It lay on the left bank of the Balikh River, a tributary of the Euphrates, astride the international route from Mesopotamia to Egypt. It was to remain important to the Patriarchal families for three generations, after which the contact was lost. At Haran, Abraham received the divine call to leave his family and continue the journey. Arriving in Canaan, he was promised by God that he would become the father of a great people and that his posterity would inherit that very land. These dual promises were reaffirmed repeatedly to each of the Patriarchs.

Abraham's journey has been placed against a background of wide tribal migrations throughout the Near East, including that of the frequently mentioned Northwest Semitic Amorites, which often occurred throughout the millenniums. The Egyptian "Execration

Texts" of the early 2nd millennium B.C., written on clay figurines, reflect conditions in Canaan when seminomadic elements were settling down and some chiefs had Amorite names. In the ethnically diverse land of Canaan, it was the "iniquity" of these Amorites which first had to reach its ultimate degree before Abraham's descendants could inherit the land.

Abraham's obedient response to the divine summons was an act of faith, as was his trust in the ultimate fulfillment of the promises he received, even though he was temporarily driven to Egypt by a famine in Canaan. This quality of faith found its ultimate expression in his unprotesting submission to God's test—rescinded at the last moment—that he sacrifice his son on Mount Moriah. His other character traits, as expressed through the narratives, are hospitality to strangers such as he offered to his three unexpected visitors in the plains of Mamre, compassion for other human beings even for the wicked inhabitants of Sodom, a fierce sense of justice even to the extent of remonstrating with God about the impending fate of that city, as well as loyalty to his kinsfolk displayed when he mounted a military operation to rescue his captive, estranged nephew Lot from foreign invaders. Abraham's character confirms the central Biblical premise that the fate of society depends on its moral obligation and actions towards its fellow man.

Abraham's son and heir, Isaac, was a rather passive individual, far less dynamic than his father. His pastoral peregrinations were confined to a narrow region, mainly to Beersheba and adjacent areas in the Negev. He, alone of the Patriarchs, never left his ancestral land, engaged in small-scale agriculture, and remained monogamous. His wife, Rebekah, presented him with twins, Esau and Jacob. The latter, the younger son, with the connivance of his mother, took advantage of his father's failing eyesight to hoodwink his father into granting him the parental blessing that normally would go with the first-born status. When the deceit was discovered, Isaac acquiesced in the transference of the birthright. All in all, this Patriarch is depicted as a passive, peace-loving, and mild person.

This episode transformed Jacob's character and the course of his life. Having incurred the fierce enmity of his brother Esau he was compelled to flee his parental home for the distant abode of his uncle Laban in Haran. On the way, he took refuge for the night at Bethel and experienced a theophany in which he was vouchsafed divine protection and reaffirmation of the Covenant with Abraham. His life in Haran proved to be twenty years of trial and tribulation, laboring as a shepherd for Laban. In the course of this period, he was tricked into marrying Leah, his uncle's older daughter, before he could marry the younger Rachel, who alone was the love of his life.

Eleven sons and one daughter were born to Jacob in Haran through his two wives and two concubines. The sons are the eponymous, or name-giving, ancestors of the tribes of Israel. Without doubt, their maternal affiliations reflect status within the broader confederation of Israelite tribes. The archives uncovered at Mari (Tell Hariri), the strategic town on the middle Euphrates in Syria with its dominant Amorite population, similarly record confederations of seminomadic tribes and of sub-groupings within the larger association, while intertribal alliances are expressed in terms of brotherhood. One of the Semitic tribes, the Banu-Yamina, or "southerners," were predators who caused constant trouble to the king of Mari. Similiar in name was Benjamin, the youngest son, born to Rachel in Canaan soon after the family returned from Haran. He is described in Jacob's last blessing as a spoiler, "a ravenous wolf" who consumed his foe.

The rest of the biography of Jacob chronicles the kidnapping of his daughter Dinah by a prince of the important city of Shechem. Her brothers responded with a murderous, punitive assault on the city. This operation may well preserve a memory of pre-conquest military activity on the part of Israelite tribes inside Canaan. In his old age Jacob also experienced the kidnapping and sale into Egyptian slavery of his son Joseph by his own brothers, an event that eventually led to the migration of Jacob and his family to Egypt, where the Patriarch died.

. . . walk before me and be thou perfect.   — Gen. 17:1

Out of the Genesis narratives, three religious motifs emerge which run as a consistent thread throughout the Pentateuch.

FAITH

The theological history of the Hebrews begins with the unquestioning faith of one man who left his father's house in Haran for an unknown land at the command of an unseen God. In Canaan, the land to which God brought Abram, a new faith could grow, far away from the repressive gods of the east. When God granted the childless Abram a son of his own, "he believed in the Lord, and he counted it to him for righteousness," Gen. 15:6. Such faith is embodied in the dignity of a kneeling suppliant, shown in an ivory figure from Alaca Höyük, c. 1700 B.C. (*opposite*). In distant lands, faith would sustain Jacob in Haran and his son Joseph in Egypt who rose to greatness, second only to pharaoh.

COVENANT

In return for unconditional faith, God made a unilateral Covenant with Abram, vowing that his descendants would inherit the land "from the river of Egypt unto the great river, the river Euphrates, " Gen. 15:18. Although God foretold that the Hebrews would sojourn in Egypt four hundred years, the memory of the Covenant remained their hope. When the Patriarchs crossed the Jordan River (*overleaf*), it represented a spiritual break with the past. The sun illumines the mountains of Gilead where Jacob, returning from Haran to Canaan years after he fled from his brother Esau, acknowledged, in the spirit of the Covenant, that the God of Abraham and Isaac had protected him during his exile.

PROMISE

Eventual nationhood and seed without number were God's promises to Abram when he entered Canaan. Abram the nomad would be called Abraham, the father of many nations. Elements of Ugaritic royal epic appear in Genesis as Abraham and Sarah were to found a royal line. God promised Abraham, "kings shall come out of thee, " while Sarai's name was changed to Sarah meaning "princess," from whom would come "kings of people," Gen. 17:6, 15-16. God's promises to the Patriarchs were made in the sparsely inhabited areas of Canaan where they settled. In an atmosphere of nomadic solitude, a lone goatherd tends his flocks in the parched and rolling hills of Judaea, west of the Dead Sea (*pp. 126-7*).

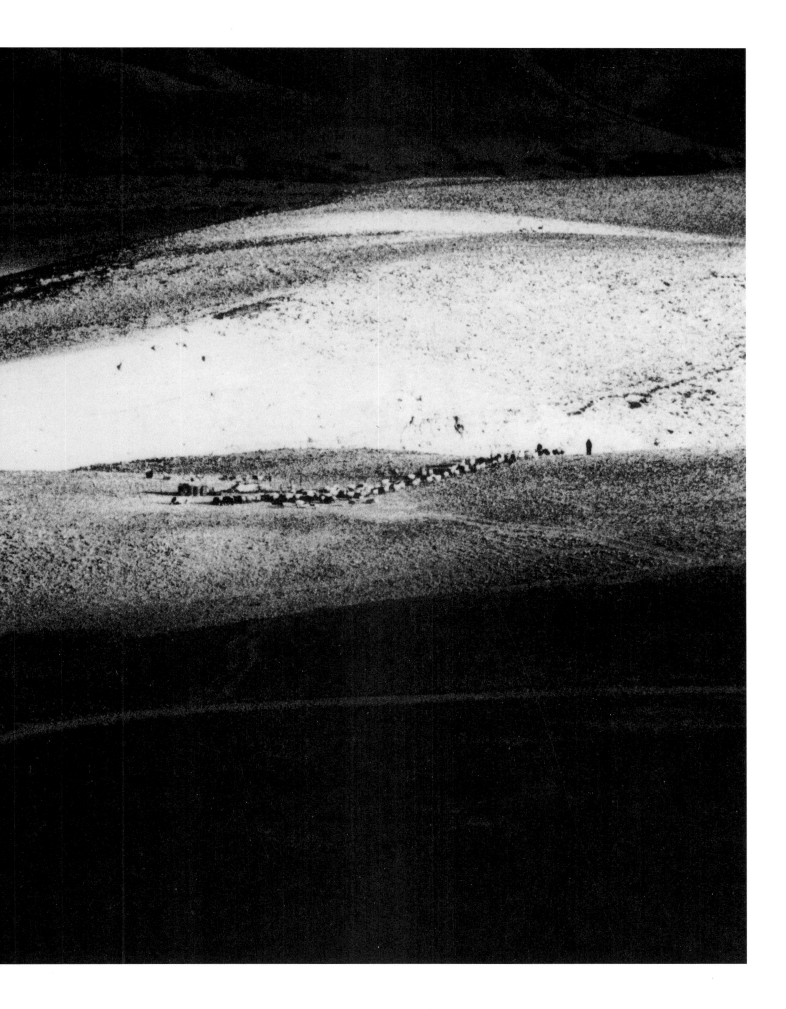

The sign of the Covenant between God and Abraham was the circumcision of the males in his household. Ishmael was circumcised at the age of thirteen years and Isaac when he was eight days old. The ritual still prevails today in the Hebrew and Moslem religions. Circumcision was practiced in ancient Egypt, Syria, and Phoenicia probably as a ceremonial act of purification of people in the service of their god. A relief from a 6th Dynasty tomb at Saqqara (*right*), 3rd millennium B.C., shows priests performing the operation on boys standing before them. The seated priest (*center*), exclaims, "Hold him, that he may not faint away." His assistant (*far left*), answers, "Do your best." According to the Phoenician priest Sanchuniathon, possibly of the 6th century B.C., the god El was circumcised and forced his followers to do the same.

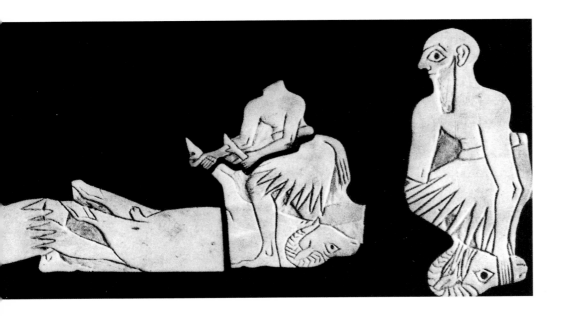

The binding of Isaac (the Akedah), Gen. 22, was the ultimate test of faith when God commanded Abraham to sacrifice his divinely granted son and heir. An ivory from the Temple of Shamash in Mari (*left*) first half of the 3rd millennium B.C., indicates how the test was resolved when a ram was substituted at the final moment. Abraham's trial was one of spiritual obedience, making the actual sacrifice unnecessary. The interpretation of the Akedah was that God valued human life above all. The pagan ritual of child sacrifice as a means of placating the gods who controlled the forces of nature and well-being was thereby banned by the Hebrews.

THE FAMILY

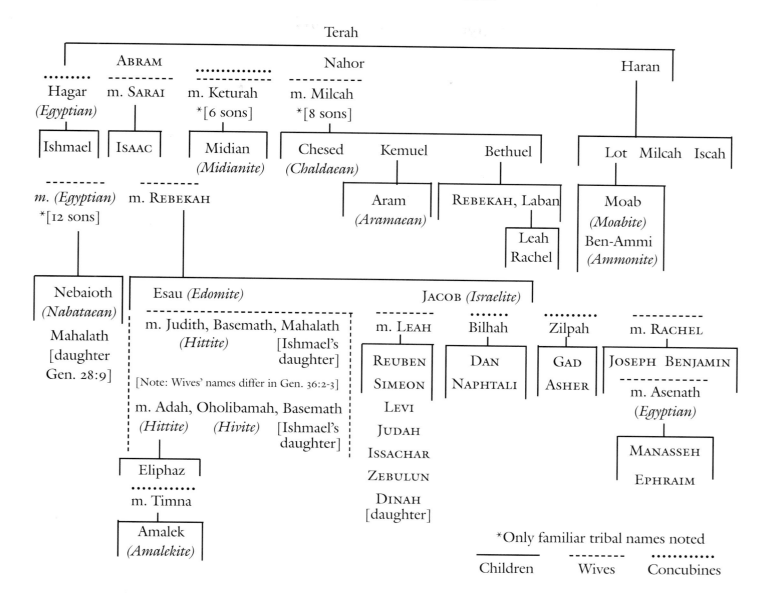

Through the use of genealogies, the mixed races in Canaan (*italicized* above), were explained in terms of one family related to Abraham. The genealogies, believed to have been compiled during the United Monarchy, c. 1000 B.C., are a valuable view of Israel's political relationships and attitudes at that time (some of which remain today in the volatile Middle East). In a burst of national pride, the Israelites emerged as the true heirs of the Patriarchs, claiming their pure blood ties to their Semitic Aramaean kinsmen, as depicted in the taking of brides from their area for Isaac and Jacob. Their cousins were the Egyptians and North and South Arabian tribes through Abraham's sons of lower social status by his concubines, Hagar and Keturah. The concubinage of Keturah whom Abraham married after Sarah's death is inferred in Gen. 25:6 and definitely stated in I Chronicles 1:32. The despised Moabites and Ammonites east of the Jordan were the sons of the illicit union between Abraham's nephew Lot and his daughters after the destruction of Sodom and Gomorrah. Jacob / Israel outwitted his twin, Esau / Edom, two rival nations portrayed as competitive brothers at a time when Israel had subjugated Edom, fulfilling the divine prophecy of their birth, "The elder shall serve the younger," Gen. 25:23. Finally, the twelve tribes, individual clans pictured as the sons of Jacob, were melded into the nation of Israel after forty years of wandering in the Sinai desert and their ultimate settlement in Canaan.

Chosen Sons

The choice of the Hebrews as the people of the Covenant destined for nationhood was confirmed through a series of extraordinary events. Sons would be divinely granted to three previously barren wives, thereby renewing the Covenant to every generation: "And the Lord visited Sarah," Gen. 21:1; "And Rebekah his [Isaac's] wife conceived," Gen. 25:21; and, "God remembered Rachel," Gen. 30:22. Although the Matriarchs would give birth to the spiritual heirs to the Covenant, their methods were far from kind as they sought the Patriarchal blessing for their preferred sons. A rare domestic scene of female figures on an Akkadian cylinder seal, 3rd millennium B.C. (*above*), might be fancifully imagined as Sarah, with Isaac on her lap, *right*, sending Hagar, her Egyptian bondwoman, *center*, into the wilderness so that her son Ishmael, "a wild ass of a man," would not share in the rights of inheritance, Gen. 21:10. Rebekah later would trick her husband, Isaac, into giving his blessing to their son Jacob rather than to Esau. Evolving religious concepts are evident in the reactions against paganism, as Ishmael, born of an Egyptian mother, was denied a place in his father's house, and intermarriage, such as that of Esau with two Hittite women, who were a "bitterness of spirit" to his parents.

NEW FAITH IN OLD SHRINES
— Demythologizing the Nature Religion of Canaan

Canaanite cult sites were taken over by the Hebrews and adapted to their own sacred traditions. The standing stone, or *maṣṣebah*, of Shechem, modern Tell Balatah, dating from the end of the Late Bronze Age, probably was the main cultic symbol of the temple. In the nature religion of Canaan, such a pillar was considered the lodging of a deity. The Hebrews erected a stone only as a witness to God's appearance, or theophany, at a site or at the conclusion of a treaty. Abram erected an altar in Shechem when God promised the land to his seed, Gen. 12:7, as Jacob did when he purchased land from Hamor the Hivite, Gen. 33:19-20. The name of El then was combined with an attribute or special experience of the Patriarch. Jacob called the altar "El-elohe-Israel," El the God of Israel.

Life-giving waters in the parched regions of Canaan, such as the sanctuary-oasis of Kadesh-barnea (*above*), in the southern wilderness, were thought to harbor supernatural powers. To the Hebrews, those forces who revealed themselves to individuals at wells or rivers were not water gods but angels of the Lord who prophesied their destinies. The fugitive Hagar at the well between Kadesh and Bered was promised numerous descendants and the birth of a son, Gen. 16:10-11. At the ford of the Jabbok, east of the Jordan, Jacob wrestled with "a man" until dawn. When the stranger changed Jacob's name to Israel, it was a forecast of the nation yet to be. Jacob called the place Peniel, "for I have seen a divine being face to face," Gen. 32:31.

For I have a tale that I would tell you . . . a tale of tree(s) and a whisper of stone(s) . . .
—*The Palace of Baal*

Trees inhabited by goddesses was another pagan concept demythologized by the Hebrews. In Canaan, the tree, or sacred pole, was called the *asherah*, symbolizing the goddess, Asherah, the source of life and fruitfulness. A fertility goddess in Cretan-Mycenaean dress who feeds two rampant goats on an ivory box from Minet el-Beida, 14th century B.C., is thought to be a Mycenaean variation of the Canaanite art motif of rampant goats feeding on the tree of life. The oracular terebinth tree sacred to the Canaanites is mentioned at various sites in Genesis. But when Jacob buried the idols under the terebinths of Shechem when he returned to Canaan, Gen. 35:4, it was an act of purification and a rejection of polytheism.

FROM MYTH TO REALISM

Literary parallels drawn from the epics of Ugarit show how the Biblical writers translated mythical events into human terms. The Patriarchal lives were placed in a family context, the unit which the Hebrews considered their best chance of survival in an alien world.

For Baal — Lordship

The virgin Anat . . . lifted up her voice and cried: "Be gladdened, Baal! . . .
A house shall be built for you like your brothers and a court like your kinsfolk."

—The Palace of Baal

Baal's most fervent wish after he triumphed over the sea god, Yamm, was for a house, or shrine, of his own that would establish his place among the gods. When El finally granted his wish, Baal's cult in Ugarit became official. The house would cover "a thousand tracts" and be built on Mount Saphon, modern Jebel el-Aqra (*above*), north of Ugarit. This Canaanite high place where the gods assembled was the equivalent of the Greek Mount Olympus. The clouds which float above the summit evoke the memory of Baal as the Rider of the Clouds, provider of life-giving rain. Baal's earthly abode was the temple (*below*), dedicated to him in Ugarit in the early 2nd millennium B.C. Among its remains is an altar in front of the cella, the inner room.

For Abram — A Son

What wilt thou give me, seeing I go childless. . . . And, behold, the word of the Lord came unto him, saying. . . "he that shall come forth out of thine own bowels shall be thine heir."   — Gen. 15:2, 4

After Abram's victory over the four kings of the east, Gen.14, he refused any reward from Melchizedek, king of Salem. The Patriarch's only wish was for a son and heir. This was granted by God with the promise that his offspring would be as numerous as the stars. In his warrior role, Abram might have resembled the bearded figure holding an adze. The imposing statue from Telloh dates from the 21st century B.C.

For Huray
—Divine Wet Nurses

The [wife whom you] take, O Kret. . . she shall bear the lad Yassib, one that shall suck the milk of Athirat, one that shall drain the breasts of the virgin [Anat], the suckling nurses of [the gods].

— *Epic of Kret*

In the Ugaritic epics, the theme of wanting a son was realized through El's advice and favor to the kings Dan'el and Kret. As kings were El's intermediaries, their sons must be divinely attended. Huray, Kret's wife, might have nursed Yassib, but as the royal son, he was to be suckled by the goddesses Asherah and Anat. On an ivory bed panel from Ugarit (*left*), two princes are nourished from the breasts of a winged goddess, probably Anat. The local artist synthesized prevailing styles: the goddess wears Syrian robes, an Egyptian Hathor coiffure, and a Hittite solar disk above her horns of fertility. Progeny also were desired by the gods themselves. Asherah, the wife of El, was the mother of seventy sons, but Anat, with no children of her own, resorted to other means. In the poem, *Anat and the Heifer*, the goddess gave to Baal, her brother and lover, who had taken the form of a bull, a heifer who would bear them a son (*see p. 139*). The theme recalls the barren wives, Sarai and Rachel, and Leah when she stopped bearing, who gave their handmaids to their husbands to bear for them. It was Anat's love for Baal, "like the heart of a [heifer] (yearning) for her lamb," and their symbolic mating as bull and heifer, which assured the fertility of the animal kingdom. Jacob's twelve sons, on the other hand, assured his posterity. His descendants one day would form the core of a new nation, divided into territories according to the inheritance inferred by Jacob's deathbed blessing of his sons in Egypt (*see pp. 234-5*)

For Sarah
—Motherhood

And she said,
"Who would have said unto Abraham,
    that Sarah should have given children suck?
For I have borne him a son in his old age."
And the child grew, and was weaned.

— Gen. 21:7-8

Although the divinely promised birth of
Isaac was in the Ugaritic epic tradition, in
the Biblical world of real people, Sarah
would nurse her own son, unlike Huray,
opposite page, whose baby would be nursed
by goddesses. Such an extraordinary event
in the life of the aged and barren Sarah
would reassure the Hebrews of God's grace
and answer the question he posed to her, "Is
anything too hard for the Lord?" Gen. 18:14.
A standing bronze figure of a woman
nursing her baby, *right*, from Horoztepe,
c. 2000 B.C., denotes the special role of
motherhood for Hebrew women—to
replenish their small numbers by bearing
many offspring in an age when infant mortal-
ity, low female life expectancy, and disease
severely diminished populations. The chastity
of women within the family unit would make
them worthy daughters of the Covenant.
The only episode of harlotry in Genesis was
that of Tamar with Judah, her father-in-law,
Gen. 38. But here the onus was on him.
Judah had not respected the law of levirate
marriage by which he should have given his
youngest son as a husband to the twice-
widowed, childless Tamar in order to "raise
up seed" for his deceased first-born son, Er.
Levirate marriage strengthened family ties
and was a means by which Israel survived the
impact of Canaanite culture. When Judah
realized that the motive of Tamar, now
pregnant by him, was to preserve the family
name by providing progeny, he admitted,
"She hath been more righteous than I."

For Children—Expectations

Trees of life in the form of stylized palms that flank the figures on the ivory bed panel of Ugarit (*above*), symbolize fertility and good fortune, such as having children who would perform their household and religious chores faithfully. Two dutiful offering bearers are a boy (*second from left*), carrying a goat with arched horns, and a girl before him, perhaps a princess, holding a vase and scepter ending in a lotus flower. In the Ugaritic *Tale of Aqhat*, girls must draw water from wells, as Rebekah and Rachel did in Haran, gather fodder for the animals, and know something of divination. But it was in the respect which a son owed to his deceased father that the Ugaritic and Patriarchal customs most agree. For Dan'el, a son meant "One to stand as steward of his father's god in the sanctuary. . . of his ancestors, one to free his spirit from the earth, to protect his tomb from the dust." Jacob's request in Egypt to be returned and interred in the family sepulcher of Machpelah in Hebron affirmed the Patriarchal ideal of being reunited after death with one's father. The obedient son Joseph promised Jacob, "I will do as thou hast said."

SOCIAL CUSTOMS—*Insights from Nuzi*

The obligation of a barren wife to provide her husband with a surrogate to bear children for her was one of the many laws of the Hurrians recorded in the Nuzi texts in the Akkadian language, which confirm the social customs of the Patriarchs. By the middle of the 2nd millennium B.C., these energetic Hurrians had settled in upper Mesopotamia in the Patriarchal area of Harran, and in northern Syria, including Ugarit. In Gen. 36:21, they are the "children of Seir" in Edom, east of the Wadi Araba. This particular law is reflected in the Biblical narratives when Sarai offered Hagar to Abram, and Rachel and Leah gave their handmaids to Jacob to do what the Hurrian wife, Kelim-ninu, must do (*italics* below, right), if she cannot have children for Shennima.

From Nuzi—A Barren Wife's Obligation

Furthermore, Kelim-ninu as wife to Shennima
　　has been given;
if Kelim-ninu bears (children)
Shennima shall not take another wife;
　　but if Kelim-ninu does not bear, Kelim-ninu a
　　woman of the land of Lullu (i.e., "a foreign
　　handmaid") *as wife for Shennima shall take;*
as for the (concubine's) offspring,
Kelim-ninu shall not send (them)
　　away. Any sons that out of the womb of
　　Kelim-ninu to Shennima may be born,
all the lands, buildings, whatever
their description, to (these)
sons are given.
In case she does not bear a son, then the daughter
　　of Kelim-ninu of the lands and buildings one
　　(portion of inheritance) shall take.

From Ugarit—A Mythological Reflex

An echo of the Nuzi law of maternal surrogacy is seen in the Ugaritic myth
in which Anat gave Baal a heifer to mate in her stead, (*see p. 136*)

And the Virgin Anat lifts her eyes
She lifts her eyes and sees
Yea she sees a cow.
And she proceeds in walking
Proceeds in walking
And proceeds in dancing
[Among] fair ones
Among lovely ones [　]
[　] to Baal Anat gives [　]

Anat later brought Baal the news:

For a bull [is b]orn unto Baal,
Yea a buffalo to the Rider of Clouds.

Bride Price and Dowry
—A Nuzi Nuance

In the Nuzi texts, different words for marital arrangements, *terhatu* for a bride price, and *mulag* for a dowry, clarify two Biblical episodes. The bride price was a transaction made by the groom's family for the bride which linked the two as future kin. Often it was the bride's brother who received the bride price which, in turn, would be given to his bride at the proper time. The gifts which Abraham's servant gave to the fair Rebekah, her brother Laban, and her mother after the girl agreed to return to Canaan and marry Isaac were considered part of the bride price (Hebrew: *mohar*). Shechem promised it for Dinah, no matter what the amount, Gen. 34:12. The dowry, on the other hand, was the property a bride received from her father when she married, an advance on her share of the inheritance from his will. The decision of Rachel and Leah to leave their father's house followed their bitter realization that Laban had no inheritance for them. The Nuzi custom of labor in exchange for a bride also is seen in Genesis as Jacob, with no means of his own, agreed to work seven years for Rachel.

Although the Nuzi texts came from a Hurrian city of the 15th century B.C., such documents usually reflected customs in use over a wide geographic area and from centuries past. A beauty from Ebla (*above*), of the previous millennium, would have received a worthy bride price from her intended groom.

And the servant brought forth jewels of silver, and jewels of gold, and raimant, and
gave them to Rebekah; he gave also to her brother and to her mother precious things.

— Gen. 24:53

Highly crafted jewelry of gold and carnelian, and a bronze mirror to admire the effect, were the
kinds of gifts included in a bride price. Buried in tombs of once thriving coastal cities of the Late
Bronze Age, the baubles were found in Deir el-Balah, south of Gaza, while the decorative mirror
with the handle in the form of a woman is from Acre (Biblical Accho), to the north.

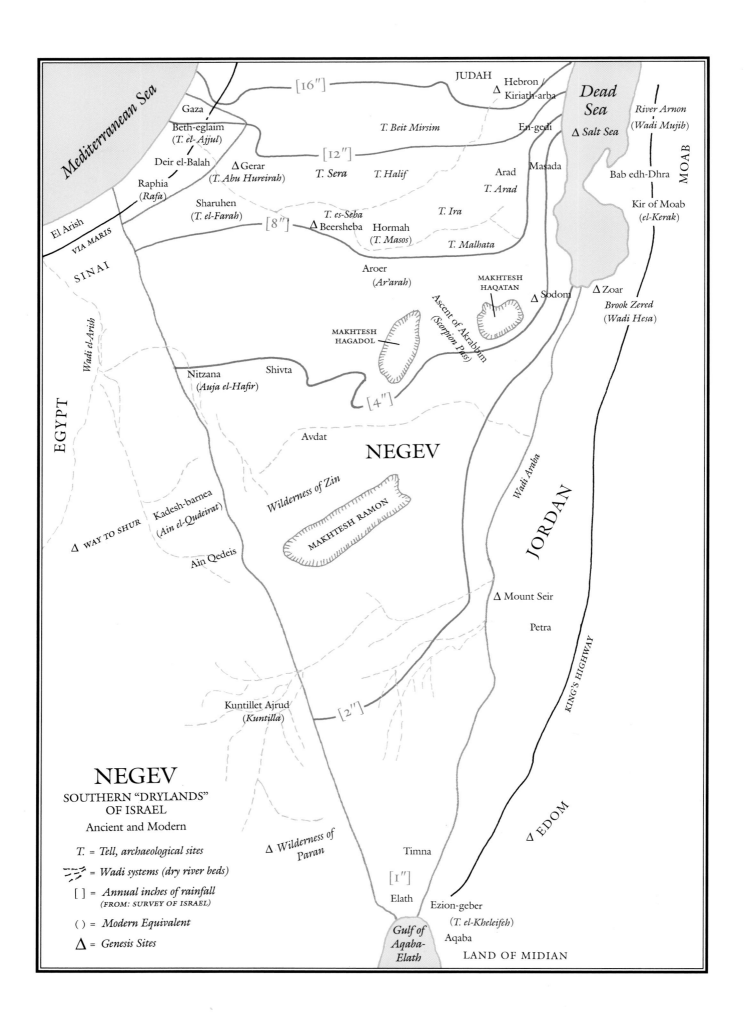

Mediterranean Sea

JUDAH

Dead Sea

△ Hebron / Kiriath-arba

River Arnon (Wadi Mujib)

MOAB

[16″]

Gaza

Beth-eglaim (T. el-Ajjul)

T. Beit Mirsim

En-gedi

△ Salt Sea

Deir el-Balah

[12″]

Raphia (Rafa)

△ Gerar (T. Abu Hureirah)

T. Sera

T. Halif

Arad

Masada

Bab edh-Dhra

T. Arad

Kir of Moab (el-Kerak)

Sharuhen (T. el-Farah)

T. es-Seba

T. Ira

El Arish

[8″]

△ Beersheba

Hormah (T. Masos)

VIA MARIS

T. Malhata

SINAI

Aroer (Ar'arah)

MAKHTESH HAQATAN

△ Sodom

△ Zoar

Brook Zered (Wadi Hesa)

Ascent of Akrabbim (Scorpion Pass)

EGYPT

MAKHTESH HAGADOL

Wadi el-Arish

Nitzana (Auja el-Hafir)

Shivta

[4″]

Avdat

NEGEV

Wilderness of Zin

MAKHTESH RAMON

Wadi Araba

JORDAN

Kadesh-barnea (Ain el-Qudeirat)

△ WAY TO SHUR

Ain Qedeis

△ Mount Seir

Petra

KING'S HIGHWAY

Kuntillet Ajrud (Kuntilla)

[2″]

NEGEV

SOUTHERN "DRYLANDS" OF ISRAEL

Ancient and Modern

T. = Tell, archaeological sites

= Wadi systems (dry river beds)

[ ] = Annual inches of rainfall (FROM: SURVEY OF ISRAEL)

( ) = Modern Equivalent

△ = Genesis Sites

△ Wilderness of Paran

Timna

[1″]

Elath

Ezion-geber (T. el-Kheleifeh)

Gulf of Aqaba-Elath

Aqaba

△ EDOM

LAND OF MIDIAN

142

THE PATRIARCHAL AGE:
Biblical Archaeology and the Test of Time

Within the boundaries of the Negev, the southern "dryland" of Israel, archaeologists and Biblical scholars have addressed the provocative question, "When was the Patriarchal Age?" or, as some ask, "Was there a Patriarchal Age at all?"

The questions relate to a continuous dialogue concerning the definition of the branch of studies called "Biblical Archaeology" and the scope of its geographic area. In its broadest sense, the leading American scholar William F. Albright included all the lands mentioned in the Bible. Biblical Archaeology was thus "coextensive with the cradle of civilization." His chronology included everything from 10,000 B.C. to the present. Some argue that there is no Biblical Archaeology before the Israelite occupation, c. 1250 B.C. Still others see no evidence of an occupation and state that Israel's history begins with King David's United Monarchy, c. 1000 B.C. Before that, they claim, all is legend.

The Biblical Negev extends about thirteen miles north and south of modern Beersheba. It was there that Abraham dug a well and made a covenant with Abimelech before planting a grove and calling on the name of the Lord, Gen. 21:30-33. Excavations in the Negev over the years illustrate how continuing archaeological field work amends those conclusions previously arrived at by scholars working in the same area:

In the 1950s, the archaeologist Nelson Glueck assigned the period of Abraham to the Middle Bronze Age I, 21st—19th centuries B.C., based on pottery remains found during extensive surface surveys of the Negev. Other scholars believed that the mention of kings and of cities in Genesis, such as Bethel, Hebron, and Gerar, was a more accurate reflection of the urban society of the Middle Bronze Age II, 19th—16th centuries B.C.

By the mid-1970s, after eight seasons of excavations at Tell Beersheba, about two-and-a-half miles east of the modern city, the team led by Yohanan Aharoni of Tel Aviv University (report on following page), found no Middle Bronze remains. The Patriarchal Age was moved forward to the Iron Age I, 13th-11th centuries B.C., corresponding to the tell's Strata IX and VIII, or the settlement period. Dr. Aharoni thought that a well on the eastern slope of the mound (*p.145*), was the one which Abraham dug, and that the find of a horned cultic altar, 8th century B.C. (*right*), indicated that Beersheba was a sanctuary site.

A decade later, in a Tel Aviv University report on the excavations, *Beersheba II*, Ze'ev Herzog, the team field director, acknowledged that the tribal way of life described in Genesis accorded with the semi-sedentary nature of the finds from Stratum IX, thus placing the "historical events which formed the backgrounds to the legends of Abraham and Isaac at Beersheba (Gen. 21; 26). . . between the second half of the 12th century and the first half of the 11th." In the same report, Anson Rainey, the team's educational director, suggested that the tribal-pastoral elements in the Biblical tradition were in some way equivalent to the nomadic herdsmen, known in Egyptian sources as the "Shasu," who were in the Negev and northern Sinai from Ramesside times.

Meanwhile, archaeologists continue their inquiries into the Patriarchal traditions, combining their synthesis of archaeological data with the historical sources in order to illuminate the Bible in its original setting.

Beersheba — (Tell es-Seba)

Yohanan Aharoni (*left*), late chairman of the Department of Archaeology and Ancient Near Eastern Cultures at Tel Aviv University, directed extensive excavations in Beersheba in southern Israel from 1969 to 1975. This site, so intimately associated with the Patriarchs, was on the main caravan route from Egypt to the Negev in the Beersheba Valley. Aharoni's conclusions on the dating of the Patriarchal Age based on his finds are described in his article, below, "Nothing Early and Nothing Late: Rewriting Israel's Conquest," from *Biblical Archeologist*, May 1976, vol. 39, no. 2.

[Ed. note: The Negeb, as spelled here, derives from the root *n-g-b*, "to be dry, " or, the dry region. Negev with a "v " is the way it is pronounced in modern Hebrew. An ancient mound, or tell, here is "tel," a usage in Israel with Hebrew names.]

In the entire northern Negeb no remains were found of the Middle Bronze Age I (also known as the Intermediate Bronze Age). This is in direct contrast to the assumption of certain scholars who would date Abraham to that period and picture him as leader of the donkey caravan trade. The Middle Bronze Age I settlements in the modern central Negeb (the Wilderness of Zin) require another explanation, since it has long ago been observed that they are not situated on trade routes at all, nor did they have any connections with Egypt. The Biblical tradition places Abraham in the more northerly Biblical Negeb and especially at Beersheba, and here there are no traces of the Middle Bronze Age I culture. As a result of the Beersheba excavations another interpretation of the Patriarchal stories is mandatory. Both on the tel itself and in its immediate vicinity there are no remains earlier than the conquest period, and the nearest site that yielded remains of the Middle Bronze Age is Tel Masos, twelve kilometers to the east. Although it is true that the Biblical narratives do not mention any pre-Israelite settlement at Beersheba (such as, for example, at neighboring Gerar or Hebron), nevertheless the Patriarchs are not depicted as pure nomads who would have left no material traces behind them. Moreover, it is to

Beersheba that the Patriarchal tradition attributes a cult site and a well, and it is now possible to identify this well with considerable certainty. Since the digging of this well did not antedate the settlement period, it therefore seems certain that neither can the Patriarchal narratives associated with Beersheba refer to an earlier period. We cannot enter into the question of the antiquity and historical background of the Patriarchal stories, nor do we wish to claim that they do not contain earlier elements, but it would seem that these traditions are not made up of a single fabric but are a compilation of traditions originating in different periods. The excavations at Beersheba have now proven they include references to events that could not possibly have occurred prior to the 13th or 12th centuries B.C.E. Naturally, this also explains the anachronisms in these stories, such as the designation of Abimelech, king of Gerar, as king of the Philistines. We should look upon the Biblical narratives relating to the Patriarchs . . . as a collection of traditions covering a long period and different groups whose chronological position cannot be established according to their literary sequence in the Bible, but only on the basis of external criteria, particularly the archaeological evidence. In the present case, the Patriarchal narratives relating to Beersheba belong to the settlement period.

One of the most astounding finds at Tel Beersheba is the well discovered in the area. The wells of Beersheba, as elsewhere in the Negeb, were usually dug along the river bed at levels where they would be filled by winter floods. To have dug a well on the heights of the mound was therefore an unusual undertaking involving exceptional efforts. This well has a circular shaft, about two meters in diameter, the upper section being lined with stones and its continuation hewn into the solid rock. According to the pottery retrieved from the shaft, this well was utilized until the beginning of the Roman period. But when was it originally dug? . . . its age may be determined with a high degree of certainty on the basis of its position in relation to the surrounding structures. During the Monarchy the well was just outside the city gate and may therefore be compared to the well by the gate of Bethlehem from which water was drawn for David during the Philistine threat (II Samuel 23:15; I Chronicles 11:17). However, there are several indications that the well at Beersheba precedes the fortifications there, and that it originated with the earliest Israelite settlement: (1) the outer city wall makes a deviation in the vicinity of the well, a sign that its position was taken into account; (2) the earliest structures were built around the well, likewise taking its existence into consideration; (3) near the well was found a surface belonging to one of the earlier strata of the settlement, covered by horizontal layers of sedimentation resulting from the water that had been spilled there over a long period of time.

Once we had established that the well belonged to the earliest Israelite settlement, we were able to deduce with reasonable certainty that this was the well attributed to the Patriarchs (Gen. 21:25; 26:25); One of the major problems with which we were involved at Beersheba throughout the excavations was the location of the cult site and temple mentioned repeatedly in the Bible. In the fifth season, a large horned altar was discovered which had been dismantled, evidently following the religious reforms of Hezekiah. However, if the sanctuary were on the tel, and undoubtedly associated with an earlier sanctified site, how did the Biblical tradition become attached to the well dug there by Abraham and Isaac, the tamarisk tree and the altar? Since wells are usually dug alongside the river bed, is it conceivable that the site of worship would be remote from the well? As soon as we had discovered the ancient well on the heights of the tel, and moreover, located beside substantial buildings of the earliest Israelite settlement, the problem was easily solved. The tremendous efforts involved in digging this well were made in connection with a place of worship that by its nature required a continuous supply of water; one can therefore understand the great impression this well made upon the ancients.

The well in Beersheba associated with Abraham's oath, was dug with iron tools obtained from the Philistines who inhabited the coastal areas to the west.

Portfolio: Biblical Memory

Within the Fertile Crescent, local tradition holds fast to the memory of the Patriarchs who followed this green arc of land from Mesopotamia to Egypt. The following picture portfolio illustrates some of these sites in Turkey, Syria, Israel, and Jordan, with a view of the Kaaba in Mecca, Saudi Arabia, which Moslems claim was built by the Prophet Abraham, the Friend of God.

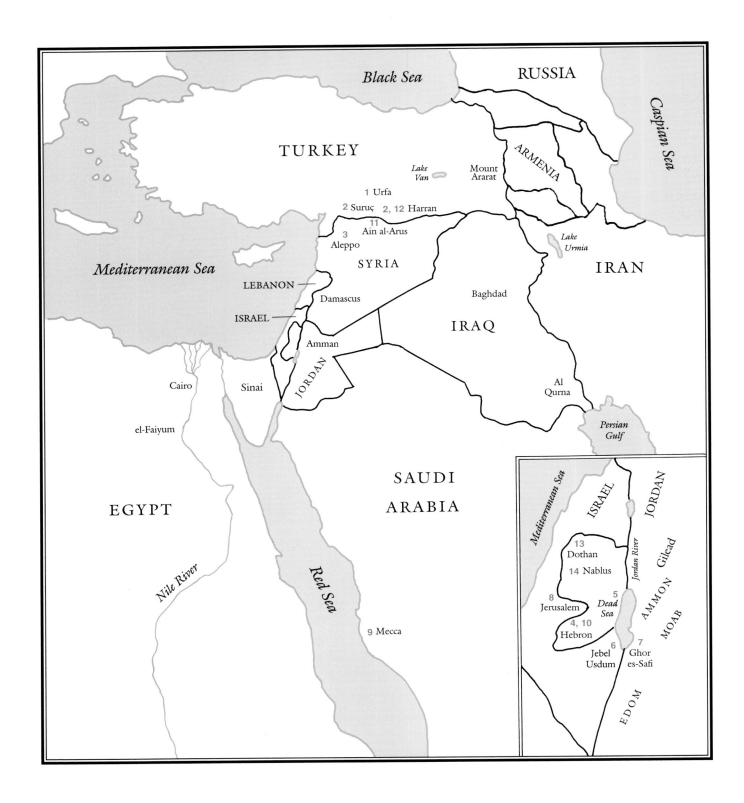

The city and site numbers, below, correspond to their geographic locations on the map (*opposite*). Page numbers in parenthesis are those corresponding to the following picture portfolio. As these relate to legends of a later time, the names of Abraham and Sarah are used throughout, as they were divinely changed after Genesis 17:5, 15.

1. URFA (anc. Edessa, mod. Şanliurfa, or "glorious Urfa"), Turkey. (*p. 149*): Although Ur of the Chaldaeans is called the land of Abraham's origins, Gen. 11:31, his legends are strong in Urfa in southeastern Turkey. Visits to the Abraham Mosque complex require that men, to the left, women, to the right, remove their shoes before entering "the cave where prophet Ibrahim was born."

   Below: Two Roman columns of the 3rd century A.D., standing tall on the ancient citadel above the city, are called by the local inhabitants the "Throne of Nimrod," after the "mighty hunter" of Biblical fame, Gen. 10:9. Legend tells that this tyrannical founder of Urfa catapulted Abraham from the high citadel into a fire below as his punishment for having destroyed all of the city's idols with an ax.

   (*p. 150*): The tears of the people watching Abraham burn in the fire formed the Pool of Abraham next to the Halil-ür-Rahman mosque, to the right. According to legend, the logs of the fire turned into carp. Due to the sacred nature of the golden fish which stock the pool, they are forbidden to be disturbed by passersby. Reflecting in the waters are the pillars of the mosque, *left*, built in 1721 by the Ottoman governor, Rizvaniye Ahmet Pasha.

2. HARRAN (anc. Carrhae), Turkey. (*p. 151*): This city some twenty-eight miles southeast of Urfa was the area called by Abraham "my country," known to the Patriarchs as Aram-naharaim, or Padan-aram, the route of the Aramaeans. Visions of Sarah, Rebekah, and Rachel in Biblical Haran are evoked by a modern-day shepherdess here framed against the archways of the Seljuk citadel in this walled city, which was a caravan stop on the Euphrates Valley trade route.

   Below, left: Legends of Abraham surround the very stones which dot Harran's fields. Medieval travelers were told of a rock, then in a mosque, against which the Patriarch used to lean, and of another in a sanctuary (Mashhad as-Sakhra), where he sat while tending his sheep.

   Below, right: SURUÇ, Turkey. Patriarchal origins are detected in the city names of the region. Suruç, between Harran and the Euphrates, recalls Serug, Abraham's great-grandfather.

3. ALEPPO, Syria. (*p. 152*): On top of the tell where the Citadel al-Qalah now stands, it is said that Abraham camped and milked his cow on the way to Canaan. The Arabic name for Aleppo is Halab, derived from *halib*, "milk."

4. HEBRON, Israel, West Bank. (*p. 153*): The six-hundred-year-old Oak of Abraham on the grounds of the Russian monastery, on the northern outskirts of the city, is shown as the one under which Abraham pitched his tent and where he was visited by three angels in human form, Gen. 18:2, who proclaimed that Sarah was to bear a child.

5. DEAD SEA, Israel. (*pp. 154-5*): Called in Arabic, Bahr Lut, the Sea of Lot, it descends to its lowest point about 1,292 feet below sea level. The salt pillars rising from its lifeless waters recall the Biblical destruction of the evil Cities of the Plain where Abraham's nephew Lot lived with his family. The curative powers of the saline waters gave rise to another legend, that Abraham's aged wife, Sarah, bathed in the Dead Sea before Isaac was conceived. The mountains of Moab loom beyond in Jordan.

6. JEBEL USDUM (Mount Sodom), Israel. (*p. 156*): The pillar of salt rising on the southwestern shore of the Dead Sea elicits the memory of the ill-fated wife of Lot who turned to witness the destruction of Sodom and Gomorrah and became this very pillar. Some believe that the formation waxes and wanes with the moon.

7. GHOR es-SAFI, Jordan (*p. 156,* below) Visitors and pilgrims enter "Lot's Cave" through a Byzantine church located in the cliffs of the southern Ghor above the Dead Sea. After the destruction of Sodom and Gomorrah, Lot fled to such a cave, where his daughters, anxious to repopulate the earth, conceived sons by him, the progenitors of the Moabites and Ammonites

8. JERUSALEM, Israel. (*p. 157*): The "lofty country" where God told Abraham to sacrifice Isaac was the land of Moriah, three days journey from Beersheba, traditionally on the city's Temple Mount. In an airview looking north, the golden dome above the octagonal Mosque of Omar, called the Dome of the Rock, shines over the old walled city.

   (*pp. 158-9*): Within the Mosque of Omar, marble colonnades surround the massive rock said to be the one on which Isaac was bound, before the angel of the Lord stayed Abraham's hand. The rock is claimed as the foundation marking the center of the earth. A subterranean cave called the Well of Souls is where the dead are believed to assemble for prayers.

9. MECCA, Saudi Arabia. (*pp. 160-1*): Moslem tradition changed the site of Abraham's trial of faith from Mount Moriah in Jerusalem to the Kaaba in the Sacred Mosque of Mecca, where it was Ishmael, the first-born son, revered as a patriarch of Islam, who was to be sacrificed. The large square Kaaba, draped in black with gold-embroidered verses from the Koran, is said to have been erected by Abraham on God's instructions, while the stone within the glass case (*right*), is the one on which Abraham stood while building the Kaaba with Ishmael. To the left of the drapery (not seen) is the sacred Black Stone of meteoric origin, placed there by Abraham and worshiped as the most holy object in Islam.

10. HEBRON, Israel, West Bank. (*p. 162*): The Tomb of the Patriarchs is seen through the trees from a near-by hill. It contains velvet-draped cenotaphs traditionally identified as those of Abraham, Isaac, and Jacob, their wives Sarah, Rebekah, and Leah, and, some say, Adam and Eve, who lived in Hebron after their expulsion from Eden. The site marks the Cave of Machpelah, which Abraham purchased from Ephron the Hittite as a family burial place, along with the surrounding fields and trees, for four hundred pieces of silver. A mosque joined to the building makes the complex a pilgrimage place for Moslems and Jews, albeit a volatile one.

11. AIN al-ARUS, Syria (*p. 163*): The "Well of the Fiancee" in northern Syria, two miles below the Turkish border, is considered to be the place where Abraham's servant emissary either rested on his way to Haran to find a bride for Isaac or where he actually met Rebekah. A shrine of the moon god was at the site, which is a source of the Balikh River.

12. HARRAN, Turkey. (*p. 163,* below): Bir Yaqub, Jacob's Well, also called Rebekah's Well, once was a gathering place where, tradition maintains, Rebekah met Abraham's servant and where Jacob rolled away a stone for Rachel so that she could draw water for her flocks. The well, now abandoned, is outside the city walls about a mile to the northwest in the Harran plain. Water troughs alongside the well would have been used by the servant's camels after their long journey from Canaan.

13. DOTHAN, Israel, West Bank. (*p. 164*): Jacob's sons pastured their flocks in the fertile valley on the route through northern Samaria, which Midianite, or Ishmaelite, caravans would have traversed on their way to Egypt. The dry well in the field, *foreground*, is shown as the one in which Joseph was placed and later removed by his jealous brothers, who then sold him to a passing caravan for twenty pieces of silver.

14. NABLUS, Israel, West Bank. (*p. 165*): The Jami el-Khadra, the Mosque of Jacob's Mourning, also called the Green Mosque, is thought to stand on the spot in this town of ancient Shechem where Joseph's blood-stained coat was brought to Jacob. A small room to the right of the courtyard is shown as the place where Jacob sat down and wept for Joseph.

Gen. 12:1 Now the Lord said unto Abram: "Get thee out of thy country, and from thy kindred, and from thy father's house. . . ."

Gen. 12:2 "And I will make of thee a great nation. . . ."

Gen. 12:3 "And I will bless them that bless thee,
and him that curseth thee will I curse . . ."

Gen. 12:5   And Abram took Sarai his wife, and Lot his brother's son, and all their substance that they had gathered, and the souls that they had gotten in Haran;

Gen. 12:5   and they went forth to go into the land of Canaan . . .

Gen. 18:1-4 And the Lord appeared unto him by the terebinths of Mamre. . . . and, lo, three men stood over against him. . . . and he ran to meet them. . . . and said: "My lord. . . pass not away, I pray thee, from thy servant. Let now a little water be fetched, and wash your feet, and recline yourselves under the tree."

Gen.19:24 Then the Lord caused to rain upon Sodom and upon
Gomorrah brimstone and fire from the Lord out of heaven;

Gen. 19:25   and he overthrew those cities, and all the Plain, and all
the inhabitants of the cities, and that which grew upon the ground.

Gen.19:26   But his wife looked back from
    behind him, and she became a pillar of salt.

Gen. 19:30   And Lot went up out of Zoar,
    and dwelt in the mountain, and his two
    daughters with him; for he feared to
    dwell in Zoar; and he dwelt in a cave,
    he   and his two daughters.

Gen. 22:2 And He said: "Take now thy son, thine only son, whom thou lovest, even Isaac, and get thee into the land of Moriah; and offer him there for a burnt-offering upon one of the mountains which I will tell thee of."

Gen. 22:4 On the third day Abraham lifted up his eyes, and saw the place afar off.

Gen. 22:9   And they came to the place which God had told him of; and Abraham built an altar there,

and laid the wood in order, and bound Isaac his son, and laid him on the altar upon the wood.

Koran, Sura 2:127 And when Abraham and Ishmael were raising the foundations of the House, (Abraham prayed): Our Lord! Accept from us (this duty).

Koran, Sura 37:102   He [Ishmael] said: O my father! Do that which
thou art commanded. Allah willing, thou shalt find me of the steadfast.

Gen. 23:19   And after this, Abraham buried Sarah his wife in the cave of the field
of Machpelah before Mamre—the same is Hebron—in the land of Canaan.

Gen. 24:2   And Abraham said unto his servant, the elder of his house, that ruled over all that he had. . .

Gen. 24:4   "But thou shalt go unto my country, and to my kindred, and take a wife for my son, even for Isaac."

Gen. 29:1   Then Jacob went on his journey and came to the land of the people of the east.

Gen. 29:2   And he looked, and behold a well in the field. . . and the stone upon the well's mouth was great.

Gen. 37:23   And it came to pass, when Joseph was come unto
his brethren, that they stripped Joseph of his coat, the coat of
many colors that was on him;

Gen. 37:24   and they took him, and cast him into the pit—
and the pit was empty, there was no water in it.

Gen. 37:34   And Jacob rent his garments, and put sackcloth upon his loins, and mourned for his son many days.

An Oral Memory — Tales of the Sinai Bedouin

Gathered around the campfire after a day's field work, Western scholars sometimes heard the local Sinai Bedouin recount the traditions of their religion. Biblical stories take on different shadings as the Bedouin adapt them to the life of their stark desert home. In the immense study, *Ordnance Survey of the Peninsula of Sinai*, by Captains C. W. Wilson and H. S. Palmer, published in England in 1869, another eminent Orientalist of the field team, E. H. Palmer, wrote of the "curious" Bedouin idea of Creation:

Bedouin of
Jebel Musa.

In the beginning God created man; and when He had made him he turned him not adrift, but created also for his use the camel and the ass, the sheep, the goat, and the ibex which is in the mountains. And the Lord taught him to sow and reap, and to milk camels, and gave him, moreover, the axe wherewith he might fell the trees. And the Lord made small birds when he was wroth with man, to eat up the seed which he had sown and spoil the young crops and the fruit, that man might be humbled from his pride. Then God made the serpent and He made it deaf one month and blind one month alternately, that it should not harm mankind. But, when man forgets his Maker, then the serpent stings him. Times and seasons, too, did God create for the service of man; and if the Lord wills it man prospers, but when He wills it, He can make him poor indeed.

The remains of ancient Egyptian mining expeditions to southern Sinai for turquoise were recorded by Sir W. M. Flinders Petrie in his book *Researches in Sinai*, 1906. A fellow scholar, C. T. Currelly, included the Bedouin version of the casting out of Abraham's Egyptian concubine, Hagar, and their son, Ishmael. Currelly noted, "Only one thing seemed well fixed in their minds - namely, that all of their own faith were going to heaven and all others were not, a theological position in which they do not stand alone."

Bedouin wife,
Serabit el-Khadim.

The prophet Abraham turned Ishmael and his mother from the tents. Together they wandered forth into the desert, till the water-skin was empty. Gradually the boy grew weaker and weaker. At last he could go no further. Twice had his mother left him and rushed eagerly on, to find that the soft blue pool she saw in the distance was but a mirage. Sadly she came back to face the death she now knew to be in-evitable, but could not remain near him in the final agonies. That she might not see him die, she went a short distance away, but she turned her eyes, how-ever, to the spot, and saw him raise one foot and bring it down on the earth, when suddenly a spout of water sprang from where his heel had struck. She rushed back and put some to his lips.

V

EGYPT
The Nurturing Land

———

CYRUS H. GORDON

A DISTINCTIVE LAND with a distinctive culture, Egypt was called in antiquity the "gift of the Nile." Egyptians were defined as the people who drank the waters of the Nile. Habitable Egypt is basically the long, narrow Nile Valley as far south as Aswan. It is very fertile and heavily populated. A few oases, notably the Faiyum, can also support an agrarian population. At the north end it opens into the Delta, which forms a large, well-watered triangle. At the south end it goes first into Nubia and then into inner Africa. Accordingly, Egypt was conditioned geographically to develop a distinctive civilization, as it was impossible for outsiders to enter it except at the north and south ends. The two flanks along the river were protected by formidable deserts.

Since the Nile produced enough water for rich productivity, the Egyptians were able to foster the notion of a happy life on earth that was worth continuing in the future. They hoped to continue their pleasures—eating, drinking, fishing, hunting, taking trips on boats, and playing various games—in the future life and left us an extensive portrayal of their expectations in their funerary art.

The early Hebrews, like the Babylonians, the Greeks, and others, looked at things differently. The post-mortem state was not regarded as happy. At best it was rather gloomy. Outside Egypt the ancient Near Easterners might find rest after death, but no active joy. The development of thought—we can call it the history of ideas—in most of the Old Testament does not indicate a happy afterlife, not even for those who deserved it. In Genesis Jacob assumes he will descend into Sheol, the Hebrew for Hades. At this early period no Hebrew looked forward to the afterlife. This did not change until the end of the Old Testament period. The best statement of it is in Daniel, Chapter 12, where it is predicted that the virtuous dead will be resurrected for eternal bliss, and the wicked, undeserving dead will reap eternal damnation. During the sojourn in Egypt, the Hebrews temporarily adopted some Egyptian customs such as embalming or mummifying the dead. Jacob and Joseph were embalmed. However, in their own land the Hebrews gave this up in keeping with their abhorrence of corpses or any dead or diseased tissue. The ancient Hebrews had no taste for the cult of the dead and gradually divested themselves of Egyptian and other funerary rites.

The first highly developed period of Egyptian history is known as the Old Kingdom in the 3rd millennium B.C. There were developments before that but not of a truly historic nature with abundant written records. The Egyptians created the greatest and most enduring monuments of stone architecture the world has ever known. The earliest monumental, free-standing stone building is the Step Pyramid of Saqqara built by Imhotep, a kind of Renaissance man, who was an architect, an author of Wisdom Literature, a physician, a royal counselor, and statesman. His Step Pyramid built for Pharaoh Djoser still stands, a wonder to behold. Later there came the larger pyramids at Giza (of Cheops, Chephren, and Mycerinus), but the outstanding one, and the turning point in architectural history, is the Step Pyramid at Saqqara.

Wisdom Literature was one of the literary, moral, and ethical accomplishments of Imhotep. This form of literature continued to develop and crossed national and linguistic boundaries easily since it deals with universal rather than regional or, as we would say in religious matters, denominational concerns.

With its open borders at its northern and southern extremities, Egypt was open to immigrations which on occasion grew to the proportions of invasions. There were two main periods of such invasions. They are called the Intermediate Periods. The First Intermediate Period occurred after the Old Kingdom in the latter part of the 3rd millennium B.C. The general breakdown of order was lamented by the Egyptian Ipuwer who included, among other woes, the influx of foreigners in the Delta. The Second Intermediate Period took place after the Middle Kingdom towards the end of the first half of the 2nd millennium B.C. The invaders of the Second Intermediate Period are generally called the Hyksos. They had to be expelled so that Egypt could control its own native destiny again.

The Middle Kingdom flourished in the early centuries of the 2nd millennium B.C. One of the accomplishments during that period was the writing of short stories of an entertaining nature. These had little to do with religion or resurrection but were designed to provide entertainment and good reading matter. They constitute the world's first literary prose.

The most famous of those tales is the *Story of Sinuhe*. Sinuhe was an official in the court of Amenemhet I, the first pharaoh of the 12th Dynasty. Sinuhe was returning from a royal expedition to Libya when news came that Amenemhet had died. His son and successor, Sesostris I, who had been Sinuhe's superior in the field, rushed back to the capital in order to secure the kingdom. But Sinuhe, fearing an unpredictable shake-up, panicked and fled from Egypt into Canaan. In spite of his success in the employ of an important sheikh at an oasis in Syria, Sinuhe felt homesick and wanted to return to his native land. His recall by Sesostris, who became the pharaoh on the death of his father, was a very happy moment in the life of Sinuhe. He left everything behind—his wife, his position, his children—put his house in order, and went back to die in his native Egypt. The king erected a tomb for him and endowed him with everything necessary to insure a happy afterlife.

This is a typical Egyptian story. While the outside world might be of interest to visit, the Egyptians regarded it as not fit to live in. Only Egypt by the banks of the Nile was the place for any first-class human being. Nonetheless, Sinuhe gives a vivid description of Canaan during the period of the Middle Kingdom. Both the prose style and the theme of wandering and return have close parallels to the Patriarchal narratives. Sinuhe and Joseph are successful in their adopted lands but long to return home and eventually to be buried in their native countries.

The Hyksos who ruled during the 15th Dynasty were composed of different ethnic groups under a united leadership. They included Semites, Hurrians, and others.* They introduced the horse-drawn chariot, which revolutionized the art of war and marked a permanent change in Egyptian capability in warfare and in Egyptian life in general. The Hebrew infiltration of the eastern Delta that ended with the Exodus, traditionally in the 13th century B.C., should not be identified with the Hyksos occupation. The Hyksos ruled Egypt, the Hebrews did not. Their departures from Egypt were centuries apart.

Egypt entered its Empire period, or New Kingdom, after the Hyksos were expelled in the mid-16th century B.C., thanks largely to the advances in military science learned from them. Ahmose I, the first pharaoh of the 18th Dynasty, is generally given credit for ridding Egypt of the invaders. The 18th Dynasty had a number of important pharaohs. One unique pharaoh was a woman, Hatshepsut, who engaged in interesting exploits, including explorations in the Horn of Africa. She imported and transplanted trees bearing incense into Egypt, as it was highly prized. Events during her reign are seen on murals in her temple at Deir el-Bahri.

One interesting detail indicates the social tie between Egypt and Canaan, including ancient Israel. Egyptian has no word for "queen." Hatshepsut ruled as a pharaoh and often was depicted on her monuments with a beard. In Canaan, as we know from the Ugaritic tablets, the chief woman in the royal courts was the "Great Lady " who came into her own only when her son had succeeded to the throne. In Israel and Judah too there is no such person as a queen, a *malkah*, which one can check by reading the books of Kings and Chronicles. As in Ugarit, the important woman in the royal court was the mother of the crown prince whose influence increased after the death of her royal husband when her son came to power. The title for this woman, far from being queen, is a *gevira*, the "grand lady" in court.

After the great pharaohs of the 18th Dynasty, notably Thutmose III, who invaded Palestine and left records of his assault on the great fortified city of Megiddo, there was a gradual decline, ending in the reigns of Amenhotep III and his son Amenhotep IV, the religious heretic Akhenaten of the Amarna Age. The latter suppressed the leading religious force in

---

*Ed. note: Regarding the origins of the Hyksos, excavations at Tell el-Dab'a-Qantir (Avaris and Piramesse), in the eastern Nile Delta, confirm the existence of a largely Canaanite (Asiatic) population with a distinctive Syro-Palestinian culture, beginning with the Middle Kingdom into the Second Intermediate Period. Dr. Manfred Bietak of the University of Vienna, the director of the excavations, wrote that Egyptian, or Egyptianized, and Canaanite populations lived side by side. Led by a local Asiatic king, perhaps Salitis, 1650 B.C., the Asiatics established Hyksos rule over nearly all of Egypt.

Egypt, namely the cult of Amon, originally the god of Thebes. When Thebes was the religious capital of a world empire, Amon was combined with Re, the sun, identified with life, to become Amon-Re, the god of the universe. Akhenaten despoiled the priesthood of Amon-Re and elevated Aten, the sun disk, to the position of Master of the Universe, which approximates monotheism.

✗	In the international atmosphere of the Near East, increased contacts between peoples of the region encouraged monotheistic trends whereby they might come to believe that the world was ruled by one god, often the head of their particular pantheon, whom they called by different names depending on their particular language. To the extent that Akhenaten's "monotheism" is a product of the same general international period of the Amarna and Ramesside ages that also produced "Mosaic monotheism"—but only to that extent—Hebrew and Egyptian "monotheism" are historically related. In no case has the one been borrowed from the other. What is clear from Genesis is that it reflects an age of internationalism and sophistication. As Sinuhe explained his exile in Canaan as "the plan of God," so Joseph and pharaoh speak of "God" who rules the universe, the one who was above all other local and national deities.

The 19th Dynasty in the 13th century B.C. inaugurated the Ramesside Age. Ramses II, its greatest ruler, was the king who outlived his first twelve crown princes. It was only the thirteenth, Merneptah, who succeeded to the throne after him. Merneptah's name is actually preserved in the Old Testament. In the period of the conquest of Joshua, there is a name, Me-Neptoah, which is not Semitic. It is a form of Merneptah. The full place-name is Ma'ayan-Me-Neptoah, which means "the spring of Merneptah," referred to in Joshua 15:9 and 18:15. Merneptah left a famous stele in which the people of Israel are mentioned for the first time in extra-Biblical sources. He claims to have wiped out and destroyed Israel, a boast which was contradicted by subsequent history.

Shortly after this period, copper mines in southern Palestine were exploited by the Egyptians. At a place now called Timna, discovered by Nelson Glueck in 1934, copper mines were found which belonged to the Egyptians who had a temple there and who left monuments with inscriptions. The turquoise mines and quarries in southern Sinai, such as those at Serabit el-Khadim, were also exploited. It is entirely likely that the laborers employed by the Egyptians in Sinai were Semites. Alphabetic inscriptions have been found carved on the rock walls near some of the mines. The script has been called Proto-Sinaitic and regarded as a progenitor of our modern alphabet. The most probable reading in the Sinaitic inscriptions remains B^{C}LT, "Baalat," the feminine counterpart of the Canaanite god Baal. The texts are still obscure and should not be regarded as the primary source of the Hebrew alphabet. Ugaritic has that distinction.

Toward the end of the 2nd millennium B.C., we have the best written example of Wisdom Literature in Egyptian, the *Wisdom of Amenemope*. Its advocacy of honesty, efficiency, reliability, and flawless character as the key to success is common to Wisdom Literature in general, including the Biblical Book of Proverbs. The most specific connection between Amenemope and Proverbs is that the authors of both state, "I have written for you thirty (chapters)." Both aim at teaching us to be wise, industrious, studious, and prudent, so that we may avoid the pitfalls of folly and live successful lives.

In the 10th century B.C., pharaoh's daughter married King Solomon. We read in I Kings 9:16 that pharaoh conquered the city of Gezer, which then was in Canaanite hands, and turned it over to his daughter and her husband as part of her dowry. Solomon's son and successor, Rehoboam, in his fifth year, suffered an invasion by Pharaoh Shishak (Shoshenq I), who stripped the temple of its treasures. Absolute synchronisms are rare in Scriptures, but this provides one which cannot be contested, for Shishak was not only reigning in the fifth year of Rehoboam but specifically had a Canaanite campaign in that time. In Genesis, where any king of Egypt is simply called "pharaoh" without his particular name, it is impossible to set up synchronisms. Joseph interpreted pharaoh's dreams, but there is no way of determining which pharaoh is meant. Comparisons of this kind have no historic significance, but they confirm the authenticity of the cultural milieu stated in the source. The Joseph story marks the culmination of the charming prose developed in the Middle Egyptian romances.

Toward the end of the 7th century B.C., Pharaoh Necho II went forth to oppose the Neo-Babylonian forces and to help his allies, the Assyrians. This was an age of restorations. The Babylonians wanted to restore the Babylonian empire. The Egyptians under Necho were trying to restore the empire of Thutmose III which reached to the Euphrates River. Indeed, on this particular campaign, Necho was headed for the Euphrates when he was confronted by the Judaean king Josiah, who actually lost his life by an arrow shot by the Egyptians in the battle around Megiddo.

The Biblical author in II Chronicles 35:21 has Necho telling Josiah not to block his way because Necho has no grievance against him. But Josiah had other plans. He too was planning a restoration of all Israel, the north as well as the south, into his kingdom which had its center in Jerusalem, where the God Yahweh was worshiped in the Temple. Chronicles tells us that God, speaking through the mouth of Necho, told Josiah that unless he desisted and abandoned his opposition to Necho, God (Elohim) would destroy Josiah. The text continues that when Josiah was killed it was because Josiah had refused to harken to the word of God from the mouth of Necho. This fits the psychology of the times. In this international period, as in others before it, all sophisticated people worshiped the God of the universe who transcended all national and local gods. The Egyptians call that god P'n*t*r, pronounced *pa-necher*, "The God," and this is the way Elohim is used in this particular passage. Scripture attributed the true word of the true God to the Egyptian Necho, whereas the messianic king Josiah occupying the throne in Jerusalem was spiritually too obtuse to realize this.

For the interplay of art and texts, Egypt has better illustrations of ancient life than any other culture in the area. In the *Book of the Dead* are vignettes—drawings or paintings—showing various scenes that were important for the process of resurrection and eternal life. One of them is called "The Weighing of the Heart," in which the heart of the deceased is weighed against the feather, symbolizing truth. If one's heart is true, he has overcome one of the important obstacles to salvation. The Hebrews did not leave artistic records worthy of the name. Their record is verbal. In Scriptural poetry we have an epithet of God who weighs, or tests, the heart and kidneys. God in his scales tests the organs of our integrity and character. This was something expressed pictorially and verbally by the Egyptians but only verbally by the Hebrews.

There are hundreds of instructive examples where illustrations from Egypt show graphically the concepts of the Old Testament. Egypt gives us more material to work with than most of the countries in the Bible World.

DIVINE KINGSHIP

The order and dignity of the Old
Kingdom is reflected in the statue of
Chephren (*facing page*), the fourth
king of the 4th Dynasty, c.2550 B.C.
The falcon god, Horus, spreads his
protecting wings behind Chephren's
throne, indicating the divinity of the
king, who was known as the Son of
Re, the creator sun god, or the living
Horus, embodiment of good. The
divine powers of the king were
described for the children of the
Chief Treasurer of Amenemhet III
on a 12th Dynasty stele from Abydos.
These same powers were attributed
by the Hebrews to their one God:

> He is Perception which is in
>   men's hearts.
>
> He has filled the two lands
>   with strength and life.
>
> The king is a *ka* [vital force].
>
> He who is to be is his creation.
>
> The begetter who creates
>   the people.
>
> He whom he hates will bear
>   woes.
>
> He whom the king has loved
>   will be a revered one.

The children then were urged to
serve the king faithfully:

> If ye do this, your persons
>   shall be unblemished.
> Ye will find it (so) forever.

It was the king's responsibility to dispense *ma'at* (justice) in his
realm, personified by Maat, the goddess of law and truth, known
by her ideogram, the feather of truth, as shown in a bas relief
from the tomb of Seti I, 19th Dynasty (*above*). During times of
political chaos, the ensuing disorder meant that Maat, at least for
the moment, had been cast out. The gods communicated directly
with the king, who guided Egypt's destiny, but, unlike the Hebrew
God, only indirectly and impersonally with man.

SUN AND NILE

Hail to thee, O Nile, that issues from the earth,
and comes to keep Egypt alive.

The annual inundation of the Nile, according to the ancient hymn quoted above, and the daily rebirth of the sun were the two dominant forces of Egyptian life. Looming in the desert beyond the reach of the river which floods the marshy plain before it, the "Bent, " or "Rhomboid" pyramid (*near right*), and the "Red" Pyramid (*far right*), built in Dahshur, south of Memphis, for Snefru, the founder of the 4th Dynasty, stand as witnesses to the life or death of the land, which was determined by its proximity to the Nile. A servant (*below*), is seen doing the routine chore of raising life-giving Nile water for his master's garden by means of a *shaduf*, a bucket suspended from a weighted beam, from a wall painting in the Ramesside tomb of the head sculptor, Apy, in the workmen's village of Deir el-Medina at Thebes. Simple astronomical observations of the stars allowed the Egyptians to predict the rise of the Nile with fair accuracy, while their solar calendar of 365 days reflected the agricultural year: Inundation, Growth, and Harvest. When the Nile did not rise due to a lack of rainfall from central Africa or melting snow from the Ethiopian highlands, famine occurred, such as the seven lean years foretold in the dreams of Joseph's pharaoh, Gen. 41:1-7.

THE VIZIER

I judged [poor and] rich (alike).
I rescued the weak from the strong. . . .
I defended the husbandless widow.
I established the son and heir on the side of the father.
I gave [bread to the hungry], water to the thirsty, meat
    and ointment and clothes to him who had nothing. . .
I was innocent before God. . . .
I did not per[vert justice] for reward.
I was not deaf to the empty-handed. . . .
I never accepted anyone's bribe.
           —Tomb 100 of Rekhmire, Thebes

Egypt's government evolved into an intricate bureaucracy run by officials accountable to the king. Second in command was the vizier, such as Rekhmire, who served the 18th Dynasty pharaohs Thutmose III and Amenhotep II. In his vizier's robe, holding the baton of authority, Rekhmire and his mother partake of the meal of the dead (*above*), from a wall painting in his tomb in the hill of Sheikh Abd el-Qurna at Thebes. His son, the erased figure before them, consecrates the offering. The standards of justice (quoted above), which Rekhmire raised "to the height of heaven," reflect the office of Joseph. During the 18th Dynasty, the increased scope of government required two viziers, one at Thebes in the south and one at Memphis in the north. Joseph would have lived in the Delta nearer to Goshen where his family had been invited to settle. Rekhmire's other titles confirm his role as "the ears and eyes of the sovereign":

IN THE ADMINISTRATION OF THE KINGDOM
Mayor of the City (of the residential capital, Thebes)
Administrator of the nomes
Superintendent of the two treasuries of gold and of silver
Superintendent of archives
Head of the Six Great Houses (of Justice)
Confidential controller in the royal administration
Steward of the palace
Superintendent of stewards

IN THE ADMINISTRATION OF AMON
Administrator of all works in Karnak
Superintendent of works
Superintendent of crafts
Superintendent of the workshop of Amon
Chief scribe of the temple offerings of Amon

PRIESTLY TITLES
Father and favorite of the god
Priest of Maat
Greatest of seers in the Great House
Sem Priest
One who establishes rules for the temples of Upper
    and Lower Egypt

—and— Inevitable Taxes

Agriculture was the basis of Egypt's economy and the taxation of its produce a main source of income. During the New Kingdom, all of the land belonged to pharaoh with the exception of the temple estates. It was this new system of land ownership following the expulsion of the foreign Hyksos Dynasty that is attributed in Genesis to Joseph's wise policy of buying all privately owned land for the king in exchange for food during the seven-year famine. To the Hebrews, the land belonged to God, the sole legitimate owner, who could dispose of it at will. Officials of the Treasury, with its subdivisions of granary and herds, have come to a country estate to assess the crop yields owed to the royal storehouses, as shown on a wall painting (*below*) in Tomb 69 of Menna, a scribe of fields of Amenhotep III, at Sheikh Abd el-Qurna, Thebes. The diligent

surveyors attended by their menials, *upper register*, measure the height of the grain to determine its readiness for harvest and subsequent tax revenues, using ropes knotted at intervals. A peasant couple, *center*, carry other taxable items to the collectors. According to established lists, these included grain, jars of honey, oil, wine, loaves of bread, and livestock, such as the donkey, being urged on by a boy with a stick, *right*, and a goat, which he holds under his left arm. Menna stands in a papyrus hut, *lower register, right*, while receiving two jugs of wine. Scribes sitting and standing behind him record the amount of grain being scooped in baskets by the field hands. The horse and chariot, *facing page*, elements which the Hyksos introduced into Egypt, patiently wait for Menna to complete his day's work.

Nomes and Gods of Egypt

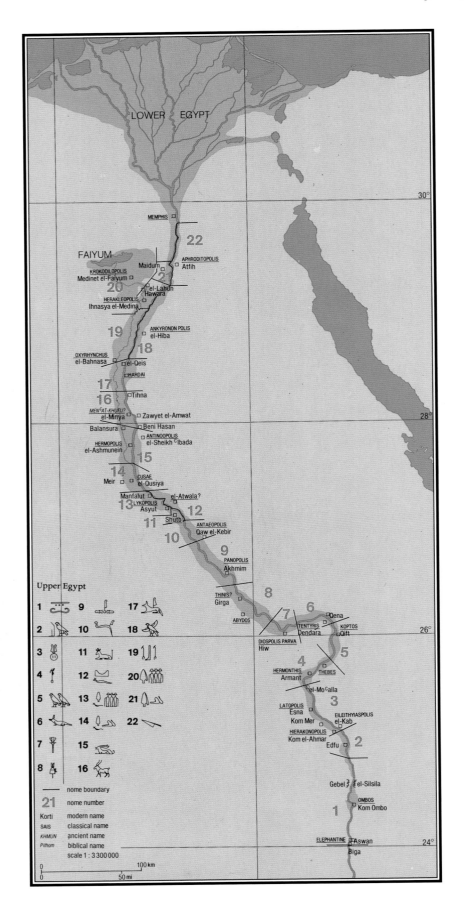

LOWER EGYPT

30°

MEMPHIS

22

FAIYUM

APHRODITOPOLIS
Maidum Atfih

KROKODILOPOLIS
Medinet el-Faiyum

21

20

el-Lahun
Hawara

HERAKLEOPOLIS
Ihnasya el-Medina

19

ANKYRONON POLIS
el-Hiba

18

OXYRHYNCHUS
el-Bahnasa el-Qeis

HARDAI

17

16

Tihna

MEN^CAT-KHUFU?
el-Minya Zawyet el-Amwat

Balansura Beni Hasan

ANTINOOPOLIS
HERMOPOLIS el-Sheikh ^CIbada
el-Ashmunein

15

14 CUSAE
Meir el-Qusiya

Manfalut el-Atwala?
13 LYKOPOLIS
Asyut 12
11 Shutb
ANTAEOPOLIS
10 Qaw el-Kebir

9
PANOPOLIS
Akhmim

Upper Egypt

THINIS? 8
Girga

ABYDOS 7 6
TENTYRIS Qena
Dendara KOPTOS
Qift 26°

DIOSPOLIS PARVA
Hiw

5

4
HERMONTHIS THEBES
Armant
el-Mo^Calla

LATOPOLIS 3
Esna
Kom Mer EILEITHYIASPOLIS
el-Kab
HIERAKONOPOLIS
Kom el-Ahmar
Edfu 2

Gebel el-Silsila

OMBOS
1 Kom Ombo

ELEPHANTINE Aswan 24°
Biga

1	9	17
2	10	18
3	11	19
4	12	20
5	13	21
6	14	22
7	15	
8	16	

— nome boundary
21 nome number
Korti modern name
SAIS classical name
KHMUN ancient name
Pithom biblical name
scale 1 : 3 300 000

0 _____ 100 km
0 _____ 50 mi

28°

In order to control the resources of Egypt, the land was divided into provinces, called nomes by the Greeks, encompassing the 750 miles of navigable river from the Mediterranean to the First Cataract at Aswan. Often, hereditary nomarchs administered the 22 nomes of Upper Egypt (*left*), and the 20 nomes of Lower Egypt (*facing page*), each with its own god and ensign. The prominent nomes were associated with the powerful gods of creation, such as Amon of Thebes (*above*), whose double-plumed headdress towers above his crown. He was lord of the Scepter, or Waset nome 4 in Upper Egypt, derived from the *was*-scepter, symbol of dominion. He was the breath of life who "abides in all things."

Nomes of Joseph's World

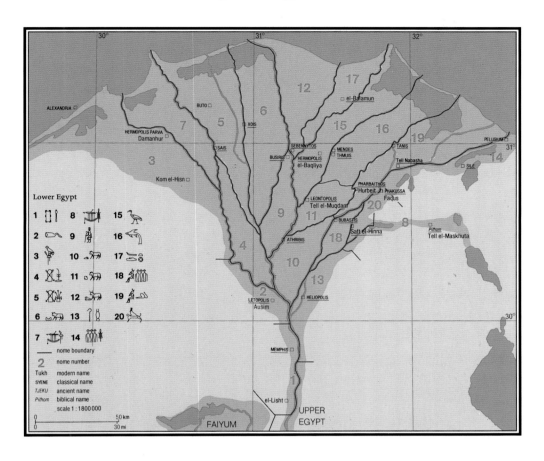

To the north, the Nile fanned out into several branches to form the fertile Delta, now referred to as Lower Egypt due to its position on the lower reaches of the river. The accessibility to the Delta through the Sinai made it the first area to be affected by any foreign influx from Asia, such as the Hyksos from Canaan, who were entrenched in their capital of Avaris on the Pelusiac arm of the Nile by the 17th century B.C. The land of Goshen, called by Joseph's pharaoh the "best of the land," now is believed to be in the area of Avaris and Piramesse in the Sethroe nome 14, modern Tell el-Dab'a-Qantir. Prior claims have included the Wadi Tumilat in the Eastern Harpoon nome 8, or the Arabian nome 20. Biblical requisites for Goshen were for a place removed from Egyptian settlements and influence, with adequate pastureland to sustain the flocks which Jacob brought with him from Canaan. To the southwest was On, the Greek Heliopolis, nome 13, the realm of Re, the sun god who, combining his solar disk with the falcon head of Horus (*above, right*), was known as the righteous Re-Harakhte. In this center of learning, Joseph married into its priestly family. Memphis was the White Wall nome l, the first capital which King Menes chose at the junction of Upper and Lower Egypt after the two lands were united, c. 3000 B.C. Its creator god, Ptah, gave the world its form. An ancient text relates, "He fashioned the gods. . . he founded nomes, he set the gods in their seats of worship." On a stone relief (*right*), Ptah wears a fitted cap and holds a scepter combining the *was*, *ankh*, and *djed* pillar, symbolizing authority, life, and stability. Within the city fortress, the young Joseph might have been imprisoned before being summoned by a troubled pharaoh to interpret his dreams.

MAGIC AND THE AFTERLIFE
— In the Realm of Osiris

Eternal life after death was the wish of every Egyptian, and magic was the means to achieve it. In the earliest religious texts written in hieroglyphs on the antechamber of the pyramid of Unas at Saqqara (*facing page*), this last king of the 5th Dynasty was identified with Osiris, the resurrected god of the dead. Many ritual incantations were to be spoken by the spirit of Unas as he ascended to heaven to be united with Re, the sun god. By the 18th Dynasty, these Pyramid Texts formed the basis for the *Book of the Dead* which was placed in each tomb and contained formulas to overcome any evil spirit which might deter the deceased from passing safely through the Underworld into eternal life. In the Papyrus of Ani, the royal, scribe, c. 1250 B.C., produced at Thebes, Osiris is pictured swathed in white funeral wrappings (*right*),as he receives the verdict that Ani has been judged virtuous. On the lotus facing him are the four sons of Horus. To the Hebrews, the place where the souls of the dead gathered was Sheol, a joyless subterranean dwelling from which there was no return.

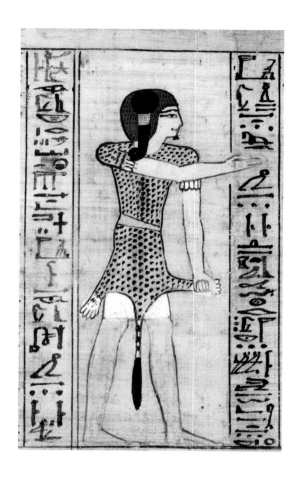

The rituals of the *Book of the Dead* were recited by special priests who were part of a complex hierarchy beginning with the king and descending in order through his delegate, the high priest, into every facet of Egyptian religious life. The Papyrus of Ani illustrates the Sem priest Iunmutef in his imposing leopard skin (*left*), wearing the side lock of Harpocrates, or Horus the child. Iunmutef introduces Ani to the gods and pleads his innocence: "He hath not sinned against any gods. Grant ye that he may be with you for all time." The Sem priest also performed the ceremony of the "Opening of the Mouth and Eyes, " which was intended to restore normal human functions to the deceased. His body then could "dwell with the company of the great gods in Annu, " (On, or Heliopolis). It was in this early theological center that scribe-priests first transformed the Pyramid Texts into the rituals of the new Osirian funerary cult. By contrast, the sons of the Patriarchs buried their fathers in a simple act of filial respect without benefit of priestly intermediaries or elaborate magical rites.

Views of Eternity

The lifetime pleasures enjoyed by New Kingdom dignitaries were painted on their tomb walls in preparation for their entrance into the glorious afterlife. Such murals were intended to promote the happiness and well-being of the deceased as he viewed the people he once loved sharing in the activity he most enjoyed. For Nakht, the Scribe of the Granaries, c.1425 B.C., these included his favorite sport of marshland hunting in the company of his family. On the mural from his Tomb 52 in the Theban necropolis at Sheikh Abd el-Qurna, Nakht stands tall in a papyrus skiff, *facing page*, hurling ebony throw-sticks at water fowl in flight. Behind him, his wife, Tawi, holds his waist, while his seated daughter steadies his right leg. His other children watch intently. The landscape is symbolic of the mythical Reed Marshes beyond the eastern horizon described in the Pyramid Texts and the *Book of the Dead* where ample birds and fish would have provided Nakht with food and recreation. The desire of the Egyptian to take his wealth and comforts with him after his death was the kind of materalism which the Hebrews rejected. Theirs was a moral criterion for happiness, originating with the Garden of Eden, by which man's actions determined his fate during his lifetime. Only good deeds on earth made man worthy of contentment and long life, with no thought of the hereafter.

SCIENCE AND WISDOM
—In the Realm of Thoth

Out of the world of magic, the infant science of medicine emerged through a process of observation and reasoning, guided by Thoth of Hermopolis, the god of magic, wisdom, and healing. Diseases and their remedies were recorded, probably as early as the Pyramid Age, again through the aegis of Thoth who, as the inventor of writing, was the patron god of physicians and also of the scribes whose writing schools these future doctors attended before studying in the medical centers of the great temples. Some of the introductions to the prescriptions collected in the Papyrus Ebers, *below*, c.1550 B.C., written in hieratic invoke the protection of the deities. Thoth, thought to be the author of the Papyrus, advised Re in the patient's recovery, while Osiris and his wife, Isis, "great in sorcery," delivered him from "everything bad and evil and vicious." A physician's marginal note commends an effective incantation, "Really excellent, (proved) many times." To the Patriarchs, their one God alone could bring plague on pharaoh or cure a barren wife.

In the Papyrus Ebers, the study of the heart was called "the beginning of the physician's secret." As the source of life and intelligence, the heart was the only organ which was left in the body during the embalming process. In the *Book of the Dead*, it was Thoth who declared that the deceased was righteous when his heart balanced equally with Maat's feather of truth. This need for a favorable judgment in the afterlife, in the spirit of Maat's truth and Thoth's wisdom, resulted in a heightened sense of social justice and consideration to others in the Middle Kingdom. One of Thoth's forms was the baboon, symbol of equilibrium. As the moon god, measurer of time and the seasons, Thoth wears a crescent moon and sun disk on a statuette, probably of serpentine, *opposite*, from el-Amarna, late 18th Dynasty. A scribe sits cross-legged before him contemplating the writing invented by Thoth without which mankind would have forgotten the arts and sciences which he gave it.

The scribes who honored Thoth were the preservers of great writings which would endure longer than the pyramids. Lines from "In Praise of Learned Scribes," in the Papyrus Chester Beatty IV, Thebes, c. 1300 B.C., affirm their craft:

> More effective is a book than a decorated tombstone. . . .
>
> A man is perished, his corpse is dust, all his relatives are come to the ground—(but). . . .
> Though they are gone and their names are forgotten, it is writing that makes them remembered.

Scribes were a critical element in perpetuating the ethics of the Hebrews. Although the Egyptians had sacred texts, they never established a body of canonized books, as did the Hebrews, with the obligation to teach them to their children.

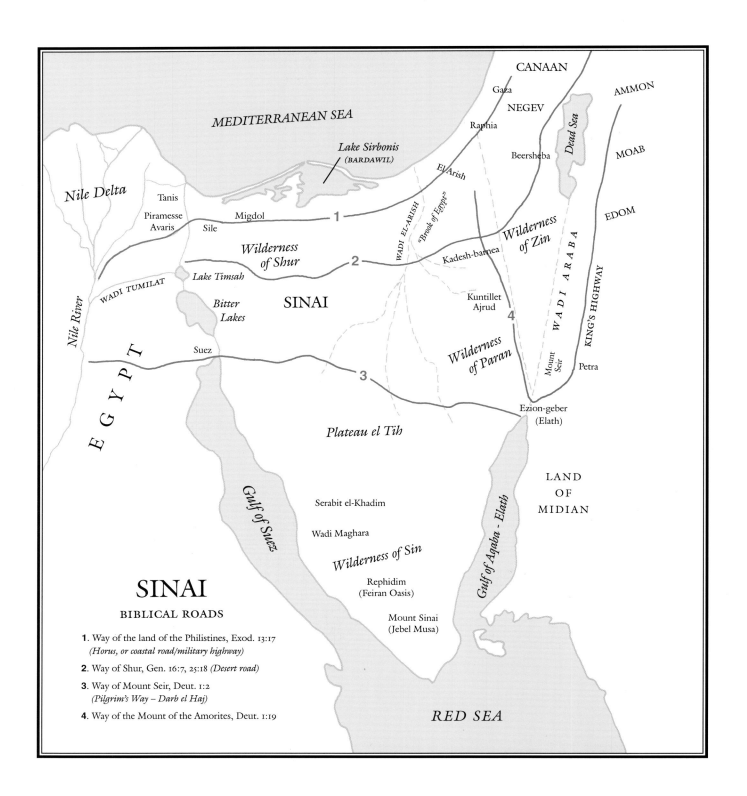

MEDITERRANEAN SEA

CANAAN

Gaza

NEGEV

AMMON

Raphia

Lake Sirbonis
(BARDAWIL)

Dead Sea

MOAB

Nile Delta

Tanis

El Arish

Beersheba

EDOM

Piramesse
Avaris

Migdol

1

Sile

Wilderness
of Shur

Wilderness
of Zin

Kadesh-barnea

WADI EL-ARISH

"Brook of Egypt"

2

WADI TUMILAT

Lake Timsah

SINAI

Kuntillet
Ajrud

4

WADI ARABA

KING'S HIGHWAY

Nile River

Bitter
Lakes

Wilderness
of Paran

Mount
Seir

Petra

EGYPT

Suez

3

Ezion-geber
(Elath)

Plateau el Tih

LAND
OF
MIDIAN

Gulf of Suez

Serabit el-Khadim

Wadi Maghara

Gulf of Aqaba - Elath

Wilderness of Sin

SINAI

BIBLICAL ROADS

1. Way of the land of the Philistines, Exod. 13:17
   (Horus, or coastal road/military highway)

2. Way of Shur, Gen. 16:7, 25:18 *(Desert road)*

3. Way of Mount Seir, Deut. 1:2
   (Pilgrim's Way – Darb el Haj)

4. Way of the Mount of the Amorites, Deut. 1:19

Rephidim
(Feiran Oasis)

Mount Sinai
(Jebel Musa)

RED SEA

THE MANY PATHS OF SINAI

Through the years, archaeological discoveries have confirmed that the Sinai was a vital land bridge between Asia and Africa, an area of ethnic diversity, and a holy place. In the Genesis tradition, the northern Sinai road was traversed by the Patriarchs seeking sustenance in the fertile Nile Delta in times of famine. Along this road, Joseph was brought as a slave by a merchant caravan to his ultimate destiny as the preserver of his people.

Surveys in the northern Sinai have identified hundreds of ancient sites with large populations and industrial centers. Forts, or depots, on the coastal road serviced passing caravans, and silos filled with grain supplied armies transiting on this active merchant artery. The Hyksos who came from Canaan through the Sinai ruled in the Delta by the 17th century B.C., thereby ending Egypt's political isolation. With their expulsion some hundred years later, Egyptian forces, spurred on by patriotic revenge, expanded the Empire as far north as the Euphrates River. Canaan became an eastern extension of Egyptian culture. Trade was a royal monopoly. In lands new and strange to them, Egyptians and Canaanites shared each other's gods.

The Egyptians called the Sinai nomads "Shasu," each tribe lord of its own territory, which over the centuries was determined by oral law and tenancy or, less peacefully, by prolonged blood feuds. Their nomadic nature was that of Abraham's first-born son, Ishmael, "his hand against every man, and every man's hand against him." In the Wilderness of Paran, bordering on eastern Sinai, Ishmael and his Egyptian wife raised their twelve sons, called "princes," or tribal chiefs, under divine protection. Their territory eventually extended from Havilah in Arabia, to Shur "that is before Egypt." This admixture of Egyptian and nomad accords with the long relations between them.

In the southern Sinai the ultimate cultural synthesis occurred. Egyptians, Semites, and the indigenous population shared their lives and beliefs for the duration of each royal mining expedition to the rich copper and turquoise mines of Wadi Maghara and Serabit el-Khadim, from the Old Kingdom to Ramesside times. In the mining area nomadic smiths plied their trade. The tradition of metalworking in Genesis relates to Cain's descendant, Tubal-Cain, the forger of copper and iron instruments. His name is associated with the Kenites, the wandering smiths, whose territory was the Sinai, the Negev, and the Wadi Araba.

An early form of the alphabet, called Proto-Sinaitic, 15th century B.C., was discovered on votive statues in the temple of Hathor at Serabit. As the forerunner of the simplified Phoenician alphabet, it was an important factor in the advance of civilization. Opinions differ as to the originators of the inscriptions, but since they were written in Canaanite characters, some scholars assume that they could have been Semites, either captives or slaves, residing in the Delta where the Hyksos previously were entrenched, who were part of the labor corvées in the mines.

Various finds at Serabit confirm that the southern Sinai was a holy place known to the Semites centuries before the traditional date of the Exodus, the latter half of the 13th century B.C. These include the sacred shrine of the native goddess of the Serabit plateau and the Hathor temple on the same site, which was expanded by successive pharaohs. Memorials to Egyptian gods and the Semitic deity named in the deciphered Proto-Sinaitic script also serve as evidence of its holy nature. Sculptures found at Serabit of Egyptian rulers who acknowledged the solar Aten indicate that Akhenaten's form of religion reached into the Sinai and probably was known to the Semitic laborers.

On a mountain undefiled by pagan gods, which late tradition locates fifty miles south of Serabit, Moses, like Joseph a Hebrew steeped in Egyptian culture, received the Law. The 6,500 foot peak of Mount Sinai was a fitting backdrop to the children of Israel who wandered in the wilderness at a time when, without ritual trappings, man was closest to his God. The Prophets of Israel would remember this time in Sinai as the "nomadic ideal" of freedom, equality, and mutual responsibility before the conquest of Canaan and Israel's nationhood brought their less exalted influences.

Along the Route of Trade

A caravan, possibly a Semitic tribe, brings kohl, the favorite black eye paint of the Egyptians, as shown on a wall painting copy from the tomb of Prince Khnumhotep of the 12th Dynasty, c.1890 B.C., at Beni Hasan in Middle Egypt. The imaginative and colorful weaving of the robes suggests the ornamented coat given by Jacob to his favorite son, Joseph, which fired his brothers' jealousy. Bellows and anvil transported on donkey back confirm that the men were skilled in metallurgy, recalling the semi-nomadic Kenites of the Midianite clan who were active in the copper-rich wadis of the Araba, south of the Dead Sea, and in the southern Sinai. These caravans crossed the northern Sinai coastal road, as did the Ishmaelites who brought young Joseph to Egypt.

Remains of Canaanite buildings found in Avaris, Tell el-Dab'a (*left*), once the Hyksos capital, attest to a foreign presence in the eastern Delta. The circular structure (*foreground*), was a grain silo. A flourishing copper industry existed near Avaris in the 18th century B.C., which would have benefited from the skills of these Semites. According to the above scene, they took their metalworking tools with them.

Barbarians from outside have come to Egypt. . . . Why really, the entire Delta marshland
will no (longer) be hidden. . . . Behold, it is in the hands of those who did not know it, as
well as those who knew it; foreigners are (now) skilled in the work of the Delta. . .

—*The Admonitions of Ipuwer* [from: Papyrus Leiden I 344, recto]

The Egyptian scribe Neferhotep (*right*), holds a scroll announcing the arrival in the caravan of thirty seven
Asiatics ['Aamu], from the land of Shutu, probably Gilead in Transjordan. Their leader is Ibsha (*center*),
bending over a wild goat behind Khety, the Egyptian Overseer of Hunters. Ibsha is called heqau-khasut, or
"ruler of a foreign country," the same term used by the Egyptians for the Hyksos invaders a century later. In
the hieroglyphs, *above*, *left*, a determinative sign for the word 'Aamu is a captive with hands tied behind him,
indicating that this element was an enemy whom the Egyptians once had defeated. The Hyksos occupation
sometimes is considered the period when Jacob and his sons settled in Goshen.

The infiltration of Asiatics
in the Delta bemoaned
by Ipuwer the prophet
(quoted above), after the
political collapse of the
Old Kingdom, 22nd
century B.C., also spread
southward. The Papyrus
Brooklyn (*right*), lists
some servants in a Theban
household of the 18th
century B.C. as male
or female Asiatics. The
women were weavers;
the male jobs included
brewer, cook, tutor—and
overseer—as Joseph was
in Potiphar's house.

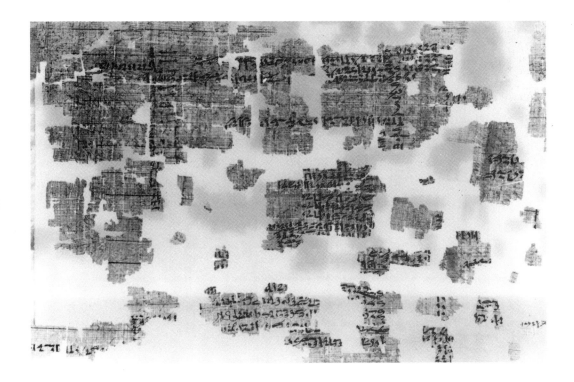

The Reach of Empire—Egypt Rules the East

Through the fortress of Sile near El Qantara on Egypt's northeastern frontier, Thutmose III, the great 18th Dynasty conqueror and founder of the Egyptian empire in Asia, marched his armies eastward to Canaan along the Sinai coastal road. After seventeen campaigns over land and sea routes during a twenty-year period, Thutmose annihilated the last nucleus of Hyksos power in Asia. His victory at Megiddo, c. 1457 B.C., was recorded on a relief from the seventh pylon of the temple of Amon in Karnak (*above*). Wearing the crown of Lower Egypt, the dominant figure of Thutmose holds his Asiatic prisoners by the hair while preparing to smite them with his mace. The god Amon, *upper right corner* (partly destroyed), witnesses the scene. Below him, the goddess of the West leads figures of conquered chiefs toward Thutmose by a rope. They each surmount elliptical rings with names of their cities written in hieroglyphs. The text describes these "mysterious lands of the marshes of Asia," two of which had Biblical overtones—Jacob-El, and Joseph-El. Large numbers of prisoners and hostages did forced labor in Thebes, the same fate attributed in Exodus to Jacob's descendants during their four-hundred-year sojourn in the Egyptian Delta.

In the wake of conquest, Egyptians in Asia combined the worship of the local gods with their own in order to insure the protection of both. At Beth-shean, one of the cities captured by Thutmose III after the fall of Megiddo, the Egyptian builder Amenemapt, and his son Paraemheb, set up a stele (*above, right*), in the temple of the local god Mekal, whom the Egyptians equated with Seth, the god of frontiers and foreign lands. Father and son bring lotuses and offer a mortuary prayer to the seated god, who wears Asiatic dress and a conical, horned cap with trailing streamers. He holds the Egyptian *ankh* in his right hand, and the *was*-scepter in his left. Mekal was a form of Reshef, the Canaanite god of heat and pestilence, reflecting Beth-shean's unhealthy climate. The Egyptian representation of Mekal as a human differed from his Canaanite form as a sacred stone column, or *maṣṣebah* (*below, right*), from the same site. With this intermingling of deities, there began an openness to new beliefs that enabled the religious revolution of Akhenaten's solar monotheism to succeed, although briefly, a century later.

In the Land of Mines

(*Opposite page*) Memorial steles on which the Egyptians recorded their mining expeditions to Sinai still stand in the Temple of Hathor in Serabit el-Khadim, eroded over the millenniums by the fine sand blown by the east wind across the mountainous plateau. The steles mention the men of Retenu (Syria and Palestine), and the 'Aamu, an Egyptian term for the Asiatics. Some claim that it was their foreign custom of raising such devotional steles in high places which the Egyptians adopted in Serabit.

The Egyptians identified the local goddess of Serabit with Hathor, the Lady of the Turquoise, protector of miners. In turn, the Semites who also worked in the mines called her Baalat, their own principal goddess, writing her name on a squat votive figure (*right*), in a simplified alphabet, applying Semitic consonantal values to Egyptian hieroglyphs. As this Proto-Sinaitic script was mastered by the common man, religious thought no longer was dictated solely by educated priests and scribes.

New Faith in Sinai

The discovery in Serabit of a statuette of Tiy (*above*), who was sympathetic to the worship of the solar Aten in the 14th century B.C., confirms that the religious heresy of her son Akhenaten reached into the remote Sinai. A commoner by birth, Tiy was the power behind the throne during Egypt's periods of building and prosperity in the reign of her husband, Amenhotep III, as the "Great King's Wife" and as advisor to Akhenaten. In the center of her crown on this green steatite head, Tiy's name appears in the cartouche between two winged cobras. The serpent uraei on her forehead are emblems of sovereignty in her role as the chief consort of Upper and Lower Egypt. The royal support of Atenism was a prelude to the conflict with the priests of Amon in their stronghold at Thebes.

The countries of Syria and Nubia, the land of Egypt, Thou settest every man in his place. . . All distant foreign countries, thou makest their life (also). . .

—*Hymn to the Aten*

Egypt's expanded foreign empire required a new god with a universal vision of the world. Akhenaten adopted the Aten, the solar disk, an abstract form of the sun god Re-Harakhte of Heliopolis, and based his rule on *ma'at*, the principle of truth. All nations were regarded as children of the Aten. On a limestone balustrade from the Great Palace of the Pharaoh's new residence in Akhetaten, *opposite*, modern el-Amarna, the Aten's protective rays end in blessing hands. They offer the *ankh*, the breath of life, to Akhenaten and his wife, Nefertiti, here followed by their eldest daughter, Meritaten. As the heavenly king, the Aten was depicted with the uraeus of kingship and an *ankh* in the lower center of the disk. This scene of the royal family bringing offerings to the Aten betrays the weakness of the religious revolution itself. Atenism was the personal fanaticism of Akhenaten, with very little appeal for the masses. His dream—a fleeting attempt to change the ingrained beliefs of Egypt—finally failed.

Despite the return to the religion of Amon and the restoration of his temples by Akhenaten's successors, a few remnants of Atenism persisted. On the lower part of a limestone tablet of Ramses I (*above*), found in the temple of Serabit el-Khadim, this first Ramesside pharaoh is called the "prince of every circuit of the Aten," and ". . . ruler of all that the sun's disk (Aten) embraces." The influence of the Aten, even a half century after Akhenaten, suggests that his form of monotheism could have been known to the Semitic laborers and nomadic smiths, possibly from Arad in southern Canaan, who worked in the turquoise and copper mines. The Sinai was to sustain other people and ideas when a "mixed multitude" accompanied the Hebrews in their exodus from Egypt. After a forty-year sojourn in the wilderness, these elements were forged into the people of Israel.

SINAI — The Southern Mines

Sir William Matthew Flinders Petrie (*left*), seen at Abydos, one of the more than fifty sites he excavated both in Egypt and Palestine for more than half a century, has been called the father of modern archaeology, based on his early systematic arrangement of Predynastic Egyptian material in a technique called "sequence-dating." In 1905, he continued his work in the southern Sinai at Serabit el-Khadim, copying inscriptions made by ancient sculptors who had accompanied the royal mining expeditions of Egyptian and Semitic laborers in their search for turquoise. In a Semitic cave-shrine, Petrie identified features of worship in use earlier than the Mosaic system, concluding that Mosaism was a continuation of older ritual, "a monotheistic reformation of existing rites." His report, "The Egyptians in Sinai," following, was reprinted in *The Great Archeologists*, ed. Edward Bacon, Illustrated London News and Martin Secker & Warburg, Ltd., 1976. His cited dates have been modified since original publication.

July 20, 1905

Far back in prehistoric times the savage who wandered over the wild desert mountains of Sinai picked up little scraps of sky-blue stone which pleased his fancy. These were doubtless preserved by being stuck into holes in his weapons and objects of wood, as the Bedawin do now; and these decorated things were traded over into Egypt. The prehistoric man of Egypt demanded more, and a trade in turquoise sprang up, and provided the turquoise beads which were treasured for necklaces in the Nile Valley about eight thousand years ago. The primitive workers doubtless extracted the stones from the sandstone rock by means of the flint-scrapers, such as are found by hundreds in the old mine heaps. These workings are at about five days journey from Suez, in the midst of a desert bare of food and water. When Egypt passed into a settled form of unified government, under the dynasties, the early kings would not leave this supply of jewels unclaimed. So in Sinai, as far back as about 4500 B.C., there are figures of the Egyptian king smiting the natives and of the general who headed the expedition. These are the oldest sculptures known.

In ancient times every place had its deity, and especially such a region as the mines, where all success depended on mysterious chance. If you wished to succeed in your search for these little blue specks among the masses of rock, you must begin by propitiating the goddess of the turquoise. A cave in the top of the rock over the mines was cut out for a shrine and here the goddess Hat-hor of *Mafkat* (turquoise) was worshiped by all miners who came there. To get the guidance of the goddess, no doubt dreams were the favorite mode, as was commonly the custom in Syria. And accordingly we find dozens of shelters on the top of the hills over the mines where pilgrim miners might sleep, and where they put up their Bethel stones in token of their vision, as Jacob did. At a later time the Egyptians built cubicles for such dreamers in front of the shrine of the goddess. The Egyptians called her Hat-hor, [their] general name for foreign goddesses. Tall tablets of stone were put up to record the expeditions of the miners who were sent out from Egypt, principally by the kings of about 2500 B.C. This temple is now known as Serabit el-Khadim, or "the heights of the fortress". . . .

Though the existence of the temple had been known long ago and many travelers had visited it, yet it had never been excavated, and even much of the plan of it was unknown. On clearing it, the whole of the walls were found, and the pillars which showed the original height. The heads of the goddess Hathor are on the tops of the pillars of about 1500 B.C. . . .

A large number of statuettes and tablets were dedicated by miners and officials, and hundreds of objects in blue glazed ware, bearing the names of the kings from about 1550 to 1150 B.C. . . . And both in the temple and at some of the mines are inscriptions in an unknown writing which was probably one of the forerunners of the Phoenician alphabet.

Serabit el Khadim
Above: Stone shelters before the Hathor temple.
Below: Hathor pillar in the temple.

THE LUXURY OF EGYPT

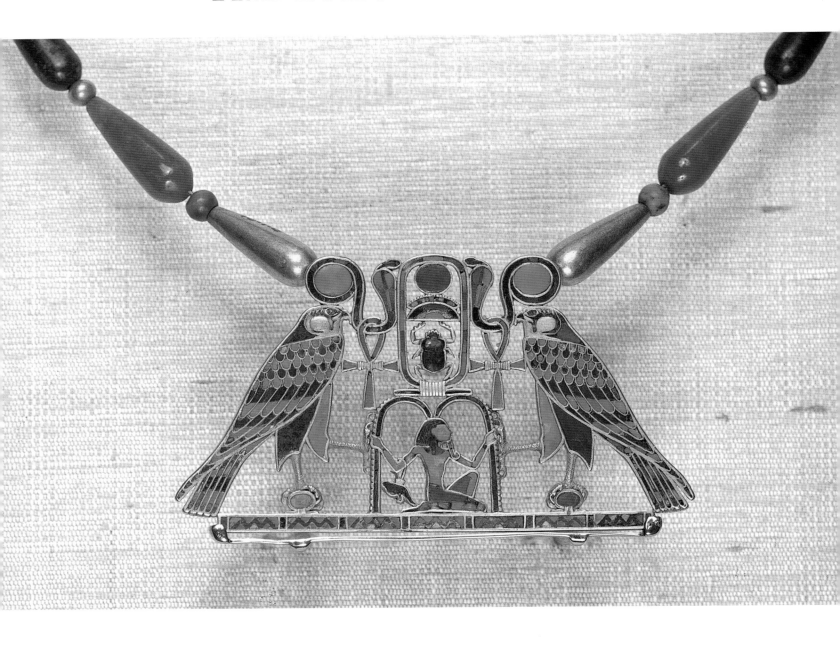

Princess Sithathoriunet, daughter of Sesostris II of the 12th Dynasty, must have been pleased with the success of a mining expedition which had been sent to the Sinai in search of turquoise. The "noble stone" was destined for her exquisite pendant which contained 372 carved bits of turquoise, lapis lazuli, carnelian, and garnet inlaid on a gold base. Two falcons flank the cartouche of Sesostris, below which is a kneeling deity grasping two palm strips representing years. The hieroglyphs express the wish that the sun god Re-Harakhte grant the king life for hundreds of thousands of years. Although Joseph, as vizier, was part of such luxury in the royal court, his family remained as shepherds in Goshen where they were permitted to settle by a grateful pharaoh, Gen. 45:18.

VI

JOSEPH

Prelude to Nationhood

Genesis 37-50

———

NAHUM M. SARNA

BEAUTIFUL OF FORM and fair of face, Joseph, the Hebrew slave who became vizier of Egypt, was divinely chosen as the instrument of his people's protection in a foreign land before their ultimate return to Canaan. The story of Joseph actually forms the transition between Patriarchal and national history.

Joseph himself is not a Patriarch, for he experiences no revelation from God and is vouchsafed no divine promises. Yet the narrative of his life is the longest, fullest, and most coherent in the Book of Genesis told in seemingly secular terms. The setting is authentically Egyptian. It betrays both a familiarity with Egyptian culture and a knowledge of some Egyptian technical terms. The storyteller weaves familiar human themes—the rivalry of brothers, a father's grief over the loss of a child, fraternal repentance for shared wrongdoing, and final reconciliation—into a drama with the underlying Biblical concept that events were preordained in God's overall scheme of things.

The story opens with the family living in Canaan. At age seventeen, Joseph is at odds with his brothers, the ill feeling between him and them having been bred by his father's show of favoritism toward him, especially as it expressed itself through a gift of some kind of ornamented tunic, apparently a prestige symbol. The hostility was exacerbated by Joseph's dreams of lordship over his brothers. When Joseph dreamed of celestial bodies bowing to him, Gen. 37:9, his father knew that it reflected his son's aspirations to greatness. Jacob, the tribal father, was the sun; Rachel, his wife, although deceased, was the moon; and their eleven sons, the stars. Dreams, it must be remembered, were taken seriously in the ancient Near East as portents of future developments. Dreams play a fateful role in Joseph's biography.

Jacob's sons were pastoral nomads moving from place to place according to the seasons. On one occasion when they were far from home, his father sent Joseph to visit his brothers and report on their welfare. This assignment turned out to be ill-fated, for as soon as the brothers saw him from afar, all their pent-up hostility towards him vented itself in a conspiracy to murder him. However, Reuben, the eldest brother, managed to persuade the others not to take his life but to throw him into a pit. A passing caravan on the way down to Egypt inspired the idea to sell Joseph into slavery, where he was purchased by a certain Potiphar, who is described as a courtier of the pharaoh. The king is never identified by name, an omission that complicates the problem of placing Joseph within a historical context. The title "pharaoh," incidentally, simply means "great house," referring to the royal palace and used to indicate the ruling monarch. The name "Potiphar" is most likely an abbreviated form of the Egyptian Pa-di-pa-re, meaning "the one whom Re (the sun god) has given."

During his years in slavery, Joseph impressed his master by his intelligence, industry, and integrity and was promoted to become overseer of Potiphar's household. This development is illuminated by an 18th century B.C. inventory of servants on an Egyptian estate. It lists nearly eighty such with their respective occupations. Several are Semites from Asian countries, and it is clear that many of these had supervisory roles performing skilled jobs inside the master's house.

The narrative continues with a report that after a while Potiphar's wife attempted to seduce Joseph, but he consistently resisted her advances. Faced with circumstances which could have been of immediate benefit to him, Joseph's nobility of character in remaining loyal to his master and denouncing the intended wrong as "a sin against God" proved his worthiness to be the instrument of divine providence. Finally, the woman falsely accused him to her husband, who threw him into prison. This item is a distinctly Egyptian touch since imprisonment was not used as a punitive measure in the Near East outside of Egypt.

This story of Joseph and Potiphar's wife has an interesting parallel in the popular Egyptian *Story of Two Brothers*, in which the wife of one brother makes amorous advances to the younger, unmarried brother living in the same house. When the young brother-in-law rejects her, she slanders him. In the Egyptian version of the story, however, the married man goes in murderous pursuit of his brother but finally is convinced of the falsity of the charge and returns home to slay his wife. Unlike the Biblical story, the Egyptian narrative was intended merely as entertainment and is spiced with all kinds of mythical details and some morally repugnant features.

In prison Joseph won the confidence of the chief jailer, who put him in charge of other prisoners. Among these were two high officials at the court, designated respectively "the cupbearer" and "the baker" to the king. The former title, especially, is known from Egyptian sources to have been that of the holder of an important office in pharaoh's palace, one which embraced a wider role than the name implies, for he often served as confidant of the king. Joseph once found both former officials to be deeply troubled by their dreams. The interpretations he put on them turned out to be verified by future developments, so that the reinstated cupbearer was able some years later to mention Joseph to the pharaoh as an expert interpreter of dreams when the king, too, experienced puzzling and worrisome dreams. The native magicians are called *ḥartumim* in the Bible, a designation that is most likely a loanword from Egyptian. These professionals were unable to satisfy the pharaoh in explaining the meaning of his dreams, which is why Joseph, attributing dream interpretations to God, was summoned to the palace.

Joseph's solution to the royal dreams as portending seven years of agricultural bounty to be succeeded by seven years of famine greatly pleased pharaoh. The motif of seven-year famines is widely documented in the literature of the Fertile Crescent and appears several times in Egyptian texts. The discretion and wisdom of Joseph's solutions for dealing with the coming developments so impressed pharaoh that he elevated the Hebrew to the position of vizier of Egypt. Pharaoh transferred to him his signet ring, had him robed in fine linen, placed a gold chain about his neck, and put at his disposal a horse-drawn chariot, an element which had been introduced to the country by the foreign Hyksos in the late 18th century B.C. All these tokens of investiture have local coloration, being mentioned in connection with the installation of Pharaoh Necho by the Assyrian king Ashurbanipal in the 7th century B.C. Further, Joseph was given an Egyptian name. This recalls the analogy of another Semitic foreigner, Ben-Ozen, from the area of Lake Tiberius, who was appointed to high office by Merneptah and was similarly endowed with an Egyptian name.

During the years of plenty, Joseph had the surpluses of grain stored in specially prepared granaries to be rationed out during the subsequent lean years. When these latter occurred, famine also struck not only Egypt but also the surrounding countries, and Egypt became the breadbasket for the region. Jacob sent his sons from Canaan to purchase grain, and, unbeknownst to them, they found themselves face to face with their brother, the vizier, who recognized them but did not reveal his true identity. This was the first of three encounters by means of which Joseph took the opportunity to test his brothers' integrity and to assay their moral development since he last saw them.

Finally satisfied that they had undergone a genuine change of heart, Joseph revealed himself to them, arranged an audience with the pharaoh, and obtained permission for the entire family to settle in Egypt in the "land of Goshen." This name is not found in Egyptian sources and appears to be Semitic. It must have been close to the border of Canaan and particularly suited to cattle breeding, the occupation of Joseph's brothers. Since Joseph went to Goshen to meet his father coming from Canaan, the accessibility of the area to the royal palace might indicate that Egypt's capital at that time was in the Delta.

The migration of Jacob's family to Egypt initiated a new and decisive phase in the history of the people. On his way down to Egypt, Jacob received a theophany at Beersheba by which he was promised that his offspring would become "a great nation" in that land and eventually would return to Canaan. This undoubtedly refers to the fact that the sons of Jacob as named are the personalities of the tribe of Israel, and that the confederation of twelve tribes to form a people first appears in Egypt. In the opening lines of Exodus, a later pharaoh would refer to the many and numerous "people of Israel," the foreign element within Egypt whom he believed to be a potential threat to his country's stability.

Knowing that their sojourn in Egypt was to be of limited duration within God's plan for their eventual return to Canaan, the Hebrews in Goshen remained relatively isolated from

Egyptian life, maintaining the cohesion of their own language and traditions. Egyptian hatred of foreigners, especially of shepherds, would have served to intensify their isolation, regardless of the protection rendered by Joseph's high office.

The rest of the story of Joseph recounts the measures that he took during the remaining years of famine. These involved the nationalization of land and cattle on behalf of the crown. The contributions which Joseph made to the administration of Egypt were pointedly ignored by the pharaoh of the Exodus who "knew not Joseph."

Joseph died at the age of 110 years, which, according to several Egyptian sources, was regarded as the ideal life span. His body was embalmed, as Jacob's was before him, not in keeping with Egyptian religious rites but as a practical means of preservation until his body one day could be returned for burial in Canaan.

The years of Israel's formation as told in Genesis come to an end. From Abraham's migration from Ur, to Joseph's deathbed reminder to his brothers of God's promise to the Patriarchs, events are seen as part of a grand design. A morally awakened people within the ancient world would be led to Mount Sinai by Moses, where they would receive the Ten Commandments. Joseph, the "fruitful bough" of Jacob's last blessing, had sustained the Hebrews in Egypt for their ultimate destiny of nationhood in the land of Canaan.

JOSEPH'S WORLD

How effective they are, thy plans,
O Lord of eternity!

The faith of young Joseph, in whom pharaoh found the "spirit of God," may be reflected in the words of the Hymn to the Aten, quoted above, and in a limestone relief of hands raised in praise to the god, *opposite page*, both from the tomb of Ai, Akhenaten's officer in el-Amarna. The Amarna Letters record a time of tribal strife in Canaan, as mirrored in the attack on Shechem by Jacob's sons, Gen. 34, and symbolized by the lunate-handled sword, *right*, from Alalakh (Tell Atchana). Both Ai's tomb and the sword date from the 14th century B.C.

Joseph was born in Haran (ancient and modern Harran), a center of moon worship, which had a Hurrian population within the kingdom of Mitanni at its height in the 15th century B.C. A century later, the Hittites from Anatolia controlled the region, adopting the Hurrian pantheon as their own. Power was to pass to the Semitic Aramaeans by the 11th century B.C. Their god was Baal Haran, an epithet of the moon god.

These ethnic and pagan elements also were found in Joseph's world. The Biblical Horites, sometimes identified as the Hurrians, lived in his uncle Esau's territory of Mount Seir in Edom, east of the Wadi Araba. Esau's marriages to two Hittite women were a source of grief to his parents. It was from Abraham's Aramaean kinsmen in Haran that a wife was chosen for Isaac and Jacob later married two sisters. Steeped in this Aramaean culture, Joseph's mother, Rachel, brought her household idols with her when she came to Canaan with Jacob. Joseph's special grace within these pagan lands was his trust in the one God of his ancestors who had guided his life for a higher purpose when, at the age of seventeen, he was brought as a slave to Egypt, a victim of his jealous brothers.

The Hebrews in Egypt

William Foxwell Albright, a major influence in Biblical Archaeology, was professor of Semitic languages at Johns Hopkins University from 1929-1958 and director of the American School of Oriental Research in Jerusalem from 1920-1929, and 1933-1936. He applied stratigraphy and pottery analysis, archaeological data, and translations of ancient texts to determine chronology and a framework for the Patriarchal narratives. The excerpt, "When Israel Was a Child," is from his book, *From the Stone Age to Christianity*, 2d ed., Johns Hopkins Press, 1957.

The Egyptian sojourn of Israel is a vital part of early Israelite historical tradition and cannot be eliminated without leaving an inexplicable gap. Most striking is the obvious relation in which the Joseph story and the later history of Israel in Egypt stand to the Hyksos movement. . . . That there was a long Semitic occupation of the northeastern Delta before the New Empire is certain from the Canaanite place names found there in the New Empire, which include Succoth, Baal-zephon, Migdol, Zilu (Sile), and probably Goshen itself. That there were a good many Semites among Hyksos officials is certain, and it is also clear that most of the Hyksos chiefs bore Semitic names, among which is Ya'qob-har (literally, "May the Mountain-god Protect"), formed with the element of "Jacob." It is impossible to separate the tradition quoted in Numbers 13:22, according to which Hebron was founded seven years before Tanis, from the Hyksos invasion of Egypt, and difficult to separate the Hyksos era of Tanis, according to which 400 years elapsed at a time shortly before the accession of Ramses I, from the 430 years assigned in Ex.12:40 for the duration of the Israelite sojourn in the district of Tanis.

In short, it must be considered as practically certain that the ancestors of part of Israel, at least, had lived for several centuries in Egypt before migrating to Palestine.

THE DESTINY OF JOSEPH

The northern stretch of the great Euphrates River in modern Turkey.

From the Euphrates —

And God remembered Rachel . . . . And she conceived, and bore a son. . . —Gen. 30:22, 23

To the southeast in Biblical Haran, made fertile by the rivers flowing to the Euphrates, Joseph was born.

—to the Nile

The rock-cut burial vaults of Middle Kingdom dignitaries halfway up the cliffs at Beni Hasan in Middle Egypt overlook modern life on the river.

God hath made me lord of all Egypt . . . . and there will I sustain thee. . . — Gen. 45:9, 11

In Tomb 3 of Prince Khnumhotep, a wall painting of a caravan of
Asiatics (*see pp. 190-1*), confirms their early trade contacts with Egypt.

From King Idrimi—to—the People of Alalakh

> My brothers. . . were older than I. . .
> none of them had the plans I had.

The theme of fraternal rivalry as told in Joseph's story also was an element in the autobiography of Idrimi, written in Akkadian on his stone statue (*right*), from his royal city of Alalakh in the same Hurrian orbit as Joseph's birthplace of Haran. On the inscription, early 15th century B.C., Idrimi described a popular revolt in Aleppo and a disagreement with his brothers which forced his exile to Canaan. Both Idrimi and Joseph ultimately reconciled with their estranged brothers. As Joseph was skilled in dream interpretation and divining from the movement of liquid in a goblet, so Idrimi could read omens in the flight of birds and the entrails of lambs. One of the diviner's tools would be similar to the ox liver model (*below*), also from Alalakh. By analyzing the chevrons and holes, usually due to parasites, the future could be foretold. But Joseph knew that it was God's plan, not divining, which directed his destiny.

— and Revenge

From Prince Lab'ayu of Shechem—to—Amenhotep III

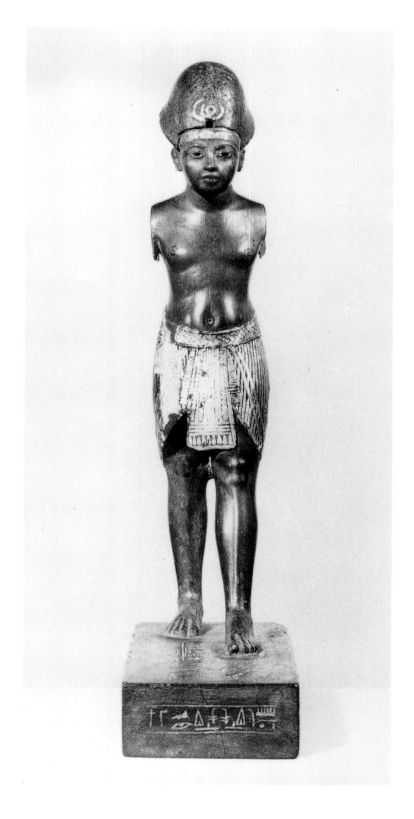

> If ants are smitten . . . they bite
> the hand of the man who smites them.

With this colorful proverb, as recorded in the Amarna Letter 252, obverse (*below*), Lab'ayu explained to Pharaoh Amenhotep III (*left*), why he had captured a neighboring town despite an existing truce. This unstable situation in Canaan of broken oaths and armed feuds was reflected in Jacob's return to Shechem from Haran. After Jacob purchased a plot of land from Hamor the Hivite, the chief's son Shechem defiled Dinah, Jacob's daughter. Even though the Hebrews agreed to the marriage of the ill-fated couple and to settling peacefully in the region if the male Shechemites would be circumcised, Jacob's vengeful sons annihilated them and sacked the city. Jacob deplored their act but on his deathbed boasted that the land which he bought from Hamor was that which he "took out of the hand of the Amorites," the local population. It was to Shechem, which became Joseph's inheritance, that the Israelites carried his remains for burial after the conquest of Canaan.

THE AMARNA AGE
—The Great Cultural Synthesis

A new blend of cultures occurred in the Amarna Age, augmented by frequent intermarriages, as the pharaohs employed capable Asian administrators at home and abroad. On a painted limestone stele from el-Amarna, a Syrian soldier in Semitic dress shares a relaxed moment with his wife, who wears a white Egyptian robe. Through a long straw held by a boy, the soldier sips beer, or barley wine, a libation also known in Sumer, Anatolia, and other northern countries. Pharaoh himself united two cultures when he arranged for Joseph, his Semitic vizier, to marry the high-born Egyptian Asenath.

Old Gods in New Lands

Even as a prisoner in Egypt the young Joseph trusted in his God, so an Egyptian, probably captured in Babylon during an Asian campaign and forced to labor as a brick-maker, etched his own sun god Anhur on a brick (*left*), c.1340 B.C., in a temple also associated with the sun. Although cosmic gods were common to both lands, only Anhur the Savior, "he who brought back the far off," could give the Egyptian hope. The brick is from Der (mod.Badrah), on the eastern Babylonian frontier.

God's permanent commitment to the Hebrews was affirmed when he promised to make of them a great nation in Egypt. The limited role of pagan deities, however, is seen when a statue of the goddess Ishtar of Nineveh was loaned by Tushratta of Mitanni to his brother-in-law, Amenhotep III, to speed his recovery from an illness. In the Amarna Letter 23 (*right*), Tushratta reminded Amenhotep that her visit was temporary. "Ishtar is my goddess, she is not yours."

The reassurance that God would go with Jacob to Egypt, Gen. 46:3, recalls the influx of foreign gods who were brought by Asian workers and merchants during the 18th Dynasty. The Canaanite Reshef not only was pharaoh's god but appealed to the common man as one "who listens to prayers." Reshef (*left*), with high cap, holds an *ankh* on an amethyst scaraboid, 18th-19th Dynasties, from Tell el-Ajjul, south of Gaza, Egypt's capital in Canaan.

The Spirit of Amarna

The Hymn to the Aten carved in the tomb of Ai in el-Amarna gave praise to the divine presence in nature. Its exalted spirit later was to echo in Hebrew song, such as Psalm 104. The Hymn was both monotheistic, naming Aten as the sole god of the universe creating and caring for all creatures with fatherly love, and life affirming, as Aten's daily rebirth illuminated the gloomy Underworld of Osiris and eclipsed the ritualistic cult of the dead. In Akhetaten, art evoked the joy of life and, true to Maat, portrayed its subjects realistically. On an enamel tile (*right*), a calf wanders among tall papyrus plants. A bird soars heavenward, on a painted pavement from the Great Palace (*below*), and Pharaoh Akhenaten lavishes affection on a daughter sitting on his lap, on an unfinished sculpture (*facing page*). The creator God of the Hebrews was above nature, and although like the Aten his rule encompassed all lands, he had a special Covenant relationship with his people.

All cattle are at peace in their pastures. The trees and herbage grow green.

The birds fly from their nests, their wings (raised) in praise of thy spirit.

. . . who giveth life to the child. . .
who comforteth him so that he cries not. . .

How manifold are thy works! . . .
O sole God, like unto whom there is no other!

JOSEPH—*With Variations on Egyptian Themes*

An awareness by the Biblical writers of Egyptian life and literary traditions is evident in the Joseph story. From tomb inscriptions, Wisdom Literature, folk tales placed in tombs and meant for the "reading pleasure" of the deceased, and ritual books, elements were adapted to conform to their own religious insights and ultimate inclusion in the Bible.

THE MODEL VIZIER

A doer of truth, a hater of deceit . . . just judge . . . whom the Lord of the Two Lands loved because of his remarkable traits . . . with the utterances of whose mouth one (the king) is satisfied . . .

This description of Ramose, who was the southern vizier of Amenhotep III and his son, Akhenaten, from his Tomb 55 in Sheikh abd el-Qurna, resembles the discretion and wisdom of Joseph, second only to pharaoh. As seen from his tomb relief, c. 1360 B.C., Ramose (*facing page*), also shared Joseph's physical attributes, "of beautiful form and fair to look upon," Gen. 39:6.

COMING OF AGE

One of the oldest collections of Wisdom Literature was that of the Vizier Ptahhotep of the 5th Dynasty. His words in the Papyrus Prisse of the Middle Kingdom guided his son in achieving the good life, for, as he wrote, "There is no one born wise." Joseph possessed the qualities which viziers encouraged in their sons—to be well-spoken, have self-control, and give good counsel. Some of Ptahhotep's advice applies to events in Joseph's life:

Family Strife

Ptahhotep knew that children often create enmity and cautioned his son in words applicable to Jacob's jealous offspring:

Do not be greedy, unless (it be) for thy (own) portion. Do not be covetous against thy (own) kindred . . . . He is a mean person who exposes his kinsfolk.

Wanton Women

Ptahhotep was firm in his warning about women, such as the comely Egyptian dancer holding a lotus (*above, right*), reflecting on the episode of Joseph and Potiphar's unfaithful wife:

If thou desirest to make friendship last in a home to which thou hast access as master, as a brother, or as a friend. . . beware of approaching the women . . . . One is made a fool by limbs of faience, as she stands (there), become (all) carnelian. A mere trifle, the likeness of a dream and one attains death through knowing her . . .

To Joseph, adultery was not only a social wrong, but a "sin against God." Morality was a universal value equally binding on all.

Marriage

When pharaoh chose a wife for Joseph, it reflected Ptahhotep's view of married life:

If thou art a man of standing, thou shouldst found thy household and love thy wife at home as is fitting.

God's Presence

As Ptahhotep believed, so did Joseph, that a divine power shaped their lives:

It is god who makes (a man's) quality, and he defends him (even) while he is asleep. . .

The Seven Lean Years

I was in distress on the Great Throne, and those who are in the palace were in heart's affliction from a very great evil, since the Nile had not come in my time for a space of seven years. —The Famine Stele, Sehel

A tale of famine in Egypt is recorded on a rock, quoted above, dating from the 2nd century B.C., on the island of Sehel near the First Cataract. A sorely troubled King Djoser of the 3rd Dynasty charged his vizier, the great architect and physician Imhotep (*left*), to find the reason why the Nile failed to rise for seven years. The early setting of the story in Djoser's reign shows a long tradition of seven lean years when the Nile remained low. Although he was so wise that he later was deified, Imhotep sought the guidance of Thoth (*above*, in his ibis-headed form), the god of wisdom and priestly lore, in the House of Life where the sacred and magic books were kept. Joseph did not need to consult such books. His knowledge came from God who would give pharaoh "an answer of peace." From the symbolism of pharaoh's dreams, Joseph quickly understood that a seven-year famine was about to afflict the land.

Grain was scant, fruits were dried up . . . .
Every man robbed his companion. . . .
The infant was wailing; the youth was waiting;
   the heart of the old men was in sorrow,
    their legs were bent, crouching on the ground,
    their arms were folded. . . .
Every[thing] was found empty.

The bitter results of a low Nile, as described in the Famine Stele, above, are shown by the emaciated figures on a relief (*below*), from the temple of Unas, 5th Dynasty, in Saqqara. The text adds that after scouring the sacred books with Thoth, Imhotep learned that the source of the Nile was "the Two Caverns" in southernmost Elephantine. Its god was Khnum, the ram-headed (*left*), who came to Djoser in a dream promising to revive the Nile. In return Djoser gave Khnum land to be tithed for his temple. Despite the literary evidence of seven lean years, the Biblical memory of Egypt was of a garden spot, Gen.13:10, in which the Patriarchs were permitted to pasture their flocks and seek sustenance during times of famine in Canaan. Such hospitality is confirmed in a report of an Egyptian frontier official of the 13th century B.C. who allowed nomads from Edom to pass through Egypt's fortified border into the Delta "to keep them alive, through the great *ka* of pharaoh—life, prosperity, health."

Interpretation of Dreams

An intricate key to dreams was used by priests especially trained in dream interpretations and rituals, as preserved in a 19th Dynasty manuscript now known as the Papyrus Chester Beatty III. In the royal court of Joseph's pharaoh, the magicians and wise men would have consulted such a *Dream Book*. But their explanations, compared to Joseph's divine insight, were of no help to the distraught ruler. Joseph understood that the seven thin cows in pharaoh's dream meant an impending famine in the land and were not the usual Egyptian symbols of the sky-goddess, Hathor, or the celestial herd in Spell 148 of the *Book of the Dead* that provided the deceased with bread and beer in the Underworld. From the Papyrus of Ani (*facing page*), the seven cows and the bull of heaven below them rest behind Re, the falcon-headed sun god with his solar disk and uraeus. Ani, with hands raised, praises Re.

The *Dream Book* consists of columns of dreams with their meanings, whether good or bad. The following examples of Egyptian dream interpretations show how they differed from those of Joseph and from events in his life. Each line begins:

IF A MAN SEE HIMSELF IN A DREAM

[SEEING] THE MOON SHINING.   GOOD: FORGIVENESS TO HIM BY HIS GOD.

When Joseph dreamed that the sun, moon, and stars bowed down to him, it not only reflected his feelings of superiority but predicted his future greatness.

SEEING A GOD WHO IS ABOVE.   GOOD: IT MEANS RICH FOOD.

Joseph's unseen God was a spiritual, rather than a material, source of strength even in his darkest hours.

COPULATING WITH A WOMAN.   BAD: IT MEANS MOURNING.

Joseph refused Potiphar's wife on the moral grounds that it was a sin against God.

PRESSING OUT WINE.   BAD: DEATH IS CLOSE AT HAND.

WHITE BREAD BEING GIVEN TO HIM.   GOOD: IT MEANS SOMETHING AT WHICH
HIS FACE WILL BRIGHTEN UP.

Completely opposite of the *Dream Book* were Joseph's correct interpretations for the royal servants in prison. From the butler's dream of pressing grapes from three branches into pharaoh's cup, Joseph predicted a good outcome. He would be restored to his position in three days. The fate of the chief baker who dreamed of birds eating white bread in three baskets on his head was bad. He was to be hanged, also in three days.

BEING MADE INTO AN OFFICIAL.   BAD: IT MEANS MOURNING.

After Joseph became vizier, all that he did prospered according to God's plan.

The formula to be recited by a man when he awakened was:

HAIL TO THEE, THOU GOOD DREAM WHICH ART SEEN (BY) NIGHT OR BY DAY.

Final Reckoning

Make holiday, and weary not therein! . . .
Behold, there is not one who departs
who comes back again!

—The Song of the Harper

[Papyrus Harris 500, c.1300 B.C.]

The pursuit of pleasure was a theme which infused society after the collapse of the Old Kingdom up to the 19th Dynasty, the traditional time of the Hebrews in Egypt. Egyptian banquets often were graced with music, such as that provided by the blind harper, shown on a wall painting from the Tomb of Nakht at Thebes (*above*). His song urged the guests to enjoy life, as it was all too short. Even the great and wise Imhotep was gone as if he had never existed. Although Joseph, as vizier, could have pursued the pleasures of the Egyptian court, he knew that his privileged position was of divine intent. When Jacob died, his sons feared that Joseph would retaliate for their earlier attempted fratricide. He then assured them, "Fear not; for am I in the place of God?" Joseph knew that although they had meant him harm, "God meant it for good, to bring to pass, as it is this day, to save much people alive," Gen. 50:19, 20.

LAST RITES

Wailing saves not the heart
of a man from the underworld.

Professional mourners, hands raised, tears flowing, cry aloud to glorify the dead and to share in the grief of the survivors, as portrayed in Tomb 55 of Ramose at Thebes (*facing page*). But as the harper warned (above), it was to no avail. The deceased still would have to be judged in the afterlife for his deeds on earth. Such mourners also would have attended the funeral ceremonies of Jacob, who was embalmed in the Egyptian manner: "And the Egyptians mourned for him threescore and ten days," Gen. 50:3.

LAST WISHES

In the *Story of Sinuhe*, this Middle Kingdom political exile who fled to Canaan expressed a great love of country, as did Jacob and Joseph in Egypt whose last wish was to be buried in the land of their fathers. Whereas Sinuhe's return to Egypt occurred during his lifetime, Joseph's remains were carried to Canaan a few centuries after his death at the time of the Exodus. Sinuhe was granted the trappings of an Egyptian nobleman:

> There was constructed for me a pyramid-tomb of stone in the midst of the pyramid-tombs. . . . Mortuary priests were given to me. There was made for me a necropolis garden, with fields in it formerly (extending) as far as the town, like that which is done for a chief courtier. My statue was overlaid with gold. It was his majesty who had it made. There is no poor man for whom the like had been done.

In sharp contrast to the luxury of Sinuhe's tomb, Jacob, the Patriarch of a nation, was buried in the modest family cave in Hebron, and Joseph, the once mighty vizier of all Egypt, was brought without pomp to Shechem. Honoring their last wishes, their sons had brought them home.

224

The Bahr Yusuf, a Nile branch in the fertile Faiyum region, seventy miles southwest of Cairo, is attributed to Joseph.

Joseph's River

In the tradition of Egyptian viziers, Joseph directed
extensive reclamation and irrigation projects on the land.

Joseph's Tomb

On the outskirts of Nablus, Joseph's traditional grave site is a modest white-domed building which has housed a religious school. The land in ancient Shechem which Jacob bought from the Hivites became one part of Joseph's double inheritance.

Akhenaten and Monotheism

Dr. John A. Wilson, the renowned Egyptologist and former director of the Oriental Institute of the University of Chicago, compares Akhenaten's religion to the monotheism of the Hebrews, in the following excerpt from his book, *The Culture of Ancient Egypt*, University of Chicago Press, © 1958. Proper names are spelled according to the original text.

Two important questions face us:

> Was Akh-en-Aton's worship of the Aton monotheism? If so, was it the world's first ancestral monotheism, and did it come down to us through the Hebrews?

Our own answer to each question is in the negative, even though such an answer may rest upon definitions of the terms, and such definitions must necessarily be those of modern distinctions.

Our modern Jewish, Christian, and Moslem faiths express the doctrine that there is one—and only one—God and that all ethical and religious values derive from that God. In the application of this definition to the Amarna religion, we see that there were at least two gods, that the Aton was concerned strictly with creating and maintaining life, and that ethics and religion derived from the pharaoh, Akh-en-Aton. It is true that the Amarna texts call the Aton the "sole god, like whom there is no other." This, however, was nothing new in Egyptian religious address. The form of expression was a fervid exaggeration or concentration, which went back to the earliest religious literature more than a thousand years before Akh-en-Aton's time. . . .

The question as to whether Atonism was ancestral to Hebrew monotheism and thus to modern expressions of religion is also difficult. This was the personal religion of a pharaoh who later became a heretic within one generation. It was not accessible to Egyptians at large. Their subsequent reaction in a fervent return to the older forms, particularly the Osirian faith and the cherishing care of little personal gods, shows how little penetration Atonism had below the royal family. Even assuming that there were Israelite slave troops in Egypt in Amarna times, there was no way by which they could learn the teaching of Atonism that there was a single, universal god, who made and continued life, toward whom the worshiper felt a warm sense of gratitude. Atonism taught that the pharaoh of Egypt was essential as the intermediary between god and people.

There is another discontinuity between Atonism and Hebrew monotheism as the latter developed, and that is the marked lack of ethical content in the hymns directed to the Aton. Akh-en-Aton's faith was intellectual rather than ethical; its strong emotional content derived from the fervor of the discoverer and convert. . . a passionate reiteration that the new was right and the old was wrong. . . . The worshiper was called upon to render gratitude for life, but was in no text called upon to render to the god an upright and ethically correct life in his social relations or in his innermost heart. . . . Nowhere do we find that rigorous insistence upon law which was central in Hebrew monotheism. . . . When the Children of Israel penetrated Canaan and settled down to work out a new way of life, their progressive religious steps were achieved through their own national religious experience as their own God-given discoveries. . . . the forms in which they are uttered may be borrowed from others, but never the innermost spirit.

EPILOGUE: *The Winds of Change*

Now there arose a new king over Egypt, who knew not Joseph.   —Exodus 1:8

After Joseph's death, the Hebrews would remember Egypt as a land where they had labored in the store cities of the pharaoh. Evidence of hostility towards the Semites in the Delta is seen on a relief from the temple of Ramses II in Tell el-Retaba in the Wadi Tumilat, the Eastern Harpoon nome. Ramses receives a short sword from Atum, identified here as the god of the eastern Delta, in order to vanquish the kneeling Syrian between them (*opposite page*). Granaries also were discovered at the site, recalling the foresight of Joseph who "laid up the food in the cities" for the impending famine.

A New Piety

THE RELIGION OF THE KING

With the restored supremacy of Amon at Thebes, a new spirit of humility arose in Egypt. Part of the coronation ceremony was the symbolic submission of the king to the god, as seen on a schist statue from Karnak (*above*). The great Ramses II kneels in total piety and commitment before Amon to whom he offers his titular name on the block which he pushes before him. This deference to the gods which existed during the Ramesside era is reflected in Genesis when Joseph's pharaoh accepted the blessing of Jacob upon his arrival in Egypt. Pharaoh knew well the power of the Hebrew God through the insights and inspired guidance of his Semitic vizier. Joseph's divine favor was confirmed in Jacob's deathbed blessing:

> The arms of his hands were made strong by the hands of the mighty God of Jacob.
>
> —Gen. 49:24

THE RELIGION OF THE POOR

The emerging personal religion in Egypt in which people found inner peace and self-awareness through their close link to the gods might have been influenced by Semitic immigrants in Egypt who brought with them a unique concept of divine mercy and human dependence. From the workmen's village of Deir el-Medina at Thebes, Egyptian artisans who built the tombs of the pharaohs in the Valley of the Kings recorded their hopes and prayers on their own steles. Nebre, the draughtsman, and his son Kha'y erected such a stele (*facing page*), in gratitude for the recovery of another son Nekhtamun. Perhaps, thought Nebre, Nekhtamun did an evil deed that caused his illness, a sentiment in sharp contrast to the Negative Confession of the *Book of the Dead* in which man admitted to no sin during his lifetime. Joseph's final words to his brothers were a reminder of God's personal commitment to bring them out of Egypt to the land he had promised to the Patriarchs.

Nebre's Stele

Nebre kneels before Amon who sits enthroned before a high pylon, on this 19th Dynasty stele found in one of the god's small temples in Deir el-Medina. Nebre's other sons, in the *right corner below him*, join in prayer. As these working-class artisans learned writing skills to adorn the necropolis monuments, they were able to express their own spiritual needs rather than accept the religious dogma of literate priests. The text confirms their gratitude to a merciful god who was a solace for their difficult existence:

> Thou art Amon, the Lord of
>   him that is silent:
> Who comest at the voice of
>   the humble man. I call upon
>   thee when I am in distress:
> And thou comest that thou
>   mayest save me;
> That thou mayest give breath to
>   him that is wretched;
> That thou mayest save me that
>   am in bondage.

But whereas Nebre's god was merely a comfort to the needy, Joseph's God was involved in his destiny. As part of God's plan, Joseph rose from slavery to glory in Egypt, ultimately to save his people.

THE PROMISE FULFILLED

God. . . will bring you. . . unto the land which He swore to Abraham, to Isaac, and to Jacob. — Gen. 50:24

Jacob's deathbed blessing of his sons, Gen. 49, became the basis of tribal territorial divisions which were finalized after Joshua's conquest of Canaan. The names of the sons who inherited land are capitalized:

THE LEAH TRIBES

REUBEN: The minor role of the first-born son was attributed to his defilement of Bilhah, Rachel's handmaid. Settled in Transjordan, north of the Arnon River, the tribe was politically unimportant.

SIMEON: For inciting the raid on Shechem, this warlike son remained in the Negev in the shadow of the Judah tribe.

LEVI: As Simeon's co-conspirator in Shechem, he did not inherit land. His tribe later came to represent the priestly class.

JUDAH: The young "lion" became preeminant after the moral default of his older brothers. His was the political center of the Southern Kingdom of a united Israel from whose tribe David, son of Jesse, was descended.

ZEBULUN: Living near the seacoast, he earned his livelihood from maritime commerce.

ISSACHAR: A "servant" among the Canaanites, he settled in the fertile Jezreel Valley to the north. In times of crisis, both he and Zebulun rallied to the Israelite cause.

[Dinah, the only daughter, inherited no land.]

The Handmaid Tribes of Leah, born of Zilpah

GAD: This brave tribe repelled frequent raids by its neighbors east of the Jordan.

ASHER: Royal courts enjoyed the delicacies supplied by this maritime tribe on the northeastern Mediterranean coast.

With Joseph's final words to his brothers, above right, he affirmed God's constant presence in the unfolding history of the Hebrews. For the Egyptians, a god's power often was defined by local political events. Seth, the god of frontiers and foreign lands, shown in human form and Asiatic dress, *above,* was honored by Ramses II on this stele found in Tanis, which commemorated the four-hundred-year jubilee of the founding of his cult. Seth became the god of the Hyksos invaders in Avaris in the 17th century B.C., was eclipsed after their defeat, and was raised again to power by the Ramessides four hundred years later. Whereas this "Stele of the Year 400" assumes Seth's transitory role, the Hebrew God was eternal. The Patriarchal tradition of Covenant, faith in one God, and family continuity were the ties that bound the diverse tribes together.

234

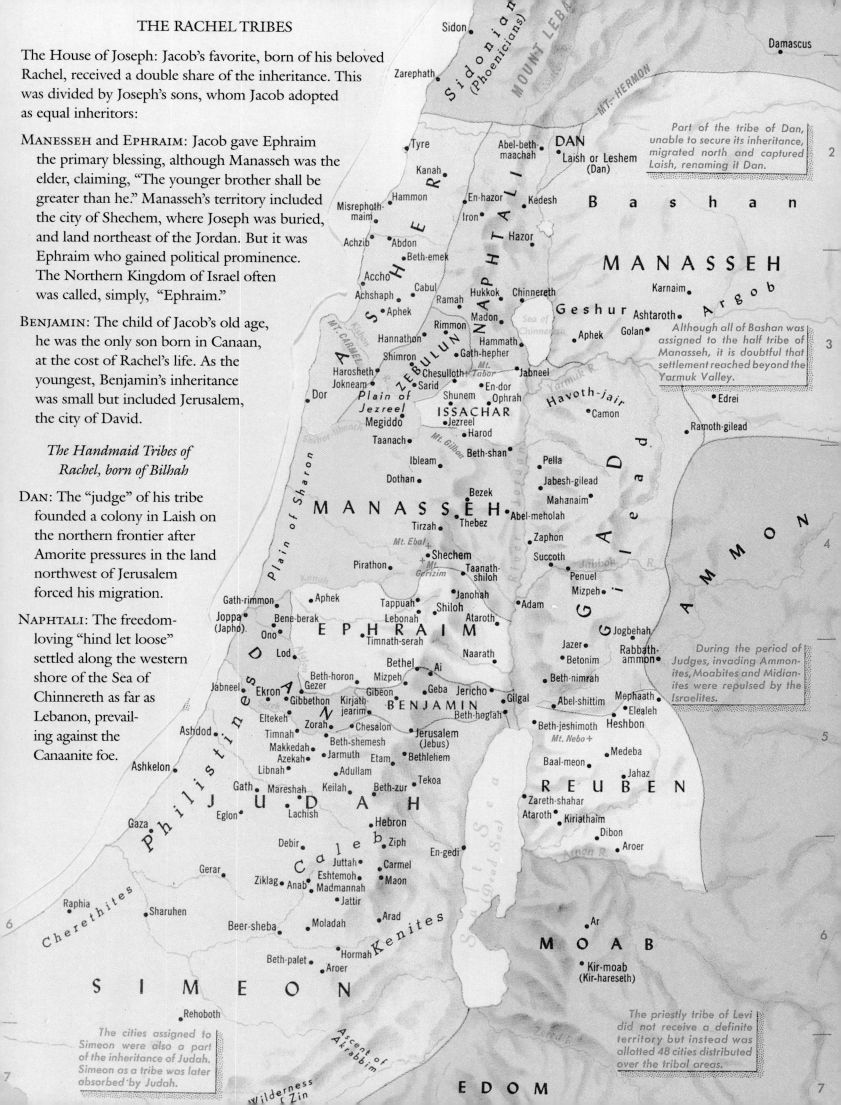

THE RACHEL TRIBES

The House of Joseph: Jacob's favorite, born of his beloved Rachel, received a double share of the inheritance. This was divided by Joseph's sons, whom Jacob adopted as equal inheritors:

MANESSEH and EPHRAIM: Jacob gave Ephraim the primary blessing, although Manasseh was the elder, claiming, "The younger brother shall be greater than he." Manasseh's territory included the city of Shechem, where Joseph was buried, and land northeast of the Jordan. But it was Ephraim who gained political prominence. The Northern Kingdom of Israel often was called, simply, "Ephraim."

BENJAMIN: The child of Jacob's old age, he was the only son born in Canaan, at the cost of Rachel's life. As the youngest, Benjamin's inheritance was small but included Jerusalem, the city of David.

The Handmaid Tribes of Rachel, born of Bilhah

DAN: The "judge" of his tribe founded a colony in Laish on the northern frontier after Amorite pressures in the land northwest of Jerusalem forced his migration.

NAPHTALI: The freedom-loving "hind let loose" settled along the western shore of the Sea of Chinnereth as far as Lebanon, prevailing against the Canaanite foe.

Part of the tribe of Dan, unable to secure its inheritance, migrated north and captured Laish, renaming it Dan.

Although all of Bashan was assigned to the half tribe of Manasseh, it is doubtful that settlement reached beyond the Yarmuk Valley.

During the period of Judges, invading Ammonites, Moabites and Midianites were repulsed by the Israelites.

The cities assigned to Simeon were also a part of the inheritance of Judah. Simeon as a tribe was later absorbed by Judah.

The priestly tribe of Levi did not receive a definite territory but instead was allotted 48 cities distributed over the tribal areas.

AT THE CROSSROADS

Through the Jordan Valley: Leaving Egypt behind. Ahead—the Promised Land.

A MEMORY OF ISRAEL IN EGYPT

This cultic credo acknowledging the events of Israel's
past was offered with the first fruits of the ground.
The "wandering Aramaean" was Jacob, whose family became
mighty under the protection of Joseph. The
rest is history.

> A wandering Aramaean was my father,
>> and he went down into Egypt,
>> and sojourned there,
>> few in number;
>> and he became there a nation,
>> great, mighty, and populous. . . .

> And the Lord brought us forth out of Egypt
>> with a mighty hand, and with an outstretched arm,
>> and with great terror, and with signs and with wonders.

> And he hath brought us into this place
>> and hath given us this land,
>> a land flowing with milk and honey.

—Deuteronomy 26:5, 8-9

ACKNOWLEDGMENTS

For their advice and insights in reconciling differing scholarly conclusions, which often included reading the full manuscript or chapters in their particular disciplines, I should like to thank: David Owen, Cornell University; Daniel Fleming, New York University; Charles Van Siclen, Egyptologist and editor; Donald Redford, University of Toronto; Robert Talbert, Virginia Commonwealth University; and two scholars who since have become emeritus at their universities, Frank Moore Cross at Harvard and Roger Wescott at Drew. Also included are David Noel Freedman, now at the University of California San Diego; Richard Fazzini, Brooklyn Museum; James Pritchard, curator emeritus, University of Pennsylvania and the University Museum of Archaeology and Anthropology; and Jack Finegan, professor emeritus, Pacific School of Religion. In Europe, my thanks to Alfonso Archi, University of Rome, and Manfred Beitak, University of Vienna. The late Alexander Shapiro, rabbi of Congregation Oheb Shalom, South Orange, New Jersey, and an editor of the Encyclopedia Judaica, provided his profound understanding of Genesis.

Grateful acknowledgment is made for permission to quote from the following works: *Ancient Near Eastern Texts Relating to the Old Testament,* ed. James B. Pritchard, 3d ed., with supplement, Princeton University Press, 1969; *Excavations at Nuzi I*, Edward Chiera, Harvard Semitic Studies V., pl. 61-2, #67, obverse, lines 16-29; and *Ugaritic Literature,* Cyrus H. Gordon, Text 67:II, lines 26-34, Rome: Pontificium Institutum Biblicum, 1949. Chaim Potok kindly allowed the use of the jacket quote from his book, *Wanderings,* New York: Knopf, 1978, p.24.

Sources of Genesis quotes are from various Bibles, including the King James Version of the Holy Bible, and J.H. Hertz, *Pentateuch and Haftorahs,* London: Soncino Press, 1938. The two Suras (pp. 160-1) are from *The Meaning of the Glorious Koran,* trans. M.M. Pickthall. New York: Mentor Books. 1955.

The archaeology reports in the Discovery sections were by the kind permission of the publishers as individually credited on their respective pages.

I am especially grateful to Erich Lessing in Vienna and Mme. André Parrot in Paris for permitting the use of photographs in their collections. Jean-Claude Margueron in Paris graciously allowed reproductions of material from Mari and Telloh as did Marguerite Yon in Lyon for material from Ugarit which appeared in Paul Geuthner's Librairie Orientaliste publications *Syria* and *Ugaritica*. Also from published sources, my thanks to Elsevier in Amsterdam, Editions Ides et Calendes in Neuchatel, and in London, the Society of Antiquaries and The Committee of the Egypt Exploration Society.

SELECTED BIBLIOGRAPHY

The following readings of general interest are suggested for each chapter.

I. MESOPOTAMIA — *Land of Myths*

ALBRIGHT, WILLIAM FOXWELL. *From the Stone Age to Christianity: Monotheism and the Historical Process*, 2d ed. with new introduction. Baltimore: Johns Hopkins Press, 1957.

BIBBY, GEOFFREY. *Four Thousand Years Ago: World Panorama of Life in the Second Millennium BC.* New York: Knopf, 1961. Reprint. Westport, Conn: Greenwood, 1983.

FINEGAN, JACK, *Light from the Ancient Past: The Archeological Background of the Hebrew-Christian Religion*, 2d ed. Princeton: Princeton University Press, 1959.

FRANKFORT, HENRI. *Kingship and the Gods: A Study of Ancient Near Eastern Religion as the Integration of Society and Nature*. Chicago: University of Chicago Press, 1948.

———. JOHN A. WILSON, THORKILD JACOBSEN, and WILLIAM A. IRWIN. *The Intellectual Adventure of Ancient Man: An Essay on Speculative Thought in the Ancient Near East*. Chicago: University of Chicago Press, 1946; Phoenix Books, 1977.

FRYMER-KENSKY, TIKVA. "God Before the Hebrews." *Biblical Archaeology Review* 8 (Sept./Oct. 1982): 18-25

GELB, I. J. *A Study of Writing: the Foundations of Grammatology.* Rev. ed. Chicago: University of Chicago Press, 1963.

GORDON, CYRUS H. *Before the Bible: The Common Background of Greek and Hebrew Civilisations.* New York: Harper & Row, 1962.

GRAY, JOHN. *Near Eastern Mythology.* Rev. ed. New York: P. Bedrick Books, 1985.

HAWKES, JACQUETTA, *The First Great Civilizations: Life in Mesopotamia, the Indus Valley, and Egypt.* New York: Alfred A. Knopf, 1973.

HROZNY, BEDRICH. *Ancient History of Western Asia, India and Crete.* Trans. Jindrich Procházka. New York: Philosophical Library, 1953.

JACOBSEN, THORKILD. *The Treasures of Darkness.* New Haven: Yale University Press, 1976.

———."Mesopotamia." Chaps. 5-7. In *The Intellectual Adventure of Ancient Man. See* Frankfort (Phoenix Books) 1977.

KRAMER, SAMUEL NOAH. *Sumerian Mythology.* Rev. ed. New York: Harper, 1961.

———. *The Sumerians: Their History, Culture and Character.* Chicago: University of Chicago Press, 1963.

LEMAIRE, ANDRÉ. "Mari, the Bible and the Northwest Semitic World." *Biblical Archaeologist* (June 1984): 101-108

LLOYD, SETON. *The Archaeology of Mesopotamia: From the Old Stone Age to the Persian Conquest.* London: Thames & Hudson, 1978.

MARGUERON, JEAN-CLAUDE. *Mesopotamia.* Trans. H. S. B. Harrison. Cleveland: World Publishing Co., 1965.

MATTHEWS, V. H. *Pastoral Nomadism in the Mari Kingdom.* American Schools of Oriental Research Dissertation Series, no. 3. Ed. David Noel Freedman. Cambridge, Mass.: American Schools of Oriental Research, 1978.

MENDENHALL, GEORGE. "Mari." In *The Biblical Archaeologist Reader,* ed. Edward F. Campbell Jr., and David Noel Freedman, vol. 2. Garden City, N. Y.: Anchor Books, 1964. Missoula, Mont.: Scholars Press (University of Montana), 1975.

MOSCATI, SABATINO. *Ancient Semitic Civilizations.* New York: Putnam, 1957.

OATES DAVID, and JOAN OATES. *The Rise of Civilization.* New York: Dutton, 1976.

OATES, JOAN. *Babylon.* London: Thames & Hudson, 1979.

OPPENHEIM. A. LEO. *Ancient Mesopotamia: Portrait of a Dead Civilization.* Rev. ed., completed by Erica Reiner. Chicago: University of Chicago Press, 1977.

PARROT, ANDRÉ. *Sumer: The Dawn of Art.* Trans. Stuart Gilbert and James Emmons. New York: Golden Press, 1961.

ROUX, GEORGES. *Ancient Iraq.* Cleveland: World Publishing Co., 1965.

SPEISER, E. A. *Mesopotamian Origins: The Basic Population of the Near East.* Philadelphia: University of Pennsylvania Press, 1930.

——. "Historiography and Historical Sources in Ancient Mesopotamia." In *The World History of the Jewish People.* Vol. 2, *The Patriarchs.* Ed. Benjamin Mazar. Tel Aviv: Massada Publishing Co., 1970.

THOMAS, D. WINTON, ed. *Archaeology and Old Testament Study.* Oxford: Clarendon Press, 1967.

WOOLLEY, C. LEONARD. *The Beginnings of Civilization.* Vol. 1, part 2 of *History of Mankind: Cultural and Scientific Development.* London: Allen & Unwin, prepared under auspices of UNESCO, 1963.

——. *Ur of the Chaldees.* Rev. and updated of *Excavations at Ur,* by P. R. S. Moorey. Ithaca, N. Y.: Cornell University Press, 1982

II. THE MISTS OF TIME — *Genesis 1-11*

ALT, ALBRECHT. *Essays on Old Testament History and Religion of Israel.* Trans. R. A. Wilson. Oxford: Blackwell, 1966.

BRIGHT, JOHN. "Has Archaeology Found Evidence of the Flood?" Ch. 3 in *Biblical Archaeologist Reader,* ed. G. Ernest Wright and David Noel Freedman, vol. 1. Garden City, N.Y.: Anchor Books for the American Schools of Oriental Research, 1975.

CHILDS, BREVARD S. *Myth and Reality in the Old Testament.* Studies in Biblical Theology, no. 27. London: SCM Press, 1960.

CORNFELD, GAALYAHU. *Adam to Daniel.* New York: Macmillan, 1961.

GASTER, THEODORE H. *The Oldest Stories in the World.* New York: Viking, 1952.

——. *Myth, Legend and Custom in the Old Testament.* Vol. 1. New York: Harper & Row, 1969.

GINZBERG, LOUIS. *Legends of the Bible.* Philadelphia: Jewish Publication Society, 1978.

GORDON, CYRUS H. *The Ancient Near East.* 3d ed. rev. New York: Norton, 1965.

GUNKEL, HERMANN. *The Legends of Genesis.* Trans. W. H. Carruth. Chicago: Open Court, 1906.

HEIDEL, ALEXANDER. *The Gilgamesh Epic and Old Testament Parallels.* Chicago: University of Chicago Press, 1946.

KAUFMANN, YEHEZKEL. *The Religion of Israel.* Trans. Moshe Greenberg. Chicago: University of Chicago Press, 1960.

KRAMER, SAMUEL NOAH. *Mythologies of the Ancient World.* Chicago: Quadrangle Books, 1961.

MOSCATI, SABATINO. *The Face of the Ancient Orient: A Panorama of Near Eastern Civilizations in pre-Classical Times.* Chicago: Quadrangle Books, 1961.

ORLINSKY, HARRY. *Understanding the Bible Through History and Archaeology.* Ithaca, N. Y.: Cornell University Press, 1960.

OTZEN, BENEDIKT, HANS GOTTLIEB, and KNUD JEPPESEN. *Myths in the Old Testament.* Trans. Frederick Cryer. London: SCM Press, 1980.

PARROT, ANDRÉ. *The Flood and Noah's Ark.* Studies in Biblical Archaeology no. 1. Trans. Edwin Hudson. London: SCM Press, 1955.

———. *The Tower of Babel.* Studies in Biblical Archaeology no. 2. Trans. Edwin Hudson. London: SCM Press, 1955

PFEIFFER, ROBERT. *The Books of the Old Testament.* New York: Harper & Brothers, 1957.

SARNA, NAHUM M. *Understanding Genesis: The Heritage of Biblical Israel.* Melton Research Center Series, vol. 1. New York: Schocken Books, 1970.

SOLLBERGER, EDMOND. *Babylonian Legend of the Flood.* 2d ed. London: Trustees of the British Museum, 1971.

THOMAS, D. WINTON, ed. *Documents from Old Testament Times.* London: Thomas Nelson & Sons, 1958.

VAWTER, BRUCE. *On Genesis: A New Reading.* Garden City, N.Y.: Doubleday, 1977.

VAN SETERS, JOHN. *In Search of History: Historiography in the Ancient World and the Origin of Biblical History.* New Haven: Yale University Press, 1983.

WRIGHT, GEORGE E., and FLOYD V. FILSON, eds. Rev. ed., with introductory article by William F. Albright. *Westminster Historical Atlas to the Bible.* Philadelphia: Westminster Press, 1956.

ZERIN, EDWARD. *The Birth of the Torah.* New York: Appleton-Century-Crofts, 1962.

III. CANAAN — *Land Between Empires*

AHARONI, YOHANAN. *The Land of the Bible: A Historical Geography,* 2d ed. London: Burns & Oates, 1979.

AHLSTRÖM, GÖSTA W. *Who Were the Israelites?* Winona Lakes, Ind.: Eisenbrauns, 1986.

BRIGHT, JOHN. *A History of Israel.* 3d ed. Philadelphia: Westminster Press, 1981.

BRUCE, F. F. *The Hittites and the Old Testament.* London: Tyndale Press, 1947.

BUCCELLATI, G. *The Amorites of the Ur III Period.* Seminario di Semitistica. Richerche 1. Naples: Instituto Orientale di Napoli, 1966.

CAQUOT, ANDRÉ, AND MAURICE SZNYCER. *Ugaritic Religion.* Leiden: E. J. Brill, 1980.

CROSS, FRANK MOORE. *Canaanite Myth and Hebrew Ethic: Essays in the History of the Religion of Israel.* Cambridge: Harvard University Press, 1973

———. ed. et al. *Magnalia Dei, The Mighty Acts of God: Essays on the Bible and Archaeology in Memory of G. Ernest Wright.* Garden City, N.Y.: Doubleday, 1976.

CULICAN, WILLIAM. *The First Merchant Venturers.* London: Thames & Hudson, 1966.

DEVER, WILLIAM G. "The Middle Bronze Age: The Zenith of the Urban Canaanite Era." *Biblical Archaeologist* 50 (Sept. 1987): 149-177.

DRIOTON, ETIENNE, GEORGES CONTENAU and JACQUES DUCHESNE-GUILLEMIN. *Religions of the Ancient East.* Trans. M. B. Loraine. New York: Hawthorn Books, 1949.

FINEGAN, JACK. *Light from the Ancient Past: The Archaeological Background of Judaism and Christianity.* 2d ed. Princeton: Princeton University Press, 1959.

FINKELSTEIN, ISRAEL. *Archaeology of the Period of the Settlement.* Jerusalem: Israel Exploration Society, 1988.

FRANK, HARRY. *Archaeological Companion to the Bible.* London: SCM Press, 1972.

GIBSON, JOHN C. L. *Canaanite Myths and Legends.* Originally edited by G. R. Driver, and published in the series Old Testament Studies under the auspices of the Society for Old Testament Study. Edinburgh: T. & T. Clark Ltd., 1977.

GORDON, CYRUS H. *Ugaritic Literature: A Comprehensive Translation of the Poetic and Prose Texts.* Rome: Pontificium Institutum Biblicum, 1949.

GRAY, JOHN. *The Canaanites.* Ancient People and Places, vol. 28. New York: Praeger, 1964.

———. *The Legacy of Canaan: The Ras Shamra Texts and their Relevance to the Old Testament.* 2d rev. ed. Supplements to Vetus Testamentum vol.5. Leiden: E. J. Brill. 1965.

GURNEY, O. R. *The Hittites.* 2d rev. ed. Baltimore: Penguin Books, 1961.

HALDAR, ALFRED. *Who Were the Amorites?* Monographs on the Ancient Near East, no. 1. Leiden: E. J. Brill, 1971.

KENYON, KATHLEEN. *Amorites and Canaanites.* London: Oxford University Press for the British Academy, 1966.

LEHMANN, JOHANNES. *The Hittites: People of a Thousand Gods.* Trans. J. Maxwell Brownjohn. New York: Viking, 1977.

MATTHIAE, PAOLO. *Ebla: An Empire Rediscovered.* Trans. Christopher Holme. Garden City, N. Y.: Doubleday, 1981.

MAZAR, BENJAMIN. *The Early Biblical Period.* Ed. Shmuel Ahituv and Baruch A. Levine. Jerusalem: Israel Exploration Society, 1986.

MITCHELL, STEPHEN. *Anatolia: Land, Men, and Gods in Asia Minor.* 2 vols. New York: Oxford University Press, 1993.

MOSCATI, SABATINO. *Ancient Semitic Civilizations.* New York: Putnam, 1958.

O'CALLAGHAN, ROGER, *Aram Naharaim: A Contribution to the History of Upper Mesopotamia in the Second Millennium B.C.* In Analecta Orientalia 26. Rome: Pontificium Institutum Biblicum, 1948.

PFEIFFER, CHARLES F. *Ras Shamra and the Bible.* Grand Rapids, Mich.: Baker Book House, 1962.

POPE, MARVIN. *El in the Ugaritic Texts.* In Supplements to Vetus Testamentum, vol.2. Leiden: E. J. Brill, 1955.

SCHAEFFER, CLAUDE F.-A. *Cuneiform Texts of Ras Shamra Ugarit.* London: Oxford University Press for the British Academy, 1939.

UNGER, MERRILL. *Israel and the Aramaeans of Damascus.* Grand Rapids, Mich.: Zondervan, 1947.

VAN SETERS, JOHN. *The Hyksos: A New Investigation.* New Haven: Yale University Press, 1966.

VAUX, ROLAND DE. *Ancient Israel: Its Life and Institutions.* Trans. John McHugh. London: Darton, Longman & Todd, 1961

YOUNG, GORDON, ed. *Ugarit in Retrospect: 50 Years of Ugarit and Ugaritic.* Winona Lake, Ind.: Eisenbrauns, 1981.

IV. THE PATRIARCHS — *Genesis 12-36*

ALBRIGHT, WILLIAM F. *Archaeology and the Religion of Israel.* 3d ed. Ayer Lectures of the Colgate-Rochester Divinity School, 1941. Baltimore: Johns Hopkins Press, 1953.

———. *Yahweh and the Gods of Canaan: A Historical Analysis of Two Contrasting Faiths.* Winona Lake, Ind.: Eisenbrauns, 1968.

Baly, Denis. *God and History in the Old Testament*. New York: Harper & Row, 1976.

Cassuto, Umberto. *The Goddess Anath: Canaanite Epics of the Patriarchal Age*. Trans. Israel Abrahams. Jerusalem: Magnes Press, Hebrew University, 1971.

Drijvers, J. H. W. *Cults and Beliefs at Edessa*, Leiden: E. J. Brill, 1980.

Finkelstein, Louis, ed. *The Jews: Their History, Culture and Religion*. 2d ed. Vol. 1. Philadelphia: Jewish Publication Society, 1955.

Gaubert, Henri. *Abraham, Loved by God*. The Bible in History, vol. 1. Trans. Lancelot Sheppard. London: Darton, Longman & Todd, 1968.

———. *Isaac and Jacob, God's Chosen Ones*. The Bible in History, vol. 2. Trans. Lancelot Sheppard. London: Darton, Longman and Todd, 1969.

Glueck, Nelson. *Rivers in the Desert: A History of the Negev*. New York: Farrar, Straus and Cudahy, 1959.

Gordon, Cyrus H. *The Loves and Wars of Baal and Anat: And Other Poems from Ugarit*. Princeton: Princeton University Press, 1943.

———. "Biblical Customs and the Nuzu Tablets." In *Biblical Archaeologist Reader,* ed. Edward F. Campbell, Jr., and David Noel Freedman, vol. 2. Garden City, N. Y.: Anchor Books, 1964. Missoula, Mont.: Scholars Press, (University of Montana), 1975.

Hooke, Samuel H., ed. *Origins of Early Semitic Ritual*. London: Oxford University Press, for the British Academy, 1958.

Irwin, William A. "The Hebrews." Chaps. 8-11 in *The Intellectual Adventure of Ancient Man. See* above, Ch. I, Frankfort (Phoenix Books) 1977.

Kapelrud, Arvid. "The Relationship Between El and Baal in the Ras Shamra Texts." In *The Bible World: Essays in Honor of Cyrus H. Gordon*, ed. Gary Rendsburg et al., 79-85. New York: Ktav Publishing House, 1980.

Kitchen, K. A. "Egypt, Ugarit, Qatna and Covenant." In *Ugarit Forschungen 11*. Internationales Jahrbuch für die Altertumskunde Syrien-Palästinas. Kevelaer, W. Germany: Butzon & Bercker, 1979.

Lloyd, Seton, and William Brice. "Harran." *Anatolian Studies 1* (1951): 77-110.

Mazar, Benjamin, ed. *The World History of the Jewish People*. Vol. 2, *The Patriarchs*. Tel Aviv: Massada Publishing Co. New Brunswick, N.J.: Rutgers University Press, 1970.

Meek, Theophile. *Hebrew Origins*. 2d ed. New York: Harper & Brothers, 1950.

Meyers, Carol. "Roots of Restriction: Women in Early Israel." *Biblical Archaeologist* (Sept.1978): 91-100.

Millard, A. R., and D. J. Wiseman, eds. *Essays on the Patriarchal Narratives*. Leicester, Eng.: Inter-Varsity Press, 1980.

Noth, Martin. *The History of Israel*. 2d ed. New York: Harper & Row, 1960.

———. *A History of Pentateuchal Traditions*. Trans. with an intro. by Bernhard W. Anderson. Englewood Cliffs, N.J.: Prentice-Hall, 1972. Reprint, Chico, Cal.: Scholars Press, 1981.

Parrot, André. *Abraham and His Times*. Studies in Biblical Archaeology, no. 14. Trans. James H. Farley. Philadelphia: Fortress Press, 1968.

Pearlman, Moshe, and Yaacov Yannai. *Historical Sites in Israel*. London: W. H. Allen, 1964.

Plastaras, James. *Creation and Covenant*. Contemporary College Theology Series. Milwaukee: Bruce Publishing Co., 1968.

Rothenberg, Beno, with Yohanan Aharoni, and Avi Hashimshoni. *God's Wilderness: Discoveries in Sinai*. Trans. Joseph Witriol. London: Thames & Hudson, 1961; New York: Thomas Nelson, 1962.

THOMPSON, THOMAS L. *The Settlement of Sinai and the Negev in the Bronze Age*. Wiesbaden: Dr. Ludwig Reichert Vlg., 1975.

VAUX, ROLAND DE. "The Hebrew Patriarchs and History." *Theology Digest* (1964): 230-239.

WEIPPERT, M. *Settlement of the Israelite Tribes in Palestine*. London: SCM Press, 1971

Wright, G. Ernest. *The Bible and the Ancient Near East*. New York: Doubleday & Co., 1961.

V. EGYPT — *The Nurturing Land*

ALDRED, CYRIL. *Akhenaten: King of Egypt*. London: Thames & Hudson, 1988

BERNSTEIN, BURTON. *Sinai: The Great and Terrible Wllderness*. New York: Viking Press, 1979.

BIERBRIER, MORRIS. *The Tomb Builders of the Pharaohs*. London: Colonnade, British Museum Publications, 1982.

BIETAK, MANFRED. *Avaris and Piramesse: Archaeological Exploration in the Eastern Nile Delta*. British Academy, vol. 65. London: Oxford University Press, 1981

BREASTED, JAMES HENRY. *The Dawn of Conscience*, New York: Scribner's, 1933.

——. *Development of Religion and Thought in Ancient Egypt*. 1912. Reprint, Philadelphia: University of Pennsylvania Press, 2d Pennsylvania paperback ed., 1986.

CERNY, JAROSLAV. *Ancient Egyptian Religion*. London: Hutchinson University Library, 1952.

CLARKE, RUNDLE. *Myth and Symbol in Ancient Egypt*. London: Thames & Hudson, 1959.

DAVID, A. ROSALIE. *The Ancient Egyptians: Religious Beliefs and Practices*. London, Boston: Routledge & Kegan Paul, 1982.

GORDON, CYRUS H. *Forgotten Scripts: Their Ongoing Discovery and Decipherment*. New York: Basic Books, 1982.

HARI, ROBERT. *New Kingdom, Amarna Period: The Great Hymn to Aten*. Leiden: E.J. Brill, 1985.

HARRIS, JOHN R., ed. *The Legacy of Egypt*. 2d ed. Oxford: Clarendon Press, 1971.

HURRY, JAMIESON. *Imhotep*. London: Oxford University Press, 1926.

IONS, VERONICA. *Egyptian Mythology*. Middlesex, G.B.: Newnes Books, 1982.

JAMES. T. G. H. *An Introduction to Ancient Egypt*. New York: Farrar Straus Giroux in association with British Museum Publications, 1979.

KITCHEN, K. A. *Pharaoh Triumphant: The Life and Times of Ramesses II, King of Egypt*. Warminster, G. B.: Aris & Phillips, 1982.

LICHTHEIM, MIRIAM. *Ancient Egyptian Literature: A Book of Readings*. 3 vols. Berkeley and Los Angeles: University of California Press, 1973-1980.

MONTET, PIERRE. *Egypt and the Bible*. Trans. Leslie R. Keylock. Philadelphia: Fortress Press, 1968

NEW, SILVA. "The Serabit Expedition of 1930: The Temple of Hathor." *Harvard Theological Review* 25 (1932): 122-129.

NEWBY, P. H. *The Egypt Story*. New York: Chanticleer Press, 1985.

OCHSENSCHLAGER, EDWARD. *The Egyptians in the Middle Kingdom*. Life Long Ago Series. New York: Coward, 1963.

OREN, ELIEZER. "The Overland Route Between Egypt and Canaan in the Early Bronze Age. Preliminary Report." *Israel Exploration Journal* 23 (1973): 198-205.

Peet, T. Eric. *Egypt and the Old Testament*. Liverpool: University Press of Liverpool, 1922.

Petrie, W. M. Flinders. *Religion and the Conscience in Ancient Egypt: Lectures Delivered at University College*. 1898. Reprint, New York: Benjamin Blom, 1972.

——. *Syria and Egypt from the Tell el Amarna Letters*. 1907. Chicago: Ares, 1978.

Pfeiffer, Charles. *Tell el Amarna and the Bible*. Baker Studies in Biblical Archaeology. Grand Rapids, Mich.: Baker Book House, 1963.

Redford ,Donald. *Akhenaton, the Heretic King*. Princeton: Princeton University Press, 1984.

——. *Egypt, Canaan, and Israel in Ancient Times*, Princeton: Princeton University Press, 1992.

Rossiter, Evelyn, *The Book of the Dead: Papyri of Ani, Hunefer, Anhaï*. New York: Miller Graphics, 1979.

Rothenberg, Beno. *Sinai: Pharaohs, Miners, Pilgrims and Soldiers*. Trans. Edward Osers. Washington: Joseph J. Binns, 1979.

Sauneron, Serge. *The Priests of Ancient Egypt*. Trans. Ann Morrisett. New York: Grove Press, 1960.

Sigerist, Henry. *A History of Medicine*. Vol. 1. Yale Medical Library Historical Publication 27. New York: Oxford University Press, 1951.

Steindorff, George, and Keith C. Seele. *When Egypt Ruled the East*. Chicago: University of Chicago Press, 1957.

Trumper, Victor L. *The Mirror of Egypt in the Old Testament*. London: Marshall, Morgan & Scott, 1931.

Williams, Ronald. "Egypt and Israel." Chap. 10 in *The Legacy of Egypt*. 2d ed. Ed. J.R. Harris, 257-90. Oxford: Clarendon Press, 1971.

Wilson, John A. *The Culture of Ancient Egypt*. Chicago: University of Chicago Press, 1951. Previous edition entitled *The Burden of Egypt*.

——. "Egypt." Chaps. 2-4. In *The Intellectual Adventure of Ancient Man. See* above, Ch. I, Frankfort (Phoenix Books), 1977

VI. JOSEPH — *Prelude to Nationhood*

Cassuto, Umberto. "Beginning of Historiography Among the Israelites." In *Biblical and Oriental Studies*, vol. 1. Trans. Israel Abrahams. Jerusalem: Magnes Press, Hebrew University, 1973.

Heaton, E. W. *Solomon's New Men: The Emergence of Ancient Israel as a National State*. New York: Pica Press, 1974.

Hermann, Siegfried. *Israel in Egypt*. London: SCM Press, 1973.

Redford, Donald. *Study of the Biblical Story of Joseph (Genesis 37-50)*. Supplements to Vetus Testamentum, vol. 20. Leiden: E.J. Brill, 1970.

Rowley, H. H. *From Joseph to Joshua*. Schweich Lectures of the British Academy, 1948. London: Oxford University Press, 1950.

Sugden, Edward H. *Israel's Debt to Egypt*. London: Epworth Press, 1928.

PICTURE CREDITS

The source of each picture is listed below, in the following order: page number, description, museum (where applicable), and photo source. Where two or more pictures appear on one page, they are separated by semi-colons. Maps and charts were prepared by Philip Grushkin, unless otherwise credited. The following abbreviations are used:

AF	Ada Feyerick
AM	Ägyptisches Museum, Staatliche Museen zu Berlin, Preussischer Kulturbesitz
Anton Moortgat VA	*Vorderasiatische Rollsiegel*. Berlin: Gebr. Mann, 1940
BM	British Museum, London
Beno Rothenberg	*God's Wilderness*. Thames & Hudson 1961; Thos. Nelson, 1962. By permission of the author
cs	cylinder seal
EG	©Editions Gallimard, L'Univers des Formes-La Photothèque
EMC	Egypt Museum, Cairo
Ernst Heinrich	*Fara: Ergebnisse der Ausgrabungen der Deutschen Orient-Gesellschaft in Fara und Abu Hatab*. Berlin: Staatliche Museum, 1931
IAA-IMJ	Israel Antiquities Authority, Israel Museum, Jerusalem
IMB	Iraq Museum, Baghdad
Jean Lauffray	Drawing by Jean Lauffray. From: André Parrot, *Le Palais: Peintures murales*. Mission Archéologique de Mari. Vol. 2. LOPG, 1958
LOPG	Librairie Orientaliste Paul Geuthner, Paris
K.R. Lepsius	*Denkmaler aus Ägypten und Äthiopien*. Berlin, 1849-59
Louvre, RMN	Musée du Louvre, Paris. Reunion des Musées Nationaux
Louvre A/O	Musée du Louvre, Antiquités Orientales
MAFM	Mission Archéologique Française de Mari. All rights reserved
MAFRO	Mission Archéologique Française de Ras Shamra-Ougarit. All rights reserved
MAFT	Mission Archéologique Française de Telloh. All rights reserved
MASUR	Mission archeologica in Siria dell' Università di Roma, La Sapienza
MMA	Metropolitan Museum of Art, New York. All rights reserved
NMA	National Museum, Aleppo
NMB	National Museum, Beirut
NMD	National Museum, Damascus
NYPL	New York Public Library. Astor, Lenox and Tilden Foundation /JD. Jewish Division; /Map. Map Division; /OD. Oriental Division
OIC	Courtesy of the Oriental Institute of the University of Chicago
SITES	Smithsonian Institution Traveling Exhibition Service
TAU	Tel Aviv University, Institute of Archaeology
UMP	University of Pennsylvania Museum of Archaeology and Anthropology
VA	Vorderasiatisches Museum, Staatliche Museen zu Berlin, Preussischer Kulturbesitz

jacket: *see page 54*

back jacket: *see page 72, Sumerian.*

frontis: Mari shepherd. NMA. Jean Mazenod. *l'Art Antique du Proche Orient*. Editions Citadelles, Paris.

I. MESOPOTAMIA—*Land of Myths*

28-9: Ur Airview. Frank J. Scherschel, with permission of Jean D. Scherschel. from: *Lost Worlds*, Horizon Books, 1962.

30: Hunt cs. Harriet Otis Cruft Fund, courtesy Museum of Fine Arts, Boston; Dumuzi cs. Anton Moortgat VA 10537.

31: Uruk vase. IMB. Hirmer Verlag, Munich.

32: An, cs detail. NMD. *Syria* 31, 1954, pl. 15. MAFM, LOPG; Uruk temple. Courtesy Salim Mahlab.

33: King List (Weld-Blundell prism, 1923.444). Ashmolean Museum, Oxford.

34: Enki, cs 202, enlargement. Pierpont Morgan Library; Eridu. From: M. Beek, *Atlas of Mesopotamia*, fig. 48. Courtesy Elsevier, Amsterdam. NYPL/Map.

35: Nippur. OIC; Naram-Sin, Louvre, RMN.

36: Stele of Vultures. Louvre, RMN; Gudea. Louvre, RMN.

37: Farmer. IMB. OIC; Artisan. Louvre, RMN; Musician. Louvre, RMN.

39: Mari tablet. Louvre, RMN; Carchemish tablet. Museum of Anatolian Civilizations, Ankara. Courtesy Turkish Information Office, NYC; Map adapted from: G.

Dossin, "Les Archives Epistolaires du Palais de Mari." *Syria* 19, 1938, fig. 2. LOPG.

40: Beasts cs. Louvre, RMN; Narmer palette. EMC; Ramses II. Foto Marburg, 86.033; Syrian cs. MMA. Collection of Mrs. William H. Moore, lent by Rt. Rev. Paul Moore, Jr. L.55.49.192; Presentation cs. BM 89126; Knossos goddess. Archaeological Museum, Heraklion, Crete.

41: Babylonian world map. BM 92687; Map drawing. From: R. Campbell Thompson, *Late Babylonian Letters*. London, 1906.

42. Ur-Nammu stele, detail. UMP. Neg. S8-8409.

43: Hammurapi stele. Louvre, RMN; Nuzi tablet. OIC.

44: Adda cs, enlarged. BM 89115.

45: Amurru cs, enlarged. Anton Moortgat, VA 712.

46: André Parrot. Courtesy Mme. Parrot; Mari airview. MAFM. From: A. Parrot, *Mari*. Courtesy Editions Ides et Calendes.

47: Shibum. NMD. Courtesy SITES, Eric F. Long.

48: Etana cs, detail. Anton Moortgat VA 3456; Kalki cs, detail. BM 89137.

II. MISTS OF TIME—*Genesis 1-11*

54: Eclipse. American Museum of Natural History, NYC. Courtesy Dpt. of Library Services. Neg. 338127.

55: Marriage cs. IMB. OIC.

56: Gods battling cs. MMA. Collection of Mrs. William H. Moore, lent by Rt. Rev. Paul Moore, Jr., L. 55.49.160; Marduk cs. BM 89589; god and victim cs. Bibliothèque Nationale 68.

57: Ur-Nammu stele, detail. UMP. Neg. S8-8429.

58-9: Investiture of Zimri-Lim, Mari. Jean Lauffray. Permission Louvre A/O.

60: Tree of life cs. BM 89308; Khafaje bowl. BM 128887.

61: Gilgamesh cs drawing. Ernst Heinrich, VA 6700; Temptation cs. BM 89326.

62-3: Shatt al-Arab. Copyright Wilfred Thesiger. By permission of Curtis Brown Ltd., London, and Wilfred Thesiger.

63: Al Qurna. Courtesy Lerner Publications Co., Minneapolis.

64: Shepherd terracotta. Louvre, RMN; Farmer cs. Louvre, RMN.

65: Offering bearers cs. Staatliche Kunstsammlungen, Dresden, ZV 2996; Statue base, Telloh. Louvre, RMN.

66: Demon terracotta. BM 22458.

67: Aqhat tablet. Louvre, RMN.

68: Caravan, Beni Hasan. From: K.R. Lepsius, vol. 4, abt. 2, pl. 133. NYPL/OD; Ur dagger. IMB. Courtesy of UMP. Neg. S-140248.

69: Abel's tomb. AF.

70: Mt. Ararat. Harry Naltchayan, Annandale, Va.

71: Deluge tablet. UMP. Neg. S8-6765; Megiddo fragment. IAA-IMJ.

72: Sumerian. UMP. Neg. N5-140244; Fara II level. UMP, Neg. F-295b; Fish, small. Ernst Heinrich, VA 6717; Fish, large. Ernst Heinrich, VA 6716; Shell. Ernst Heinrich, VA 6759.

73: Rampant bull. IMB. Courtesy of UMP; Sheep, large. UMP. Neg. N35-101548; 2 Doe. Ernst Heinrich, VA 6747, VA 6748; Boat, Fara. UMP. Neg. S8-72081.

74: Mari dove, detail. Jean Lauffray. Permission Louvre A/O.

75: Fara necklace. UMP, Neg. F284; Deity with plow cs. OIC.

76-7: Nations, tomb of Seti. From: K.R. Lepsius, vol. 6, abt. 3, pl. 136. NYPL/OD.

78: Enmerkar tablet. UMP. Neg. S8-47374; Ziggurat builders cs. Bible Land Museum, Jerusalem, seal 377, ex-coll. E. Borowski. Photo: Dietrich Widmer.

79: Lamentation tablet. UMP. Neg. G8-6563; Ur standard, peace. BM 121201. Ur. U 11164.

80: L. Woolley. BM. Ur 16425.

81: Ur ziggurat. Royal Air Force. From: L. Woolley, *Ur Excavations*. Vol. 5. Joint Expedition to Mesopotamia, BM and UMP, 1939.

82: Ur-Nammu stele. UMP. Neg. S8-61926.

III. CANAAN—*Land Between Empires*

88: Map, Canaan. Reprinted with permission of Simon & Schuster. From: Y. Aharoni and M. Avi-Yonah. *Macmillan Bible Atlas*, rev. ed. ©Carta Ltd., 1969.

89: Ebla. Courtesy of MASUR.

90: Ugarit. AF; Sphinx. NMD. From: *Ugaritica* I, 1939, pl.3, MAFRO. LOPG; Mycenaean krater. Louvre A/O. From: Claude Schaeffer, *2ème Campagne de Fouilles à Ras Shamra*, Spring 1930, pl. 3. LOPG 1931.

91: Ini-Teshup seal, fig. 35, NMD; Niqmad II seal, fig. 92. NMD. Both from: *Ugaritica* III, 1956. MAFRO, LOPG.

92: El stele. NMA. From: Claude Schaeffer, *8ème Campagne de Fouilles* à *Ras Shamra-Ugarit*, Spring 1936, pl. 17. MAFRO, LOPG 1937.

94-5: Bekaa Valley. Courtesy National Council of Tourism, Lebanon.

96: Mari screen. *Syria* 48, 1971, pl. 14. MAFM, LOPG.

97: Amorite remains, Sinai. Beno Rothenberg.

98: Byblos. Servizio Editoriale Fotografico, Turin. Art Resource, NYC.

99: Phoenician ships. From: Georges Daressy, *Revue Archéologique* III, Ser. 27, 1895. NYPL/Annex; Cedar cutting, Karnak. From: W. Wreszinski, *Atlas zur Altägyptischen Kulturgeschichte*. vol. 2, pl. 35. Berlin, 1935. NYPL/OD.

100: Seti triumphant, Karnak. Courtesy of The Committee of the Egypt Exploration Society. From: Alan Gardiner, "The Ancient Military Road Between Egypt and Palestine." *Journal of Egyptian Archaeology* 6, 1920. NYPL/OD.

101. Sinai littoral. Beno Rothenberg.

102. Execration Texts. ©A.C.L. Bruxelles.

103: Ashkelon. Jerusalem. Shechem. AF; Hazor. Courtesy Denise Gold.

104: Byblos sword. NMB. Photo: EG, *Les Pheniciens*, 1975.

105: Baalat cs, drawing. From: Pierre Montet, *Byblos et l'Egypte*. LOPG, 1928; Atanah-ili cs, drawing. From: Ernst Sellin, *Tell Ta'annek*. Vienna, 1903.

106: Warrior king, Ugarit. NMD. From: *Syria* 31, 1954, pl. 10. MAFRO, LOPG.

107 Baal stele, Ugarit. Louvre, RMN.

108: Royal couple, Ugarit. NMD. From: *Syria* 31, 1954, pl. 9 MAFRO, LOPG.

109: El statuette. Courtesy Marguerite Yon.

110: Mother goddess, Beth Yerah. IAA-IMJ.

111: Phoenician farmers. NMB. EG, *Les Pheniciens*, 1975.

112: Claude Schaeffer. *Ugaritica* III, 1956, pl. 217. MAFRO, LOPG.

113: Ugarit airview. From: Claude Schaeffer, *7ème Campagne de Fouilles à Ras Shamra-Ugarit*, spring 1935, pl .22. MAFRO, LOPG 1936.

114: Anat stele. Permission of Magnes Press, Hebrew University, Jerusalem. From: Umberto Cassuto, *The Goddess Anath*, 1st Eng. ed. 1971. credit G. Michaelides, Cairo; provenance unknown.

115: Anathoth. David Harris, Jerusalem.

116: Ai. AF.

IV. PATRIARCHS—*Genesis 12-36*

122: Orant, Alaca Höyük. Museum of Anatolian Civilization, Ankara. EG. *Les Hittites*, 1976.

124-5: Jordan River. Permission of Erich Lessing. From: *The Bible: History and Culture of a People*. New York: Herder & Herder, 1970. NYPL/JD.

126-7: Judaean hills. Kazuyoshi Nomachi, Tokyo.

128: Circumcision, Saqqara. EMC; Ram sacrifice, Mari. NMD. *Syria* 31, 1954, pl. 18. MAFM, LOPG.

130: Domestic scene cs. BM 89343.

131: Shechem. Courtesy Erich Lessing.

132: Kadesh-barnea. David Harris, Jerusalem.

133: Goddess, Minet el-Beida. Louvre, RMN.

134: Jebel el-Aqra. Ugarit. AF; Baal temple, Ugarit. AF.

135: Warrior, Telloh. IMB. MAFT.

136: Nursing goddess, Ugarit. NMD, *Syria* 31, 1954, pl. 8. MAFRO, LOPG.

137: Nursing mother, Horoztepe. Museum of Anatolian Civilization, Ankara. EG. *Les Hittites*, 1976.

138: Ugaritic ivories. NMD. MAFRO. Octopus Publishing Group Ltd., London.

139: Nuzi fragment. From the collections of the Harvard Semitic Museum; Ugarit fragment. *Syria* 17, 1936, pl. 24. MAFRO, LOPG.

140: Ebla girl. Courtesy of MASUR.

141: Canaanite jewelry. IAA-IMJ.

142: Map, Negev. Rainfall figures permission of the Survey of Israel. From: *Atlas of Israel*, Map IV/2, 1970.

143: Altar, Beersheba. TAU.

144: Yohanan Aharoni. TAU; Well, Beersheba. TAU.

BIBLICAL MEMORY—*Portfolio*

149: Urfa mosque. AF; Urfa columns. AF.

150: Urfa pool. AF.

151: Harran arch. AF; Harran field. AF; Suruç sign. AF

152: Citadel, Aleppo. AF.

153: Oak, Hebron. AF.

154-5: Dead Sea. Max and Hilla Jacoby, Berlin.

156: Salt pillar, Sodom. Werner Braun, Jerusalem; Ghor es-Safi, Jordan. Oded Borowski, Emory University, Atlanta

157: Mount Moriah, Jerusalem. Richard Cleave, Nicosia.

158-9: Dome of the Rock, Jerusalem. Dean Conger, Durango, Co.

160-1: Mecca, Saudi Arabia. Abdelaziz Frikha, Tunis.

162: Machpelah tomb, Hebron. Werner Braun, Jerusalem.

163: Ain al-Arous, Syria. AF; Well, Harran. AF.

164: Dothan, Israel. AF

165: Green mosque, Nablus. AF

166: Bedouin, Jebel Musa. From: *Ordnance Survey of the Peninsula of Sinai*, 1869; Sinai wife, Serabit el-Khadim. AF.

V. EGYPT—*The Nurturing Land*

174: Chephren and Horus. EMC. Dagli Orti, Paris.

175: Maat. Archaeological Museum, Florence, Italy.

176: Apy, Deir el-Medina. MMA 30.4.115.

176-7: Dahshur pyramids. Eliot Elisofon. National Museum of African Art, Eliot Elisofon Archives, Smithsonian Institution, Washington D.C.

178: Rekhmire, tomb 100, Thebes. MMA 30.4.79.

178-9: Menna, tomb 69, Thebes. MMA 30.4.44, Egyptian Expedition, Rogers Fund, 1930.

180-1: Map and nomes, Upper Egypt, Lower Egypt. Andromeda Oxford Ltd., Oxfordshire, England.

180: Amon of Thebes. Brooklyn Museum 37.4. Charles Edwin Wilbour Fund.

181: Re of Heliopolis. BM 60346; Ptah of Memphis. ©A.C.L. Bruxelles.

182: Unas pyramid. Victor R. Boswell, Jr., National Geographic Society.

183: Osiris, Ani Papyrus. BM 10470/4; Priest, Ani Papyrus. BM 10470/12.

184-5: Nakht, tomb 52, Thebes. Victor R. Boswell, Jr., National Geographic Society.

186: Papyrus Ebers. From: *Papyrus Ebers*, vol. 1, pl. 40. Leipzig, 1873, NYPL/OD.

187: Thoth. EMC. Courtesy Museum of Fine Arts, Boston.

190. Avaris. AF.

190-1: Caravan, Beni Hasan. From: K.R. Lepsius, vol. 4, abt. 2, pl.133. NYPL/OD.

191: Papyrus Brooklyn. Brooklyn Museum 35.1446. Gift of Miss Theodora Wilbour, from the collection of her father, Charles Edwin Wilbour.

192: Thutmose III, Karnak. A. Gaddis, Luxor.

193: Mekal stele, Beth-shean. IAA 28256; Maṣṣebah, Beth-shean. UMP. Neg. S4-140246.

194: Serabit el-Khadim. AF.

195: Votive, Serabit el-Khadim. EMC.

196: Tiy, Serabit el-Khadim. EMC; Akhenaten stele. EMC.

197: Ramses tablet, Serabit el-Khadim. EMC. From: W.M.F. Petrie, *Researches in Sinai*, Dutton, 1906.

198: W. M. F. Petrie. Courtesy the Petrie Museum, University College, London.

199: Stone shelters. Serabit el-Khadim. AF; Hathor pillar. Serabit el-Khadim. AF.

200: Pectoral. ©1983. MMA. Rogers Fund and Henry Walters Gift, 1916. (16.1.3)

VI. JOSEPH—*Prelude to Nationhood.* *Genesis 37-50*

206: Hands, tomb of Ai, el Amarna. AF.

207: Sword, Alalakh. Courtesy of the Society of Antiquaries of London. From: Sir Leonard Woolley, *Alalakh*, 1955: AT/36/4.

208-9: Euphrates River. AF.

210-211: Middle Egypt. AF.

212: Idrimi. BM 130738; Ox liver, Alalakh. Courtesy of the Society of Antiquaries of London. From: Sir Leonard Woolley, *Alalakh*, 1955. AT/47/75.

213: Amenhotep III. Brooklyn Museum 48.28. Charles Edwin Wilbour Fund; Amarna Letter 252. BM 29844.

214: Syrian soldier, AM 14122. From: Hugo Gressman, *Altorientalische Texte und Bilder zum Alten Testament*. Berlin: Vlg. Walter de Gruyter, 1927.

215: Brick, Der. IMB. Courtesy of The Committee of The Egypt Exploration Society. From: Sidney Smith, "An Egyptian in Babylonia." *Journal of Egyptian Archaeology*, vol. 18, 1932, pl. 3. NYPL/OD; Amarna Letter 23. BM 29793; Reshef seal, Tell el-Ajjul. Wilfrid Israel Museum, Kibbutz Hazorea, Israel.

216: Calf, Amarna. Louvre, RMN; Birds, Amarna, EMC.

217: Akhenaten and child. EMC,

218: Ramose. Courtesy of The Committee of The Egypt Eploration Society. From: Norman de Garis Davies. *Tomb of Vizier Ramose*, 1941. NYPL/OD.

219: Ostracon with dancer. AM 21445. Giraudon, Paris.

220: Imhotep. MMA 89.2.528. Gift of Mrs. Lucy W. Drexel, 1889; Thoth. Louvre. Larousse, Paris.

221: Khnum. BM 64532; Famine, Unas stele, Saqqara. Victor R. Boswell, Jr., National Geographic Society.

223: Papyrus Ani. BM 10470/35.

224: Harper, Nakht tomb 52, Thebes. A. Gaddis, Luxor.

225: Mourners. Ramose tomb 55, Thebes. A. Gaddis, Luxor.

226-7: Bahr Yusuf. AF.

228: Joseph's tomb, Nablus. Garo Nalbandian, Jerusalem.

229: Akhenaten. EMC.

EPILOGUE

230-1: Ramses II, Tell el-Retaba. UMP. Neg. S4-38014.

232: Ramses II kneeling. EMC. Pro-Image, Montreal.

233: Nebre stele. Formerly AM 20377, destroyed during World War II. From: Adolf Erman, "Denksteine aus der Thebanischen Graberstadt," *Akademie der Wissenschaften*. XLIX. Pl. 16. Nov. 30, 1911.

234: Four-Hundred Year stele. EMC.

235: Map Twelve tribes. ©Hammond Inc., Maplewood, N. J.

236: King's Highway. Dean Conger, Durango, Co.

INDEX

The interplay of history and Genesis required that the Index be both alphabetical when possible and chronological when necessary. "Gen." notes facts within the Biblical narrative, and "ref." is a reference to the subject rather than its specific name. **Boldface** type is used for major entries, Biblical Memory sites (usually grouped after an entry), and Discovery pages, inclusive of archaeologists, sites, and content. Page numbers in *italics* indicate illustrations, maps, and charts.

Meritaten, *196*, *197*
Merneptah, 171, 204
Mesopotamia (general): agriculture in, 64 (*see also* fertility); cities in, 25, *28-9*, *34*, *35*, 36, *72* (*see also* Mari; Nuzi); cultural interaction with, Ebla, 24-5, Egypt, 26, 84, region, 38, Ugarit, 26, 84; invaders in, 38; trade in, 39, 96; Gen., family ties to, 91 (*see also* Aramaeans), reflections of, Eden, 22, social customs, 26, 139
Mesopotamia (historic periods), **21-7** passim. *See also* Akkad; Babylon; Sumer; Ubaid; Ur; Uruk
Mesopotamian literature. *See* Sumerian, literature; Babylonian, literature
Mesopotamian, religion and beliefs: gods, 23, attributes of, 57, 60 (*see also* Babylonian, literature; Sumer; Sumerian, literature; by specific god names); New Year's ritual, 55
metals, metalworking, 68, 189, 190
Midianites, *129*, **148**
Middle Bronze Age, 96, 143, **144**
Migdol, 207
migrations, 38; of Amorites, 25, 96, 119; of Aramaeans, 85. *See also* Abraham; Jacob
Milcah, *129*
military campaigns: in Canaan, 213 (*see also* Hyksos); of Egypt, Thutmose III, 170, 189, *192*, Seti I, *100*, Necho II, 172; in Mesopotamia, 35, 36; in Ugaritic myth, 109; Gen., of Abram, 36, 135, in Shechem, 213. *See also* war; warfare
mines, mining. *See* Timna; Sinai
Minet el-Beida, 90, 133
Minoan, 40
Mitanni, 207, 215
Mizraim (Egypt), *76*, *77*, 90
Moab, Moabite, *129*, **147**, **154-5**
monotheism: of Akhenaten, 171, 193, 216, **229**; of Moses, 93, 171
moon: god, Aramaean, 207, Egyptian, 186-7, 222, Mesopotamian, 24, **148** (*see also* Ur); Gen., 24, 202, 222. *See also* individual god names
moral law, morality: in Ugarit, 92, **113**; Gen., 52, 53, 64, 75, 119, of Abraham, 120, of Joseph, 203, 219, at Sinai, 205
Moriah, land of, 93, **148**, **157**; Mount, 120
Moses, 189, 205
Moslems, modern, 128, **146**, **148**, **229**
motherhood, 136, 137
Mycenae, Mycenaeans, 38, 133
Mycerinus (Menkaure), 169
myths, 9; of Ugarit, **112**

Nabataean, *129*
Nablus, **148**, *165*, **228**
nagû (unknown lands), *41*
Nahor, *129*
Nakht, tomb of, *184-5*, *224*
names, changes of, Gen., 10, 110, 123, 204
Nanna(r). *See* Ur, moon god of

Naphtali, *129*; territory of, *235*
Naram-Sin, *35*
Narmer palette, *40*
nationhood, of Israel, 118, 189, ref. 229; promises of, 123, 130, 205
Near East (ancient), 22; ideas and customs in, 50, 51, 118, 168 (*see also* circumcision); migrations in, 119; Gen., themes in, 52, 53
Nebaioth, *129*
Nebre, 232, *233*
Nebuchadnezzar II, 27
Necho I, 204
Necho II, 172
Neferhotep, *191*
Nefertiti, *196*, *197*
Negative Confession (in *Book of the Dead*), 232.
Negau, 105
Negev(b), *142*, 143; archaeology of, **144-5**; Gen., Patriarchs in, 118, 120
Nekhtamun, 232, *233*
Nergal, 23, 105
Neribtum (Ishchali), 37
Nile Delta. *See* Delta, Nile
Nile River, 168, *176-7*, 220, branches of, *181*, **226-7**
Nile Valley, 84, 168, 198
Nimrod, 91, **147**
Nineveh, 72, 215
Ningal, 79
Ningirsu, 23, 36
Ningizzida, 65
Ninhursag, Enki and. *See* Sumerian literature
Nini-zaza, 47
Ninsun, 32
Ninurta, *44*
Nippur, *35*, 71
Niqmad II (Nigmed), 91, 107, 112
Nisir, Mount, 71
Noah: before Flood, 72, 73; after Flood, covenant and laws with, 42, 45, 53, 75; curses Canaan, 76, descendants of, *76-7*, 90-1
Nod, land of, 67
nomads: in Canaan, 38, 120; in Mari 9, 25, 39; nature of, 123, 189; in Sinai, 189, 221; nomes, *180-1*
Nubia, Nubians, *77*, 168, in Aten hymn, 197
Numbers, Book of, 207
Nuzi, customs similar to Gen., 10, 26, and laws, *43*, 86, 119, *139*, 140

Oholibamah, *129*
Old Testament: influenced by, Egypt, 168, 173, Mesopotamia, 27, Ugarit, 85, 86, **112-3**
Olympus, Mount, 134
Omar, Mosque of, **148**, **157**, **158-9**
On (Heliopolis, nome 13), *181*; in Ani papyrus, *183*; Gen., 181
oral tradition, 89, **112**, **166**

Osiris, *183*, 186; in Amarna period, 216, **229**
Ottoman, in Urfa, **147**

Pabil, in *Epic of Kret*, 109
Padan-aram, 85, **147**
paganism, 130, 133
Paghat, in *Tale of Aqhat*, 67
Palestine, 84, 113, 170, 171
Palmer, E.H. and H.S., 166
papyrus, 99. *See also* Egyptian literature, papyri
Paraemheb, *193*
Paran, Wilderness of, 189
Parrot, André, *46-7*, ref. *57*
Patriarchal Age, 143
Patriarchal narratives: precursors of, **112-3**; reflect ancient customs, 118, 119 (*see also* Nuzi); traditions, in Beesheba, 143, **144-5**, of Covenant, 234; form transition to national history, 202; tribal God in, 93
Patriarchs, *129*; assimilate El's name, 92, 131; know God's power, 186; promises to, 119, **123**, 232; sites sacred to, 116, 131; social customs of, 139 (*see also* Nuzi); wanderings of, 118, **146**; wives of from Haran, 91, *129*, 207. *See also* by individual Patriarch names; sons
Pelusiac, Nile branch, *181*
Pentateuch, 118
Persia, 27
Persian Gulf, (Lower Sea), *17*, *38*, *47*, *76*, 96
Perizzite, 95
Petrie. W.M. Flinders, 11, **166**, **198-9**
pharaoh: historic synchronism of, 172; meaning of name, 202
Philistines: as Sea Peoples, 38, 90; way of in Sinai, *100*, *188*; Gen., 84, **144**, **145**
Philo of Byblos, 98
Phoenician: cap, *104*; origins of, alphabet, 189, 199, legends, **112**; practise of circumcision, 128; ships, *99*
Pilgrim's Way (Darb el Haj), *188*
Piramesse (Qantir), 170n, *181*
Pishon, river of Eden, 57
plant of life, 61
plow, idea of origin, *75*
Potiphar, *191*, 202; wife of, 203, 219, 222
priests: in Babylon, 66; in Egypt, 195, 233, Sem, 178, *183*, conflict with Atenism, 196; in Ugarit, **112**
primogeniture, 118
prisoners: in Egypt, *100*, *102*, *192*. *See also* Joseph, in prison
promise, of God: Gen., to Abraham, 93, 107, 119, **123**, to Jacob, 215, Joseph recalls, 205, 232
Prophets: ideals of, 10, 86, 87, **112**, 189; literary sources of, **113**
Proto-Sinaitic writing, 171, 189, *195*, ref., **199**
Proverbs, Book of, 172
Psalms, 216
Ptah, *181*

sun: in Egypt, as god, 105, 171, 197, 215, 222, as life force, 176; Hittite disk *136*; in Mesopotamia, 24; Gen., 24, 202, 222. *See also* individual god names

surrogate motherhood; in Nuzi texts, 119, *139*; in Ugaritic myth, 136, *139*; Gen., 10, 86, 119, 136, 139

Suruç, **147**, *151*

Susa, 35

Sutekh (Seth), *193*, 234

Syria: archaeology in, 13 (*see also* Ebla; Mari; Ugarit); customs in, 128, **199**; ethnic elements in, 96, 139; in Aten hymn, 197, in Sinuhe, 169; **146**, **147**, **148**, *152*, **163**

Syrian, *214*, 230-1

Taanach, 105

Table of Nations, *77*

ta-denit (canal), *100*

Tamar, 119, 137

Tanis, **207**, 234

Tawi, 184-5

taxation, Egypt, 179

Tel Masos, **144**

et-Tell (Ai), *116*

Tell el-Ajjul, 215

Tell Asmar, 75

Tell Atchana. *See* Alalakh

Tell Balatah. *See* Shechem

Tell el-Dab'a (Avaris), 170n, 181

Tell Hariri. *See* Mari

Tell Muqayyar. *See* Ur

Tell el-Retaba, 231

Tell er-Rumeileh (Beth-shemesh), 114

Tell es-Seba. *See* Beersheba

Tell es-Sultan (Jericho), 114

Temple Mount, Jerusalem, **148**, *157*, *158-9*

Telloh (Girsu), 37, 65, 135

Temptation Seal, *61*

Ten Commandments, 51, ref. 189, 205

Terah, *129*

Thebes (Waset nome 4): god of, *180*; prisoners in, 192; tomb paintings from, *99*, (*see also* Deir el-Medina; Sheikh abd el-Qurna); vizier in, 178

Thel (Sile, Zilu), *100*, 192, **207**

theogony, theomachy, 50

theophany. *See* Abraham; Jacob

Thoth, 186, *187*, *220*, 221

Thutmose III, 170, 178, *192*, 193

Thutmose IV, 51

Tiamat, *56*

Tiberius, 110; Lake, 204

Tigris River, 22, 63; Gen., *57*

Tigris Valley, 71

Timna, 171; Gen., family of Esau, *129*

Tiy, *196*

Tower of Babel. *See* Babel, Tower of

trade. *See* caravans; roads

tradition: of cities, 98; of Covenant, 234; of Judaic origins, 29; written, 89. *See also* oral tradition

Transjordan, 191; Gen., territory of Reuben, 234, *235*. *See also* Jordan

tree of knowledge, 52, 57, 60, 63

tree of life, 52, *60*, 61, 62

Tubal-Cain, 68, 189

Turkey, 208; **146**, **147**, **148**, *149-51*, **163**

turquoise: pendant with, *200*; from Sinai, 171, 189, 197, **198-9**, goddess of, *195*, **199**

Tushratta, of Mitanni, 215

twelve tribes of Israel, 84-5, 120-1, *129*, 204, 234-5

Ubaid period, 34

Udm, in *Epic of Kret*, 109

Ugarit (Ras Shamra), **112-3**; alphabet in, 26, 84, 85, 171; children in, 138; gods of, 86, **113**, 114 (*see also* by individual god names; Ugaritic literature); internationalism of, 84, through trade, 90-1; king in, 86, 87, 92 *106*, *107*, *108*, 109, and wife, 170. *See also* Ras Shamra

Ugaritic, 25, 84, 85, **112**

Ugaritic literature: epics, *Aqhat*, 67, 86, 109, 136, 138, *Kret*, 85, 109, 136; myths, *Anat and the Heifer*, 136, *139*, *Baal and Mot*, **113**, *Palace of Baal*, 93, 133, 134, *Baal and Yamm*, refs. *107*, 134, *Shachar and Shalim*, 114, 116

Umma, 36

Underworld, of Osiris, 216, 222

United Monarchy. *See* Israel

Unas, 183, 221

Upper Sea. *See* Mediterranean Sea

Ur (Tell Muqayyar), *28-9*; art of, 68, 79, (*see also* Ur-Nammu, stele); moon god of, *42*, *79*, **80**, 82; ziggurat of, *29*, **80-1**; Gen., 119, **147**

Ur, Third Dynasty (Ur III), 34, 42; destroyed, 25, 38, 79, 96

uraeus, *196*, 197, 222, *223*

Ur-Nammu: laws of, 42; stele of, *42*, *57*, *82*

Ur-Ningirsu, of Lagash, 65

Urshanabi, in *Epic of Gilgamesh*, 61

Uruk (Bibl. Erech, mod. Warka), 30, *32*, 33

Usmu (Isimud), *34*, 44

Utnapishtim, in *Epic of Gilgamesh*, 48, 53, 61, 73, 74, 75

Utu (Shamash), 23, 42, 43, *44*

Utu-hegal, of Uruk, 33

Valley of the Kings, 232

Venus, 24

Via Maris (Way of the Sea), *100*, ref. *101*, 102, *103*, *188*

viziers: of Egypt, *178*. *See also* Imhotep; Ramose; Joseph

Wadi Araba, 139, 189, 190, 207

Wadi Maghara, 189

Wadi Tumilat, 181, 231

war, warfare, 23, 36, 68. *See also* military campaigns

Warka. *See* Uruk

was (scepter), *180*, *181*, *193*

Waset (nome 4, Thebes), 180

water, 10; in Canaan, 110, 132; in Mesopotamia, 22, *57*, *58-9*; Gen., 57, 119, *132*, **145**

Way of the Land of the Philistines, *100*, *188*

Ways-of-Horus, 100

Well of the Fiancee, **148**, *163*

Well of Souls, Mosque of Omar, **148**, *158-9*

Wenamon, 84, 87, 105

White Temple, Uruk, *32*

White Wall (nome 1, Memphis), 181

wisdom: in Egypt, 186 (*see also* Egyptian literature); in Mesopotamia, 60; Gen., of Joseph, 204, 219

Wilson, C. W., 166

Wilson, John A., **229**

Woolley, C. L., *80-1*

writing: in Canaan, 89, **112**; in Egypt, 186, 195, 233; in Mesopotamia, 22, 23, 84; spread of, 38, 39; in Ugarit, 84. *See also* alphabet; cuneiform; hieratic; hieroglyphs; Proto-Sinaitic

Yahweh, 86,93

Yamm, 107, 134

Yarah-Shalem (Jerusalem), 114

Ya'qob-har, **207**

Yarikh (Yarih), 114

Yassib, in *Epic of Kret,* 136

Zagros range, *38*

Zakar-Baal, of Byblos, 105

Zebulun, *129*, 234-5

ziggurat. *See* Sumer, architecture; Babel, Tower of

Zillah, 52

Zilpah, *129*; tribes of, 234, *235*

Zilu (Sile, Thel), *100*, 192, **207**

Zimri-Lim, of Mari, 46-7, 57, *58-9*

Zin, Wilderness of, **144**

Ziusudra, 52, 72

Zoar, **156**

GOOD MEDICINE

GOOD MEDICINE

The Illustrated Letters of

CHARLES M. RUSSELL

With an Introduction by Will Rogers
and a Biographical Note by
Nancy C. Russell

NEW EDITION

DOUBLEDAY & COMPANY, INC.
GARDEN CITY, NEW YORK

New edition, from new plates, 1966

ISBN: 0-385-05662-1
9 8 7 6 5

DEDICATION

"The West is dead!
You may lose a sweetheart,
But you won't forget her."—C.M.R.

THIS BOOK is lovingly dedicated to the West and to Charlie's friends. What a multitude, what a legion they were! Some of them were real saints in his eyes. And some of them were real sinners, too. And he knew it. And never cast a stone. But he would say, "My Brother, when you come to my lodge, the robe will be spread and the pipe lit for you."

NANCY C. RUSSELL.

CONTENTS

The people to whom the letters in this book were written,
with descriptive lines by Mrs. Russell

7

INTRODUCTION

I AM awful glad that Mrs. Russell is allowing the Publishers to put out a Book like this. It's sorter like putting a name on a Tombstone: if you didn't, nobody but the family would ever know who was buried there. If it wasn't for a Book like this, Charlie Russell would just go down in history as an Artist, "The Great Cowboy Painter." We that knew him would all pass by his grave and know that there was more buried there than just a Painter. But the outside world wouldn't know it. They would be liable to figure him just "Another Artist." But he wasn't just "Another Artist." He wasn't "just another" anything. In nothing that he ever did was he "just another." I always felt that all that Painting gag was just a sort of a sideline with Charlie. I don't know that there is any grounds or foundation, but most of us come to think of an "Artist" of any line as a sort of half-breed Nut. We figure that if you took their "Art" away from 'em they would be pretty naked. In other words, every time we meet one of 'em in any line of Art he might be dealing in, we want to either hear him play his fiddle, or sing us a Song, or hand him his brush and tell him to start painting. But with old Charlie, if he had quit talking to you and started painting, you would-a got sore. It wasn't what you wanted. What you wanted was to hear him talk, or read what he said. He could paint you a Picture, and send you a letter with it, and you would value the letter more than you would the picture. Why,

Charlie didn't have a single earmark on him that we associate with the "Artist." Why he could *think* twice as straight as he could draw a line with a brush. He was a Philosopher. He was a great Humorist. He had a great underlying spiritual feeling, not the ordinary customs and habits that are supposed to mark, "What the well-dressed Christian is wearing this season," but a great sympathy and understanding for the man of the world, be he "Injun" or White. I don't know what religious outfit he sorter leaned to, if any of the present organized and chartered ones. But he sure had him one, and that was a belief in somebody or something, and that somebody or something was the one that he was going to leave to judge his fellow man,—he didn't believe that he was called on to do it himself. He was Cowboy enough to know that the final roundup ain't on this range, and you are not "parted" and classified by any other Humans. One Steer don't cut out another one and decide what market he will be shipped to. That's done by a man, or somebody of an entirely different race from cattle. And that's the way Charlie figured us. No other human ain't going to tell us where we are headed for. He would have been a Great Teacher,—I wanted to say Preacher, but I wouldn't a called him that because they feel called on to advise and regulate, and Charlie didn't. He believed in "Letting alone" and figuring it out for yourself, and when you got it figured out, it wasn't necessary to announce "how you had figured it out." He kinder figured that "Reforming" comes from a conscience, and not from advice. His belief was peace and contentment, let everybody go their own way, live their own lives, so long, of course, as it didn't trespass the rights of others. He wanted to see an "Injun" let alone. He believed that he was as happy, and as great a contribution to mankind, on a Pony as he is in a Ford. He believed that an "Injun" living off the wild game of the Plains, and the fishes of the streams, and taking nothing from his fellow man, demanding no changes, might, if his example was followed, lead to a life of peace and contentment as beneficial as if you followed in the footsteps of a Wall Street broker. He had lived and associated with the Indians, and he knew that if you talked with a wise old Indian you would receive more real philosophy and knowledge than you could attending 32 Chamber of Commerce, Rotary, and Kiwanis Luncheons. He didn't believe that everything New was necessarily "Progress." He didn't think because we are going in Debt, that we are going ahead. He didn't think a "paved" street made a better Town. He knew that it only made a more comfortable town for an Automobilist to ride in. I doubt if he thought a round or two of Cocktails served to your Guests in your own home was any great improvement over going into the Silver Dollar and having a couple and not breaking any law.

He loved Nature,——everything he painted God had made. He didn't monkey away much time with the things that Man had made. He would rather paint a naked Indian than a fully clothed white man.

In people, he loved Human Nature. In stories, he loved Human interest. He ought to have been a Doctor. He wouldn't have had to use an Xray. He studied you from the inside out. Your outside never interested him. You never saw one of his paintings that you couldn't tell just what the Indian, the Horse and the Buffalo were thinking about.

If he had devoted the same time to writing that he had to his brush, he would have left a tremendous impression in that line. It's cropping out in every letter, in every line, his original observations, original ways of expressing them. He was a great story-teller. Bret Hart, Mark Twain or any of our old traditions couldn't paint a word picture with

13

the originality that Charlie could. He could take a short little yarn and make a production out of it. What a public entertainer he would have made. So few writers can tell their stuff. You are going to get a lot of it in these letters. Read between the lines. Don't just glance over the bare words. It's like his Pictures. He never painted a Picture that you couldn't look closely and find some little concealed humor in it. And that's the way with these,—every line has something more than appears on the bare paper.

It's hard for any man to tell what we did lose when we lost this fellow. No man, in my little experience, ever combined as many really unusual traits, and all based on One—Just Human. No conceit—You won't find a line or a spoken word ever uttered by him that would lead you to believe he had ever done anything that was the least bit out of the ordinary. You won't find a line of malice, hatred or envy (I haven't, as I write this, seen all the letters and contents of this book, but I just know it ain't there, for it wasn't in him). He had it in for Nobody.

I think every one of us that had the pleasure of knowing him is just a little better by having done so, and I hope everybody that reads some of his thoughts here will get a little aid in life's journey by seeing how it's possible to go through life living and let live. He not only left us great living Pictures of what our West was, but he left us an example of how to live in friendship with all mankind. A Real Downright, Honest to God, Human Being.

WILL ROGERS.

BIOGRAPHICAL NOTE

CHARLIE RUSSELL was what they call a good mixer. The gay times he was having in the big town interfered with his work, so in October, 1895, he decided to visit a friend in Cascade and fill some orders for pictures.

There was great excitement at the Roberts' home, where I lived, as a distinguished guest was expected. Charlie Russell, the cowboy artist, was coming for a visit. He knew a great deal about Indians, cowboys, and the Wild West. The Robertses had known him since he landed in Helena in 1880.

Just about supper-time, there was a jingle of spur-rowels on the back steps; then, Mr. Roberts brought his cowboy friend into the kitchen, where Mrs. Roberts and I were getting the supper on the table.

Charlie and I were introduced. The picture that is engraved on my memory of him is of a man a little above average height and weight, wearing a soft shirt, a Stetson hat on the back of his blonde head, tight trousers, held up by a "half-breed sash" that clung just above the hip bones, high-heeled riding boots on very small, arched feet. His face was Indian-like, square jaw and chin, large mouth, tightly closed firm lips, the under protruding slightly beyond the short upper, straight nose, high cheek bones, gray-blue deep-set eyes that seemed to see everything, but with an expression of honesty and understanding. He could not see wrong in anybody. He never believed any one did a bad act intentionally; it was always an accident. His hands were good-sized, perfectly shaped, with long, slender fingers. He loved jewelry and always wore three or four rings. They would not have been Charlie's hands any other way. Everyone noticed his hands, but it was not the rings that attracted, but the artistic, sensitive hands that had great strength and charm. When he talked, he used them a lot to emphasize what he was saying, much as an Indian would do.

Charlie was born in St. Louis, Missouri, on March 19th, 1864. As a small boy, he loved to hear about the pioneer life that had broken through and was supplanting the frontier with man-made civilization. He was interested in the stories of the fur and

Indian traders and the outfitting of boats that crawled up the Missouri River to Fort Benton, Montana. The levees of his home town had an irresistible fascination for the lad and he planned to run away and turn Indian fighter. School had no charm for him. He played hookey and the hours he should have been in school, he spent at the river front watching and talking with all sorts of men, unconsciously starting to build the foundation for his life work.

After several unsuccessful attempts to get West, he was sent to a military school at Burlington, New Jersey. He was made to walk guard for hours because book study was not in his mind. He would draw Indians, horses, or animals for any boy who would do his arithmetic in exchange. He loved American history, especially that of the country west of the Mississippi River. The teachers gave him up because he could not be made to study books--but pioneer life--yes, it was absorbed wherever he touched it, and made such an impression that it never left him.

When the military school failed to hold him or teach him application, he returned home. His father decided to try another way, so one day he said, "Would you like to go West, Charles? A gentleman I know is going to Montana and I was thinking of letting you go with him. You will stay but a few weeks, I imagine, until you will be glad to get back home and then go to work in school."

So, early in March, just before Charlie's sixteenth birthday, he started with Pike Miller by way of the Utah Northern Railroad and stage coach to Helena, Montana.

When they arrived there, the streets were lined with freight outfits. He saw bull teams, with their dusty whackers, swinging sixteen-foot lashes with rifle-like reports over seven or eight yoke teams; their string of talk profane and hide-blistering as their whips, but understood by every bull, mule-skinner, or jerk-line man. The jerk-line man would be astride the saddled nigh-wheeler, jerking the line that led to the little span of leaders. These teams were sometimes horses and sometimes mules, and twelve to fourteen span to a team, often pulling three wagons chained together, all handled by one line.

It was also ration-time for the Indians in that section, so the red men were standing or riding in that quiet way of theirs, all wearing skin leggings and robes. They did not have civilized clothes. The picturesqueness of it all filled the heart and soul of this youthful traveler and he knew that he had found his country, the place he would make his home; but he did not know what a great part he was to take in recording its history for the coming generations.

In Helena, Mr. Miller outfitted, buying a wagon and four horses, two of them being Charlie's. With their load of grub, they pulled for the Judith Basin country, where Miller had a sheep ranch. The wagon trails were very dim and rough and they had a hard time crossing the Crazy Mountains, as one of their horses played out. But they did arrive—a very weary outfit. Charlie said that that trip settled it with him so far as driving a team and wagon was concerned. Thereafter, pack and saddle horses were his favorite way of traveling and he never changed. He often said to me, "You can have a car, but I'll stick to the hoss; we understan' each other better."

He did not stay with Miller but a few weeks, as the sheep and Charlie did not get along at all well. When they split up, Charlie didn't think Miller missed him much, as he was considered pretty "ornery."

He took his two horses and went to a stage station where he had heard they needed a stock-herder, but word of his dislike for the sheep job had gotten there ahead of him and they were not willing to trust their horses with him, so he did not get the job.

Leading his pack horse and carrying a very light bed, Charlie pulled out for the Judith River, where he made camp and picketed his horses. He had a lot of thinking to do. As he unrolled and started to make his bed, a man's voice from out of the shadows said, "Hello, Kid! What are you doing here?"

Half scared, he turned to find a stranger sizing him up.

"Camping," he answered.

"Where's your grub?" the stranger inquired.

"Haven't any."

"Where you going?"

"To find a job."

"Where you from?"

On being told, he said, "You better come over and camp with me; I got a lot of elk meat, beans and coffee. That ought to feel pretty good to the inside of a kid like you."

So Charlie threw in with him. The man was Jake Hoover, hunter and trapper, and a lifelong friend to the boy he met there on the trail. Hoover's manner of life suited young Russell, who longed for the open country and its native people.

Jake advised him to get rid of his horses, as they were big team horses and one a mare. Jake said this country was no place for a lady-horse; if she took a notion, she would leave and take every other horse with her.

In a few days, he met a bunch of Piegan Indians and traded for two smaller horses, one a pinto, that he named "Monte." They were kids together and, when Monte died in 1904, Charlie had ridden and packed him thousands of miles. They were always together and people who knew one, knew the other. They didn't exactly talk, but they sure savied each other.

Charlie lived with Jake about two years. They had six horses; a saddle horse apiece and pack animals. They hunted and trapped, selling bear, deer and elk meat to the settlers, and sending the furs and pelts which they got in to Fort Benton to trade.

In the Spring of 1881, Charlie's father sent him money to come home. To acknowledge it, Charlie wrote a letter in which he said, "Thanks for the money, which I am returning. I can't use it, but some day I will make enough; then I will come home to see you folks."

By the Spring of 1882, he had saved enough to return to St. Louis, where he stayed about four weeks. He could not resist the call to Montana, so he came back with a cousin, Jim Fulkerson, who died of mountain fever at Billings two weeks after they arrived.

Again alone, with four bits in his pocket and 200 miles between him and Hoover, things looked mighty rocky. He struck a fellow he knew and borrowed a horse and saddle from him until he could get to his own; then, started for the Judith Basin country.

There was still a little snow, as it was early in April, but after riding about fifteen miles, he struck a cow outfit, coming in to receive a thousand dogies for the Twelve Z and V outfit up in the Basin. The boss, John Cabler, hired him to night-wrangle horses. They were about a month on the trail and turned loose at Ross Fork, where they were met by the Judith roundup.

Charlie was getting back to Hoover and the country he knew, but he'd had a taste of the cow business and wanted more. The Judith roundup foreman had just fired his night-herder and Cabler gave him a good recommend, so he took the herd. Charlie said it was a lucky thing no one knew him, or he never would have gotten the job.

When old man True asked who he was, Ed Older said, "I think it's 'Kid' Russell."

"Who's Kid Russell?"

"Why," said Ed, "it's the Kid that drew S. S. Hobson's ranch so real."

"Well," says True, "if that's 'Buckskin Kid,' I'm bettin' we'll be afoot in the morning."

So you see the kind of a reputation he had. He was spoken of as "that ornery Kid Russell," but not among cow men. He held their bunch and at that time they had about four hundred saddle horses. That same Fall, old man True hired him to night-herd beef and for the most part of eleven years, as he says, he sang to their horses and cattle.

In the Winter of 1886, there was a bunch wintering at the O H Ranch. They had pretty nice weather till Christmas. When the snow came, there was two feet on the level. The stage line had to have men stick willows in the snow so they would know where the road was. Those willows, on parts of the road, were standing in May.

There was good grass in the Fall. The country was all open—no fences. The horses went through the Winter, fat, since they could paw, breaking the snow's crust and getting through to grass. A cow won't; they are not rustlers. They would go in the brush, hump up and die; so the wolves fattened on the cattle.

Charlie was living at the ranch. There were several men there and among them was Jesse Phillips, the owner of the O H. One night, Jesse had a letter from Louie Kaufman, one of the biggest cattlemen in the country, who lived in Helena. Louie wanted to know how the cattle were doing. Jesse said, "I must write a letter and tell Louie how tough it is." Charlie was sitting at the table with Jesse and said, "I'll make a sketch to go with it." So he made a little watercolor about the size of a postcard and said to Jesse, "Put that in your letter."

Jesse looked at it and said, "Hell, Louie don't need a letter; that will be enough."

The cow in the picture was a Bar R cow, one of Kaufman's brand. On the picture Charlie wrote, "Waiting for a Chinook and nothing else."

That little watercolor drawing made Charlie famous among stockmen and was the wedge which opened up the field of history in this part of the West for him. He still did not know he was about to graduate from this School of Nature, to take up his life work.

In 1888, he went to the then Northwest Territory and stayed about six months with the Blood Indians. They are one branch of the Blackfeet tribes. He became a great friend of a young Indian, named "Sleeping Thunder." Through their friendship, the older men of the tribe grew to know Charlie and wanted him to marry one of their women and become one of them. The Red Men of our Northwest love and think of Charlie as a kind of medicine man because he could draw them and their life so well.

He learned to speak Piegan a little but could use the sign language well enough to get along anywhere with any tribe of the plains that he ever met, as the sign talk is universal among the American Plains Indians. Whether with white man or red, with a lump of wax or a few tubes of paint, he drew, painted and modelled, all his spare time, just for the satisfaction of recording what he saw and to entertain his friends. Still, he did not dream of the great work ahead of him.

In the Spring of 1889, he went back to Judith to his old job of wrangling. The captain was Horace Brewster, the same man who had hired him in 1882, on Ross Fork. All these years there had been the mixing with, studying the habits of, and drawing all the different types of men and animal life.

Living with a trapper, he got close to the hearts of the wild animals. He saw them in their own country; got to know their habits. Knew them with their young and saw their struggle against their enemies, especially Man.

But the West was changing. Stage coaches and steamboats carried the white people west, while the freighters with bull, mule and horse teams, played their great part in bringing what we call civilization to this Northwest country.

Charlie was here to see the change. He did not like the new; so started to record the old in ink, paint and clay. He liked the old ways best. He was a child of the West before wire or rail spanned it; now, civilization choked him. Even in 1889, when the Judith country was becoming well settled and the sheep had the range, he resented the change and followed the cattle north to the Milk River, trying to stay in an open range country.

In the Fall of 1891, he received a letter from Charlie Green, a gambler, better known as "Pretty Charlie," who was in Great Falls, saying that if he would come to that camp, he could make $75.00 a month and grub. It looked good, so Charlie saddled his gray, packed Monte, the pinto, and took the trail. When he arrived, Green introduced him to Mr. K., who pulled out a contract as long as a stake rope, for him to sign.

Everything he modelled or painted for one year was to be Mr. K.'s. Charlie balked. Then K. wanted him to paint from early morning until six at night, but Charlie argued there was some difference in painting and sawing wood. So they split up and Charlie went to work for himself. He joined a bunch of cowpunchers, a round-up cook and a prizefighter out of work. They rented a shack on the south side. The feed was very short at times but they wintered.

Next Spring, he went back to Milk River and once more lived the range life. But it had changed. That Autumn, he returned to Great Falls, took up the paint brush and never rode the range again.

20

We met in October, 1895, and were married in September, 1896. With $75.00, we furnished a one room shack there in Cascade, where we lived one year. There was little chance to get orders for pictures in such a small town, so we moved to Great Falls, where Charlie could meet a few travelers and get an occasional order.

Charles Schatzlein, of Butte, Montana, was one good friend. He had an art store, and gave Charlie a good many orders, making it possible for us to pay our house rent and feed, but, as Charlie said, "The grass wasn't so good."

One time, Mr. Schatzlein came to visit us.

"Do you know, Russell," he said, "you don't ask enough for your pictures. That last bunch you sent me, I sold one for enough to pay for six. I am paying you your price, but it's not enough. I think your wife should take hold of that end of the game and help you out."

From that time, the prices of Charlie's work began to advance until it was possible to live a little more comfortably.

In 1900, Charlie got a small legacy from his mother, which was the nest egg that started the home we live in. After the cottage home was finished and furnished, Charlie said, "I want a log studio some day, just a cabin like I used to live in."

That year, 1903, the studio was built on the lot adjoining the house. Charlie did not like the mess of building so he took no more than a mild interest in the preparations. Then, one day, a neighbor said, "What are you doing at your place, Russell, building a corral?"

That settled it. Charlie just thought the neighbors didn't want the cabin mixed in with the civilized dwellings and felt sure they would get up a petition to prevent our building anything so unsightly as a log house in their midst. But way down in his heart, he wanted that studio. It was the right kind of a work-shop for him, but he was worried at what he thought the neighbors would say, so said he would have nothing to do with it.

He made no further comment, nor did he go near it until one evening, Mr. Trigg, one of our dearest friends, came over and said, "Say, son, let's go see the new studio. That big stone fireplace looks good to me from the outside. Show me what it's like from the inside."

Charlie looked at me kind of queer. The supper dishes had to be washed. That was my job just then, so Charlie took Mr. Trigg out to see his new studio that he had not been in. When they came back into the house, the dishes were all put away.

21

Charlie was saying, "That's going to be a good shack for me. The bunch can come visit, talk and smoke, while I paint."

From that day to the end of his life he loved that telephone pole building more than any other place on earth and never finished a painting anywhere else. The walls were hung with all kinds of things given him by Indian friends, and his horse jewelry, as he called it, that had been accumulated on the range, was as precious to him as a girl's jewel box to her.

One of Charlie's great joys was to give suppers cooked over the fire, using a Dutch oven and frying pan, doing all the cooking himself. The invited guests were not to come near until the food was ready. There was usually bachelor bread, boiled beans, fried bacon, or if it was Fall, maybe deer meat, and coffee; the dessert must be dried apples. A flour sack was tucked in his sash for an apron and, as he worked, the great beads of perspiration would gather and roll down his face and neck.

When it was ready, with a big smile, he would step to the door with the gladdest call the oldtime roundup cook could give—"Come and get it!"

There was a joyous light in his eyes when anyone said the bread was good, or asked for a second helping of anything. When no more could be eaten, he would say, "Sure you got enough; lots of grub here."

Then the coffee pot would be pushed to one side, frying pan and Dutch oven pulled away from the fire, and Charlie would get the "makins." Sitting on his heels among us, he would roll a cigarette with those long, slender fingers, light it, and in the smoke, drift back in his talk to times when there were very few, if any, white women in Montana. It was Nature's country. If that cabin could only tell what those log walls have heard!

The world knows about his paintings and modelling, but his illustrated letters are novel because of his spelling and lack of book learning. The perfection of his humor is not of books, but comes direct from the life in the West that he lived and loved.

The State University of Montana is not prodigal in giving honors, but Charlie justified himself as the greatest student and teacher of the West in his time and so won the fourth honorary degree of Doctor of Laws ever given by that University. Charlie said, "Nature has been my teacher; I'll leave it to you whether she was a good one or not."

It will be next to impossible in a few years for anyone to recall what he said, so this book is gotten together that the many may know Charlie and his philosophy through his letters, as do the few who have received them. To those who have been kind enough to loan their letters for this purpose, I express my sincere thanks and appreciation. I am sure they will be glad to have participated in this effort to leave as a permanent record this memorial of the love of a great man for a big country and its people.

NANCY C. RUSSELL.

Publisher's Note: In the general make-up of this book the publishers have constantly kept before them the desirability of reproducing the letters of Charles M. Russell, both pictures and text, as nearly as possible in the identical manner in which they were written. Mr. Russell's own spelling, punctuation, and spacing have been followed in cases where the letters have been reproduced in type. To have prettified his text for typographical reasons would have destroyed much of the charm of the book and much of its historical authenticity. As nearly as possible the reproduction gives us the man and the artist who was so well loved by people who know and understand the old West.

In order to give a wide selection of letters and as many of the illustrations as possible, it has been necessary to delete lines or paragraphs from the letters here and there. This has been a matter of keen regret to the publishers. All deletions are indicated by ellipses.

The letters are not published in chronological order for reasons connected with the technical reproduction. As a whole the effort has been to give a pleasing relationship between color and text. Where the date of the letter appears on the picture it is not repeated in the printed text, but wherever a date appeared on the original letter it is reproduced in one place or the other. Some of the letters were not dated at all and consequently bear no dates in the book.

The only places where Mr. Russell's original spelling has not been carried out are a few instances of obvious slips of the pen where the intention of the writer would be obscured by a too faithful reproduction of the letter. Typographical consistency has been sacrificed wherever by so doing a clearer picture of Charlie Russell could shine through these pages to the reader.

WHERE TRACKS SPELL WAR OR MEAT

Nature taught her child
  To read, to write and spell,
And with her books before him
  He reads his lesson well.

Each day is but a page
  His God, the sun, has turned.
Each year, a chapter nature taught
  Her child has read and learned.

A broken twig, a stone is turned
  Disturbed by passing feet
His savage eye has caught it all
  For tracks spell war or meat.

Nature holds his Bible
  With pages open wide,
He questions not her miracles
  'Tis done; he's satisfied.

He loves his mother country
  Where all her creatures trod,
Yet he is called a heathen
  Who has always lived with God.

Courtesy of Dr. Philip G. Cole. This poem was written by Mr. Russell to go with the picture of the same title, which is here reproduced as endpapers.

Friend Joe

I have received sevral letters from you so I will answer the last one   Mame told about the talk she had with you over the fone but long range talks are like letters not like the real thing

Im sorry to here that old man Cross is sick and hope by this time hes all right.

I got a letter from Krieg a long time ago, but have not answered it yet   Im mighty slow coming across with letters but it aint becaus I dont think of my Friends you know that Joe

We went to Arizona since I saw you on a trip with the Eaton party   I saw a fiew folks like the above sketch   It is a great country wild and makes good picture stuff. the Indians are not as good as there northern brothers eather in looks ore dress but a bunch of Navajoes mounted in there country of red sand makes a good picture and for a man who likes mountians and Indians I know no better country

I was up to see Frank Linderman last fall   he has built a big cabon on Flat Head lake and is living there with his family   Its about fifteen miles above Summers it is a bautiful place   when I was there the cabon was not finished so frank and I camped in a loge and we shure had a good time.

Now joe if the three Scheuerleys do come west dont forget our camp   the lach strings out   Percy Rabon was just here and sends his regards   I wish you could see our boy jack   hes 17 months old   he runs all over the place now and it keeps both of us buisy hearding him   he has a language of his own that we don't savy.

This is a long letter for me so I guess Il close with best whishes from Nancy and I to the three of you

Your Friend
C M Russell

Miss Josephine and Mrs Trigg send regards

Dear Mr. Hart

I received some newspaper pictures which reminded me of the photographes and letter you sente me some months ago. I liked them very much. I guess you think I'm a long time saying so but you wont have to go far in this letter to find out that writing is no pass time with me its

WORK   I am average on talk but hand me these tools an I'm deaf an dum

you said in your letter you hoped I enjoyed Your play I certainly did

I have your photo hanging in my little parler an old cow puncher friend. droped in the other day an was laking at the pictures an when he run on to your photo he asked whos the Sky pilot

well if you ever drift west again which I hope you will an sight the smoke

of my camp

Come and as our red brothers say my pipe will be lit for you

June 29
1902

Yours Sincerly
CM Russell

C. M. RUSSELL
GREAT FALLS, MONTANA

Friend Theo

March 19 1920

Friend Theo

Im down here in what is called by some the worlds pick nick ground and I think thats a good name caus theyv shure picked a nick in my bank role

Early history says this country was the home range of the hold up till the law makers came and hung up a bounty for the head ore scalp of all gents of the road when they opened the law on road agents and put on a bounty everybody quit mining and went hunting and for many years Califonia was smoky and in actions resembled Bill Harts pictures   the Digger Injun lived in caves and fed on roots and acorns this vegitaron grazing made him non war like and pease loving so they dident take sides in aney of the killings   Spaniard Mexicon ore Yankee all looked alike and was much easier to get along with after they quit breathing so they just sat at the mouth of thair caves and wached thair gold loving brothers exturmanate one an other The hold ups were in the megority so at the cleanup there wasent enough reformers left to start aneything so the Diggers lived in safety for quite a while   all this happened long ago   the Bandits who wached the roads like the Digger have gon   But history repeats   the Digger has not returned but the hold up is here   his work is not as corse as it was   In days gon by he had a good horse under him and went heeled to the teeth   if he lived long it was because his guns were faster and shurer than those

28

of the law   his home was aney where he unsaddled his horse   this kind only lives in history but right now maby its his ofspring   thair lives in Califonia a hold up man that makes his Great Grand Dad look like a watermelon theif   This gent rides a Pierce Arrow ore some other wagon that causts more than 500 head of the mistang breed his Great Grand Dad rode   This new hold up dont have to sit up nights and wach the roads and trails   he owns a hotel a restraunt or a bunch of bungiloos   in these he traps and skins the tourist. To steal is to take when thairs no one looking of corse the Califonian dont do that he stands in front of you when he takes your role and thairs no law agin it. but law has changed   in early days they hung ore shot his Great Grand Dad for the same kind of worke

Theo if you ore aney of your friends ever come down to this Pick nick, bring one of them roles with a rubber band on it the kind that would choke a cow   Stay a month and Im betting you wont need a rubber   right now what I got left wouldent choak a chick a dee

with best whishes to you and yours

Your friend
C M Russell

866 Chester av north
Pasidana
Califonia

Friend Guy

I received your postal and letter an was glad to here from you

You were so bussy when I left I did not get to thank you for the good time we had at the Stampede

I came west 31 years ago   at that time baring the Indians an a fiew scaterd whites the country belonged to God   but now the real estate man an nester have got moste of it grass side down an most of the cows that are left feed on shuger beet pulp but thank God I was here first an in my time Iv seen som roping an riding but never before have I seen so much of it bunched as I did at Calgary   Ive seen som good wild west showes but I wouldent call what you pulled off a show. it was the real thing an a whole lot of it

those horses judging from the way they unloded them twisters wasent broke for grandmas pheaton, they were shure snakey an your cattel dident act like dary stock

30

to me   I dont think aney I saw had been handled by milk maids   they were shure a supprise to those old cow poneys that had been running short horns all there life. It wasent hardly fair to spring a gray hound waring hornes an Guy football ain't so gentel——the bull ring an prise fighting is som rough but bull doging those long horns makes all other dangerous sports look like nursery games

I am not alone in my praise of the Stampede   there are other men better judges than myself make the same talk.

With best whishes from
            my wife and I
                to you and yours

                                            your friend
                                            C M Russell

Nove 26
1925

Ralf Budd
Dear Mr. Budd

this is Thanksgiving day an Im thanking you for the good time you gave us last summer

turkey is the emblem of this day and it should be in the east but the west owes nothing to that bird but it owes much to the humped backed beef in the sketch above

the Rocky mountians would have been hard to reach with out him

he fed the explorer   the great fur trade wagon tranes felt safe when they reached his range

he fed the men that layed the first ties across this great west   Thair is no day set aside where he is an emblem

the nickle weares his picture dam small money for so much meat   he was one of natures bigest gift and this country owes him thanks

the picture you sent a photo of that I painted was made a long time ago   It was made to reprsent Fater DeSmit on the Missouri River

hoping you and yours are all well   I am

your friend
C. M. Russell

Mrs. R——sends best regards

Friend Bill

I am sending you the long promised sketch   it represents an old time cow dog mounted on a bronk

In this day of fancy roaping the trick hes turning aint so much. but I remember when a hand that could do this from the top of a stiff necked bronk was not classed with punkin rollers

My wife got a letter from your best half asking us to come and camp with you all   we both thank you verry much but we wont worke your range this year   wev got a six months old boy at our camp and we think hes a little young for trail work so we are going to class herd him a while   The Stork dident bring him   he had been on earth about three moons when he was thrown in my cut but hes waring my Iron now and I hope nobody ever vents it

now Bill if you ore your folks ever drift this way dont forgit my camp   theres grub and blankets for you and yors aney time   with best whishes to you all from us both

your friend
C M Russell

KIT. CARSON that rod for the Ω
is married and quit
riding
and goin to
gambling
he has win
a good hous
here in Grate Falls 
and has money in the bank he
is ~~on~~ the onley one of our old
Frenends that has raised from a
saddel blanket gambler to well to do
man behind the silver box but he

all ways was lucky you know
⚹ For what hands he held on a
blankset years ago

34

Charly Bowlegs

killed at
Dupuyer
while playing
Cards

Charley was killed by a beed
it was an old grudge
some years before Bowlegs
shot at the breed it was
in the dark and he onley
powder burnt him of corse they
never were verry fruendly so one
day when bowlegs was playing
poker he baught the drinks
the breed asked if he dident
drink to Bowlegs told him
he wasent bring booze fro Inguns
and the ball opend Bowlegs had
on a over coat and youldent
get his gun quick so he cashdin

35

C. M. RUSSELL
GREAT FALLS, MONTANA

Friend Sweet

I am returning the tin tipe an I guess you think its about time. I had a good copy made of it which I will al ways keep   it shure brings back the old days an that trip to White Sulpher over the south fork trail

If I rember right I was gide but failed an lost the blaze   you run out of Climax an was forsed to chew Durham but we made up for lost time when we reached the Burg

with best whishes to your self and Wife an all old timers

Your friend

C M Russell

The Manhatten has sent for the pigan it
is good
the Antilope s hart would be glad to smoke with many
tribes   at the big camps
but for thier moons the trails have hidden beneath
the snow
an it is not good to travel far when the poney
wares his hair long

My arms is short an cannot reach the pipe
you light for me
but our harts are together and the same
it is good

Antilope

Feb 8th
1923

Richard Jones
Friend Dick

     You will see by the sketch I am among the palms and flowers but Im still packing coal   sun shine in this country is like near beer   it looks good thats all   in most countrys flowers and palm trees mean warmth but that dont go here   Aney thing that grows here would thrive aney where in Glacier Park

     tell Bull Trout thairs lots of fishing here from shark to smelt   the ocion aint fifty yards from my door   Frank Linderman and me are going clam fishing in a fiew days   Frank lives next door   we get these with a shovel and working around a furnis so many years Im shure handy with that tool   When they fish with a shovel its a sinch Il bring back the goods   Dick I would like to step in to the Como right now   give my regards to the bunch including the young lady

     best whishes to you and yours

                    Your friend

If you have time tell me the news.   C M Russell

Address 509 East Cabrillo Boulevard Santa barbara

Friend _____ received the _____ Both send many Thanks we are as ever your friends

We dide'nt do a thing to him

Edward Borein

Frend Ed

    I got your card telling of your tye up.

    Im glad your necked.

    its the onley way to hold a bunch quitter, animals are easier found in pairs than alone.

    A he bear has no home till he ties to a lady.

    The wolf is a drifter untill the she one of his kind shows him the cave under the rim rock,

    The mules in the pack trane would leave the trail and scatter, but thairs a differnt shaped track in the trail ahead.

    its the hoof marks of the lady hoss that leads her long eared lovers to camp.

    Im hoping the tie rope will never choke ore brake.

Your friend

C M Russell.

Friend Ted

I got the picture and letter both the 9th and you and your old hoss will deck the walls of my shack always   and when ever I look at the picture my memory will drift back over trails long since plowed under by the nester to days when a pair of horse ranglers sat in the shaddoes of thair horses and wached the grasing bunches of cyuses   these cyuses had all heard the fiddle mouth harp and the maney songs sung by thair riders   even the war drum of the red men was no novelty to them   but the day I speak of it was different   every hoss with head up and ears straightened listened for one of the ranglers was a musician . . .

I remember one day we were looking at buffalo carcus and you said Russ I wish I was a Sioux Injun a hundred years ago   and I said me to Ted thairs a pair of us

I have often made that wish since an if the buffalo would come back tomorrow I wouldent be slow shedding to a brich clout and youd trade that three duce ranch for a buffalo hoss and a pair ear rings   like many I know, your all Injun under the hide and its a sinch you wouldent get home sick in a skin lodge

Old Ma Nature was kind to her red children and the old time cow puncher was her adopted son . . .

Your friend
C M Russell

Miss Josephine Dear Friend

This is a portrait
of Bills Grate Grater
Grate Gran Dad
by Renbrandt
you will now
under stand why
Bill has turned
that hair loos
he hopes some
day to look like
Grand pa
below you well
see the famely
Coat. of. armes
It is hard for a white
man to interpret think
but I would it means
to gether we are strong
though the sausage is
no stronger than its weakest
link it still hangs together
an you know how strong Dutch
chees is
the strin I think de notes joy

Your friend
C M Russell
Sept 22
1912

Smell
Smell
Smell
Smell
Cheese
Smell ant
Sour cant
Sausage rampant

41

There was a Twister at Haver[1] that hung up a bet of fifty Dollars that hed ride a certain hoss and fan him with his hat. He might of faned him but he lost his hat an then got off to look for it.

Oct 31 1917

Friend Con

I got your letter and was glad to here from you   Im sorry you have been sick I hadent heard aney thing about it till I heard from you

in your letter you said you guessed the old timers were getting scarce up here you were right   there's a lot of them chashed in latly with in the last six months Trigg, John Mathison and Dinny Dolan all good old friends

judging by the number thats snuffed out in the last fiew years that trail is well broke and plane across the big devide   it aint had much chance to grass over

I was down at Haver last 4th of July and saw quite a nomber of our old friends Bob Stewart, K Lowrie, Bill. Mackdonna, Morman Zack Larson, Babe and Oliver Tingly, Cal Shuler, Charlie Mud, Humpy Jack Davis, Bob Malone and a fiew others Kid Price wasent thair   they say he aint verry well   from what I here he leans to much on the bar   he still eatis that old joy juice   the same old kinde that Bill Noris ust to make   three swollers and the Missouria looked lik Dog Creek   it was good

[1]Haver refers to Havre, Montana, never by any chance called other than Haver in Montana.

stuff to swim cattle with but when used more than a week steady its liable to bring mooving pictures the kind that nobodys stuck to see

They pulled a riding and roping contest at Haver and some of it was good   old K Lowery said they was good riders all right but if theyd give him an ax and let him chop them nobs off thair saddle forks he dident think theyd stay so long

mos of our old cow puncher friends have got big famlies of groun up kids an when I look at them it makes me feel like Grand Pa

maby you dont know it Con but we got a boy at our house now   he was a little two months slick ere when we put our iron on him   hes a yearling past now and wer shure stuck on him   his name is Jack and he reminds me of Leslie when he was a baby

well Con I colose for this time   with best whishes to the three of you from us both

Your friend
C M Russell

If no find in 10 sleeps come back to Great Falls

Chas. Schatzlein
Butte
Mont

43

Here's to all old timers, Bob,
They weren't all square it's true,
Some cashed in with their boots on—
Good old friends I knew.

Here's to the first ones here, Bob,
Men who broke the trail
For the tenderfoot and booster
Who come to the country by rail.

Here's to the man with the gold pan
Whose heart wasn't hard to find,
It was big as the country he lived in,
And good as the metal he mined.

Here's to the rustler that packed a notched gun
And didn't call killin's sins,
If you'd count the cows and calves in his herd
You'd swear all his bulls had twins.

Here's to the skinner with a jerk line
Who could make a black snake talk,
An could string his team up a mountain road
That would bother a human to walk.

Here's to the crooked gambler
Who dealt from a box that was brace,
Would pull from the bottom in stud hoss
An' double cross friends in a race.

Here's to the driver that sat on the coach
With six reins and the silk in his grip,
Who'd bet he could throw all the ribbons away
An' herd his bronk team with his whip.

Here's to the holdup an' hoss thief
That loved stage roads an' hosses too well,
Who asked the stranglers to hurry
Or he'd be late to breakfast in Hell.

44

Here's to the 'whaker that swung a long lash
An' his bulls bawled with fear when he spoke,
He'd swear on a hill he wouldn't drop trail
If every bull starved in the yoke.

So here's to my old time friends, Bob,
I drink to them one and all,
I've known the roughest of them, Bob,
But none that I knew were small.
Here's to Hell with the booster,
The land is no longer free,
The worst old timer I ever knew
Looks dam good to me.

Sentiments of your Friend

Friend Bill:[1]

I received your letter; allso headdress and Mame got the spoon and we both send thanks.

We all had a good Christmas; got lots of gifts and we would have enjoyed having you here. You were so long coming a cross with your answer that I begin to think you had crossed the big creek an throwed in with your Duch relations agin them frog and beef eaters. That namesake of yours is sure a ware like proposition.

Young Boy and Little Bear were here the other day and wanted to know all about the ware. Little Bear seemed quite pleeased to hear that boath sides were whites and when I said that there had been over a million killed, a broad smile covered his kindly face. No doubt, he would have liked to have been thair at the hair gathering; especuly, the English killed. Thair's nothing he likes about an Englishman but his hair. In old days, his Gran Dad used it to trim leggins with it and what was good enough for that old man looks good to his grand son and I don't doubt but that Little Bear has some of these souvaniers hid away that he gathered douring the Real War in Canada. . . .

Well, Bill, I'l close for this time, hoping you and Julia a Happy New Year. Mame is in on this hoping.

Your friend

C. M. Russell

[1]Letter not dated. Written during the Great War.

Ed Neitsling   November 14
                                                        1923
    Friend Ed   I got the meat all right and its fine and I thank you verry much
I lost out on a hunting party   its the first fall Iv missed a hunt for many years but I
hope we will go again some time   I am better but am still using four legs   the frunt
ones are wooden
        give my regards to all Friends
        with thanks and best whishes to you

                                            your friend
                                            C M Russell

46

C. M. RUSSELL

GREAT FALLS, MONTANA

April 4 1922

Georg Calvert

    Friend Georg   we were all glad to here from you   Frank Linderman and I went fishing the other day   the Ocean was pulling what the sea folks call a ground swell   it was the swellist thing Iv been to in California   Bill Hall and his quartett usto sing rocked in the cradel of the deep calm and peacefull is my sleep   I was rocked all right but I wasent calm inside ore out and I dident sleep   Bills song was all right an it sounded good floating over the mohoginy about a thousand miles from salt water if I remember right I usto get in on the base but I couldent do it now and hold my dinner   that old bunch were all right but its a sinch non of them ever fished for mackril ore road a ground swell   Frank lives next door but he and his fambly leave for home in a fiew days we expect to leave about the first of may   I will tell you all about Calif when we get home

    with best whishes to you all from the three of us

Your friend

C M Russell

Feb 13
1918

Friend Ed

I got a letter from you about three years ago so I thought Id hurry up and answer it. I was down on your range a year ago last October with the Eaton party and judging from what I saw Im twenty years late   the scool teachers beet me to it. those wisdom bringers surtenly wipe all the picture out of nature but I saw a fiew like the above sketch but most of them had disgarded the dress of the savige for the beautifull garments of these white brother but Ed Im glad I wint and I whish I knew those people and there past   If I savyed the south west like you Id shure paint Navys.[1]

One camp we made I wont forget it was at a little lake in the dessert at sundown a bunch of these American Arabs droped down from the high country with about five hundred horses   most of these riders looked lik the real thing in there high forked saddles and concho belts silver ore turquis necklaces and year rings they were all hatless some wore split pants their shirts were Navyho make but its a safe bet if we could drop back in there history they would be shy the shirt   they rode short sturrips an each packed a skin rope. They were not like the Indian I know but

48

every thing on them spelt wild people and horsemen and in a mixture of dust and red sun light it made a picture that will not let me foget Arizona

I also saw a Yabachae dance of the Navys[1] that was wild and scary   I guess I been telling you things you already know but I like to unlode on men whos likes are the same as mine   I dont know when I will see you so I want you to write and tell me about the big camp   How is Marsh   do you ever see that Terrapin Bill Crawford   is Rogers still heeling fillyes at the follies   does he still loap up to your camp quirting himself down the hind leg with a paper   if he keeps that up hel get to be a ring tail. I wonder if Fred Stone when hes Lion hunting pulls that funny stuff of his   if he dos tell him I dont think its squar to shoot the big cat while hes Laughing

with best regards to yourself and the bunch from my best half and myself
Your friend
C M Russell

[1]Navajoes.

C. M. RUSSELL

GREAT FALLS, MONTANA

March 22, 1923

To My Friend Ed Borein

If hosses were health I'd comb the range
and trim every band I knew
You'd go to the end of a long long trail
with a top hoss under you

C M Russell

50

May 20 1925

Dick Bodkin
Friend Dick

judging from the way you stick in the oringe belt your warped on that country. Since you started riding for cameras your harder to locate than Kid Kurry. Jack gave me your address.

Dick I used to make fun of moove cow Boys but since I saw them worke my hats off

once an old Injun told me that it wasent the head that made men brave it was the hart if his talk was right these moove punchers has inlargment of the hart and shrinking of the head   I seen them ride down hills that I wouldent do with a ladder   Im an old man now but I still like to ride a frendly horse but I dont want no moove director to pick trails for me. I know a fiew moove men down on the screen range   Tom Mix Bill Rogers Bill Hart Neal Hart Buck Conner Harry Carey   I knew Tom Mix when he owned a saddle and a pair of spurs and if youd asked him where Holly wood was he wouldent have known if it was a line camp ore a state but Mix is a regular man and Im glad he got the coin   all the men I know down thair are good men and worth beeing friendly with   aney of them you meet give my regards to. things are about the same around here   I see your brother Jack every day   Saw your Mother and she wants you to come home and make her a visit   She looked well   you ought to come home onc and a while and see your folks   the country looks better than it hase for a long time good grass.   woldent you like to get a horse under you and ride over som real grass country and get down on your belly and drink from a cold mountion stream

with best whishes to you and yours   Your friend

Hows the little girl   C M Russell

51

May 4 1914

Friend Bill we received your letter and was shure glad to here from you London is quite a sisabol camp and hase many things of Intrist

I took in a future show the other day that skimed auey thing I've seen one of the Futis led me around an explaned making it as clear as London it self

this Futs was bilt like a wine bottle verry lady like as wore a thin beard. I think to head off regular men that might make naughty eys at him

he sprung a string of talk that sounded like them you an Maty ust to pull off

he led me up to somthing in a frame that looked like an enlarged slice of spoilt summer sausig And said this is not disintegration of Simultaneousness but Dynamie dynamism. An it did look like that. Another he showed as near as I could make from his talk represented the feeling of a bad stomach after a duck lunch

an it mighty near turned mine but I didnt smell aney limburgar

Wev been to Paris stayed onely three days Saw Seven hundred miles of pictures about the same distance in restronts sevaral Churches and Nepoilans Toom. Old Nepo has been a sleep a long time but judging from the size of the stone over him an the gards a round the French are takeing no chances on him wakeing up. no doubt his peaple loved him but think hes better of where he is an its a sinch every body else is

well Bill I'l tell you all about it when I see you an that wont be long

with best regards to you an Julie from us both your friend

C M Russell

52

Feb 24 1916

Friend Trigg

we are still in camp back of the stock yards its about thirty two years since I first saw this burg. But I remember that morning well. I was armed with a punch pole a stock car under me loded with grass eaters   I came from the big out doores and the light smoke and smell made me lonsum.

The hole world has changed since then but I have not   Im no more at home in a big city than I was then an Im still lonsum

If I had a winter home in Hell and a summer home in Chicago I think Id spend my summers at my winter home   There might be more people there but there couldnt be more smoke   But there is lots of good people here   maby it aint there fault

I suppose Great Falls will be lik Cicago some day but I won't be there

well Trigg I here the snow is all gon an I know youl miss it but youl have to bear it   You might arrange to join som poler expodation

With best whishes to yourself Mrs Trigg Miss Josephine the chickons gold fish and bird

This gose for both of us

Your friend
C M Russell

53

Will James   May 30 1924
Friend James

    I got your letter and sketch and was glad to here from you   you asked how I would handel such an animal   If I ever saw it I wouldent get close unough to handle Iv known cow punchers that saw such things after hanging around a rode ranch ore burg but non of them tuck a rope down but they used a quirt mighty nasty and as I am better with a quirt than a rope Id use the one I know best

    I have been getting your stuff in Scribners   its good both pictures and writing.
. . . I have been in bade shape for nearly a year but am better now   tryed to get on a horse the other day at Harry Carys ranch but couldent mak it   cant ride nothing wilder than a wheel chair . . .

    I appreciate your invite to come to your home and am glad you have a nice place and I will come some time   this goes both ways   I have a camp in the Glacier park where the pipe is and the robe spred for you aneytime you come . . .   you wont care much for the horses   thair all quiat old mountian horses that will pack aneything from a screaming lady to a dead bear over trails that makes mountian goat nurvis   I have been mooving around so much that I have missed our home paper and never saw the artical about you   we expect to leave here in a fiew days for Great Falls   hoping you all kinds of good luck   Your friend
Rout 3 Box 223 Pasedina Califonia   C M Russell

June 17
1923

Mike Shanon
Friend Mike

Im a long time answering your letter but if letters were money and I was called to pay up I'd be bankrupt   Since when did you turn poet   that was good stuff   if you keep that up youl be braking into booklets and the dudes will be shy a guide but judging from the fiew poets I know dude ranglers eat oftner   I think thairl be lots of people in the park this summer and as thair are still people who like to ride I hope you and your horses have all you can handle   a machine will show folks the man made things but if people want to see Gods own country thave got to get a horse under them   In spite of gasoline the bigest part of the Rocky Mountains belongs to God and as long as it dose thairl be a home for you and your kind   to me the roar of a mountian stream mingled with the bells of a pack trane is grander musick than all the string or brass bands in the world

Well Mike we hope to be in the park in a fiew days and if I see you we will talk   its easier than writing

with best whishes to you and yours from me and mine.

Your friend
C M Russell

55

55. W 42 ST
NEW YORK
JAN 29 1905

Friend Trigg as I am lonsum to night an far from my range I thaught it might help some to write you just think I am in a Camp of

Friend Trigg

    as I am lonsum to night an far from my range I thaught it might help some to write you   just think I am in a camp of four millions an I guess I know about eight it makes me fell small   It makes it strong d——— small   the whits are shure plentyfull

    Nancy and I took in a Chinees theator the other night   I guess it was good the Chinks seemed to think so, but for me it was a little better than grand opra the way those Mongoliens were painted up would make our Indian grind his teeth

56

with envy thair shure a scary looking bunch baring this and a fiew other shows
I havent seen much since I been here

but I did have a good time at the Fair the most interesting to me were the
people of the Philipines especially the Iggeroties these folks are verry primitive
forging there own weapons an weaving there own cloth but you will notice from
this sketch that the latter industry dos not take up much of thair time as there
wasent enough cloth in the hole camp to upholster a cruch they are verry small
but well bult pople an judging from the way they handle the spere or assiga if
they ever lern to handle the new gun Uncle Sam is liable to have trouble corraling
em their sirtenely a snakey looking artical an they say they aint sadisfide with no
puney suvinere like a scalp but take the hole top peace from the Adams apple up

Well Trigg, hows everything in the Falls I havent heard from there since
I left onely through Nancy an that don't tell me much of the bunch I mix with
but we expect to start home in three weeks so Il soon know.

With regards to everybody in Montana

Your friend
C M Russell
If you get time write

Sept 1st
1913

Friend MacKay

I suppose by this time you'r setteled down among the cliff dwelers

the seat you got in that money shack of you'rs is easier than the roost on the corall fence but I bet the looking aint as good

Our seats wasent strong for comfort but they were easier to hold than some of the boys had that left the shute   you savy those moving leather seats that so maney of the boys lost

I suppose by this time you'v bull doged every milk cow on that Ten a Fly ranch of yours   It will be hard to handle the de horned milkers but I dont think ear holts are bared

with best regards to your self and family from us all

Your friend
C M Russell

May 8
1925

Friend Harry

Im a long time thanking you for the Head dress you sent. but I never was fast an old Dad Time aint changed my gate   the Head dress is a good one   it is certainly a wild mans crest.

I think our red brother stole his fashion from animals and birds he knew   he saw the sage cock dance and spred his tail fethers   that's where Mr Injun got his dance bussel   he liked the war bonnet that the Canadian jay and the King Fisher wore so he made himself one but the only real American dont use much stile aney more   Unkle Sam lets him play Injun once a year and he dances under the flag that made a farmer out of him   once nature gave him everything he wanted. now the agent gives him bib overalls hookes his hands around plow handles and tell him its a good thing push it along   maby it is but thair having a hell of a time prooving it.

To people who since time began never don aney thing harder than pull a bow string ore push a skining knife nature was not always kind to these people but she never lied to them.

The red skined men are all moste gone now Harry but if fiew clothes and fancy ones means saviges we got lots of she ones now and moste of them set traps for men.

Thanking you again for the head dress—good medicine to you and yours—

Your friend

Ah wah cons[1]

[1]Indian word for antelope, and Mr. Russell's Indian name.

Feb 4th
1902

Senitor Paris Gibson
Dear Friend

no dought you will bee suprised to here from me but if you are like myself when in St Louis you will be glad to here from aney one in Montana   As I am a verry poor writer I will make a kind of Injun letter mostly pictures

I went to see the big man the other day who was on exhibition at Luthurs hall he stood seven feet ten inches and a half   he was shure big and farley bilt but his countenance appeared to bee warped caused I supose by beeing up in the wether   his

right eye looked up bear gulch while his left survade lower alkali creek   the man that owned him said he was verry inteligant but all we got is his word for it . . .

I saw Jim Dunivan the other day   Jim looks good but the gamblers dont think so   speaking of gamblers reminds me several years ago when games were wide open   I sat at a faryo layout in Chinook   the hour was lat an the play light   a good deal of talk passed over the green bord   the subject of conversation was the Indian question   the dealor Kicking George was an old time sport who spoke of cards as an industry   he I believe was born in Missouria but came to Colorado with his folks when he was a yearling an had never left the shaddoes of the rockyes   the Kicker alloud an Injun had no more right in this country than a Cyote   I told him what he said might be right but there were folks coming to the country on the new rail road that thaught the same way about gamblers an

60

he wouldent winter maney times till hed find out the wild Indian would go but would onley brake the trail for the gambler

My prophecy came true   we still have the gambler but like the cyote civilization has made him an outlaw . . .

Speaking of Indians. I understand there is a man back in your camp Jones by name who has sent out orders to cut all the Indians hair   if Jones is stuck to have this barber work done he'd better tackle it himself as no one out here is longing for the job   the Indians say whoever starts to cut thair hair will get an Injun hair cut and you know that calls for a sertean amount of hide   they clame it makes it handier to trim legons with

Bridgman who is agent at Belnap isent worring much as he owns about as much hair as a Mexicon dog an thair fixed for hair about like a sausage   the Great Falls Daly Leader has a standing bet up of twenty to one he won't loose aney.

Well Senitor as I am all up on news I will close the deal

Hers How

With best wishes your friend

61

Aug 11 1912

Friend Joe   we have just received you pictures and they are shure dandys an I want to thank you for them and all so the tom tom

I was sorry that your trip wound up with such hard luck   Iv heard of men that couldent ride a coverd wagon but I suppose yours dident have a lid on. a spring seet can go higher an hit the ground harder than most bronks   I was unloded wonce my self by one an have not forgotten   I dident brak aneything but all hinges an bolts were loosened   braking your coller bone sounds reasinable enough but are you shure that Jonson dident slip in an get your scalp before you woke   you know how strong he was after suviners   aneyway I'd like to look through his getherings just to sadisfy myself. I bet hes got Dutch hair among em.

Well Joe I will close with best whishes to you and yours

Your friend

C M Russell

April 7th
1912

Stuart Florida
Friend Trigg

    we are now in the land of flowers where things grow with out the help of man an when I look at its maney water wayes it is easy to understand why this was a favorit hangout for all sea holdups of the old days on these shores maney a ship changed her captions an he who lost command left his bones on the sands of Floridas shore

    well Trigg I will tell you all about it soon

    with best whishes to you all

Your friend

C M Russell

old time Senter fire man

Joe De Young

I received your letter also model of puncher an photo of rider you modeled I think they were good your horse was a little short in the back but if you will study proportion you will come out all right most range horses measure the same. from the top of the head to middle of the withers would measure the same as from there back to the coupling study your saddle horse he will teach you more than I could tell you in a thousand years

The picture of your Father and I with the bunch in the Silver Dollar was no good   it was so blured you could hardly tell one man from annother

You will find enclosed a photo of my self and friend   I have riddin this old boy nearly 15 years so you see hes a has been

the saddle was made in 1888 by Meany of Cheyenne   it is the old time Vacala tree   the spurs I ware Iv had for 32 years   the rawhide ranes 30 and I have been in Montan nearly 34 years   so you see the picture shows a bunch of old has beens

Yores

C M Russell

Give my regards to your Father

64

April 20 1914

Freind (Percy

here I am in old London un its Sum antique

I was up north of thir big camp the other day where stand, an old Monistary allso a wall built by the romans built I suppose to protect them from Dinny Doolins fore fathers who crosed the chanel once an a while in there bull boats healed with clubs of black thorne an stone axes to pruve to the gladitors that life wasent no lengethy pickenic

I was told that this country was also the home range of William the Conqueror a gentleman whos history would make Sitting Bull look like Brother Van

I found a pack of woods that was realy lonsum an I couldent help but wonder what would happen if the wheel of time would slip her cogs an slide back to the tenth Sentury like Mark Twains yankie

A fine chance I'd a stood in this timber afoot if Bill Conk an his bunch of killers lead of rode on to me dressed in their steel chain union suits theird ben nothing for me but take my hat off an make a squaring talk or sing God save the King

Well Percy I will have to Close as we are going out in the country with best wishes from us both to you and yors

Your friend
C M Russell

Address Dore Gallery
35 New Bond St
London

Pan handle Jack

killed at
Gild Edge
by a saloon man Pan handle
gave his gun to the buze boss
then got drunk an wanted it
back the buze boss refused
an panhandle got a winchester
and come back but it was
another case of slow

66

P. P. Johnson

killed in his ~~outlaw~~
Saloone by night watchman
at Lewistown Jonson made
his talk that he was
going to shoot up thei
watch man but when the
time come P.P was soaked and
was slow delivern the led

Aug 30
1908

Friend Percy

I was verry sorry to here of your sickness but by this time you have been trimed an if you are like I was you feeal a hole lote easyer in mind if your intearer dond feel just right

trouble shore com to you in bunches

it was tough enough when you tuck the antlers. but stepping off the goat onto the meet block is piling it up on you plenty an Im sending all that cheep stuff sinpothy I got on me   this is shure the age of impruvement an it looks like most men has to be made over   of corse I am glad to loose my apendex but I hope thers no more improvements to be made on my anatomy but I suppose we should bee thankfull that we dident live in the age when our Fore Fathers tailes became diseased an usless so were forsed to have them removed with a stone ax an I suppose if the patient was timid he was put to sleep with a club

there is not much news to tell up here an as we expect to be home in a fiew days I will close with best whishes hoping soon to see you

Your friend
C M Russell

69

Friend Kid I received your letter an was glad to here from you I have often wandered where you were since I saw you in the land of these posple

I was afraid

The Puralyes had taken you in, but I am glad you beet them to the line and are safe   this side

the old Rio Grand. wet clather in the United Stats are often mor comfurtibal than dry ones in Mexico

I saw Jim two years ago in the big camp   he was punching cows at the Hipidrome an altho he was fighting Sioux every day he wasent scared up much

the last I saw of him he was thinking of crossing the creek that layes betwin New York and Londen but as I have never heard from him I dont know whether hes still in this country ore not

now kid I hope you hit this country an if you drift on to my range dont pass my camp   the latch string is out side for you and yours

With best whishes from us both to your self and wife

Your friend
C M Russell

C. M. RUSSELL,
GREAT FALLS, MONTANA.

Chas. Schatzlein
Butte
Mont

71

C. M. RUSSELL

GREAT FALLS, MONTANA

June 30
1914

Friend Joe
        I heare you and
your better half are in
Harlam   my wife and I leave
here to morrow for Miles City   but will be
back the 6 of July   and I want you both
to come to our camp   on your way
to the park   I hope you are having a good
time . if you happen to come here before
I get back   go to the house   my nephew is there
and will take care of you   Your friend C M Russell

72

May 12
1920

Hello Will James

I got your letter and sketch and from it and other worke I have seen of yours in the Sunset I know you have felt a horse under you. Nobody can tell you how to draw a horse ore cow

I never got to be a bronk rider but in my youthfull days wanted to be and while that want lasted I had a fine chance to study hoss enatimy from under and over   the under was the view a taripan gits   The over while I hoverd ont the end of a Macarty rope was like the eagle sees grand but dam scary for folks without wings . . .

James, you say you havent used color much   dont be afraid of paint   I think its easier than eather pen ore pensol

I was down in Cal this winter and saw som fine back ground for cow pictures roling country green with patches of poppies and live oak   mountian ranges with white peaks that streach away to no where   I have never seen this kind of country used in cow pictures   Why dont you try it . . .

James as I said before use paint but dont get smeary   let sombody elce do that   keep on making real men horses and cows   of corse the real artistick may never know you but nature loving regular men will and thair is more of the last kind in this old world an thair the kind you want to shake hands with . . .

With best whishes to yourself and any who know me

Yours
C M Russell

C. M. RUSSELL

GREAT FALLS, MONTANA

April 30
1922

Friend Georg

Im a long time answering your letter but you know I never was rapid with ink I hear its been cold up home   well it aint had nothing on the oringe belt   Its don everything but snow down here   Iv been cold so long now Im numb   Its kind a like the first stages of freesing to death   its painless   Georg if you ever figer on wintering down here take my advise bring a stove and some sand coole ore belt creek with you   ladyes ore still waring furs but nothing elce much but paint   from now on nobody can tell me that he humans or more hardy than shes   if a baby doll tuck a notion she wanted an Esquemaw she'd slip on som gaus and lace and with a powder puff and lip stick she'd start for the Pole and freeze aney dog runner in his cariboo capote to death that ever traveled the Great Slave providen she don't run short of power ore rouge.

The wethers fine right now. Little Jack is shure haven a good time   he gets lots of out doors   the countrys open here and all we do is range heard him

We start home May 14 and when I get home Il tell you all about Cal   With best whishes to you all including your Grand son from the three of us

Your friend
C M Russell

R 3 Box 223 Pasidana Cal

July 9th 1910

Hellow Dutch

 how are you we expect to go to the lake about the 15th an we want you and your wife to com up

 be shure and bring your paint box I expect Goodwin soon an if you come we will shure do some painting are you doing aney modling these days

 I here Cut Banks married how dos he work in double harness

 I hope you dident loose on the fight theres shure a sore bunch over here . . .

 I had a good time East and made a littel money will tell you all about it when we meet with best whishes to you both from us both

your friend
C M Russell

75

June 17
1918

Friend Berners

I got your long letter and was glad to here from you an Im coming back fast for me with my short paper talk caus I know you must be lonsum in that medison camp   Its a wonder them plumbers dident want to put a new pump in you. but from what you tell me that medison man looked through you with out lifting the lid an tells you that laying down is the best thing for you   its no easy game but seeing Sippys such a good guesser youd better play his hunch an if its laying down you need Lake McDonald is the best bed ground in the world and my lodge is open and the pipe lit for you and yors   you know that Lake country sings the cradle song to all who lay in her lap

Old Rip Van snoozed twenty years but if Hank Hudson would open a blind pig in our big hills with one shot of his suthing surip aney human with insomnia could beet Rips record . . .

with best whishes from my best half and me to you and yors

Your friend

C M Russell

76

November 2?
1921

Guy Weadick
T
S Ranch
Longview
Alberta

Friend Guy

I got your letter and am glad to here you are doing so well with your ranch
it pleases me plenty to know that thair is so maney men and wimen that will quit a
gas wagon and a good road and ore wilen to look at the world with a horse under
em. and where you live Guy if theyl step in the middel of a hoss you can show folks
the top of America the wildest the bigest and for a Nature Lover the best part of it

In tame countrys on a good road an autos all right but if your hunting for aney
thing wilder than a Doctor take a horse

I suppose by this time your on the rode   Im sending you a book which I hope
you enjoy   My wife and I leave for Denver tommorrow morning so this is a buisy
camp   we will returne in about two weeks

Thanks for the Invite to viset the $\frac{T}{S}$ Ranch   we might do that some time   with
best whishes to you and yours from us all

Your friend
C M Russell

Magpie. Wheres that man going
Crow. Dam fi know ask the horse

Chas. M. Russell
Great Falls, Montana

Sept 24
1914

Friend Bill Krieghoff

I dont have to tell you that the above sketch is not a chees eater carring despatches for Bill Hohenzollern the second

This rider's name is also Bill an clames german breeding   he eats every thing a dutchman will which mighty nere proves it an by the gate he went I think hes Bill the first   Duck Leg if you could onley git across to them fighting folks of yours with that horse and lead a charge there woldent trees enough in France to hold the Frog eaters

well Bill were still here at the Lake but are leaving day after tommorrow for home   we have had fine wether till the last two weeks   Its been raining mighty

78

steady an now the country sogy as a wet blanket an its cold an Bill you know what that meens to the wood getters   Auston an I both miss you verry much   Mame an I went over to Kalispell on our way to Flat head Lake where we visited Linderman and his folks who were camped there   on our way back we bumped in to your old pard little Artie Larivy   every body inquired after Willie

Bob Benn and his wife spent a couple of days with us at the lake   Mrs Benn spoke of the Arte talk you sawed of to her   she said it was verry interesting but she dident savy only about half of it   I guess you sprung some of that Mazzy on her Bill

I heard it so often I can almost handel it my self but don't know what it meanes yet.

Joe Scheuerle and his wife were here with us a fiew days and we had a good time

We all so saw Mr and Mrs Crudson at the foot of the lake wating for the boat they were on there way through the park

well Bill I will close with best whishes to you and Jule also all friends from us all

Your friend

C M Russell.

IF NOT FOUND IN 10 DAYS RETURN TO C M R GREAT FALLS

Chas. Schatzlein PAINT Co BUTTE MONT

Sep 4
1908

Friend Holland

I have received sevral letters from you an I guess its time Im answering

news are short up here an I havent seen Apgar for a day or two so I havent got much to right about

tell Littel Sunshine the blood hounds have eat the last Ladrone blood raw an are now taking there seastia an the Don after a firce struggle was swollod by an allagator.   our hero spyed the reptile but to late an noting its sweled an after dinner look rased his trusty rifal an pirced its brane   after another firce strugle it sank to the depth of the lagoon with its lothsum repast never to rase again   after one long sad look our hero turned an sadly retraced his steps an marryed the widow under the spreding palms while the sweet voised pelicons sang the wedding march

80

things are verry quiet up here   since the folks left there is onley seven of us now conting the two chickons an as bakon is getting scarce I belive they will not be with us long

We have just returned from a trip to the glacier an had good wether an a fine time   the wether since has been rany an cold up to the last fiew days   it is now fine   tell Miss sun shine that the lake is still warm in spite of the cold wether

I hope Mrs Holland is getting all the tomaters I mean tommotoes she wants

people are leaving the lake every day for there homes an we will soone be getting ready our selvs

one ore two skunks have taken up quarters under the house an seem to like the place al so a number of montian rats have mooved in an by the noise they make Iv a hunch my night watches are sleeping on gard As soon as dark comes the new comers goes to work all hands   the skunks practis two steps and barn dances on the porch or in the kitchen   the rats dont seem to like our roof   all night long thair bussy making it over occasionaly stopping to gether up tooth brushes leaving rocks sticks ore old bones in exchange   they are traders who belive a fair exchange is no robery the great horned owl in the seaders at intervals askes who   no one knows so receiving no answer he keeps it up all night an at day brak flies away in disgust but returnes the next night with the same question   its to bad someone cant tell him

Well Holland as I cant think of aney more foolishness I will close with best wishes to you all

Your friend
C M Russell

May 1 1921

Friend Ed

   Mame wrote you a fiew days ago that we would make you a visit but the way things have turned we cant make it   we thought we could hold our hous another week but as thair is another party wants to get in we have to leave so we will have to put our viset off for another year   we leave here a week from to day   I wish you could com up to Montana this summer   if you do you know where my camp is   I have seen Bill Rogers quite often   met Dug Fairbanks Neal Hart Buck Conners and several other moovie folks   maney of them know you. I also saw Jim Minnick he wanted to be rememberd to you

   With best whishes to you and yours

                    from all of us

                              Your friend
                              C M Russell

Just got a paper saying Marchand is dead

C. M. RUSSELL
GREAT FALLS, MONTANA

Mr Ralph Kendall

Dear Mr Kendall

a guess you think its about time I said thank you for the book you sent me

I injoyed the book verry much

and since I red it I know why you love pictures you are a word painter your self betwine the pen and the brush there is little diffoence but I belive the man that makes word pictures is the greater

Kendal you have traveled lifes trails with your eyes open you have laughed and al so cryed, for in the book of life they are not all funny pictures

I hope you write more your country holds maney storyes

With best wlnishes to you and Yours and thanking you again

C M Russell

C. M. RUSSELL
GREAT FALLS, MONTANA

November 9, 1924

Ed. Neitzling

Friend Ed   again I thank
you for that fine hind quarter of deer
it is shure fine   thair is no meat as good
as the wild for me
I am sorry you dident have a good time on
your hunt
this fall makes two years Iv missed
I am as you know a harmless hunter but
I shure like to git out with a good bunch
the old rumitism I dont know whether that
the way to spell it or not but it is still with
me but by next fall I hope to git out
with the same good bunch we shure had
a good time   with best regards to you and
all friends
        thanking you
            your friend
            C M Russell

84

Feb 16 1919

Friend Bollinger

I received your good long letter and was glad to here from you and that you had a good hunt and brought in meat   but your rong when you think the absence of Mrs B[1] had aney thing to do with my not showing up on that hunt. but I had a hunch you and Lewis would hold that agin me   it would be a safer bet to play me the other way   four Jacks and a Queen is a good hand in stud poker but the same number of hes and a she like Mrs B aint a lucky combination and a deer hunt might turn to man slaughter   Some morning that camp might look like one of Bill Harts moovies   The onley difference some of the performers wouldent act no more   the above sketch would go good in the moovies but it would look like hell in the Great Falls ore Davenport papers   Romance is a beautiful lady that lives in the book case who can pull aney thing from a cold deck to murder and get away with it but shes got a homely sister Reality by name that hangs around all the time

this old girl aint so lucky   let som man make a killing over her and the Judge tells him where hes going and nobody knowes his address after that

Mrs B dident take the picture   som body in New York bought it   the price was three hundred   my oils run from six hundred to two thousand

With best whishes from all the Russells to you all

Your friend

C M Russell

[1] "Mrs. B" refers to a lady in no way related to either the writer or the recipient of the letter.—*Editor*.

April
1926

Frank Brown
Friend Frank

I received your nice long letter and was glad to here from you   this is the bigest moovie camp in the world   thair are more two gun men here now than the history of the west from north to south ever knew

I was at a studio the other day   they were making a dance hall seen   this dance Hall made aney I ever saw an Iv seen some that wasent real gentile but this one made Chicago Joes look like a Kindergarden and if I rember right Joe dident run a young ladys finishing school   if the old west had of been as tough as the mooves make it theyd be runing buffalo yet on the Great Falls flat yet   Jew Jake and Pike Sandusky were easy to get along with compared with these hair trigger moovie gun fighters I wouldent bet how good theyd be up aganst the reel thing but with blanks they look mighty nasty

Frank I see in the paper your going to take a hand in the straw hat perade   I hope you and the bunch have good luck but dont go to far with a straw hat   you might want to trade for a buffalo overcoat

Frank this country brags on its climet but the Cal booster dont tell that it also has chills   the old fashon kind that shakes and when it shakes it dont leave much but climet and no climet is much good that houses wont stand in   an Ingun lodge might be good but thairs no lodge pole pine in this country

with best whishes to your self and Great falls

Your friend
C M Russell

86

May 14 1914

Friend Holland

We received your letters and were shure glad to get them

We are one night out from England right now

An altho Im glad I went I did not shed maney tears leaving the home of my Ansesters

I find the Russells were pritty plenty in this land theres Great Russell St Russell Squar Hotel

Sir Russell entring the Kings Coart

Russell an all kinds of Russells in England   Iv been a littel doubtfull about my folks. I always had an Idar that the Russell tree was a scrub. but the other day I was told that Sir Sombody Russell was led to the block an had the upper end of his back bone removed by the Kings ax man who was a bussyer man them days than Fred Piper ever was on saterday night. this loping off of Sir Russells Head makes it sinch he was a Nobel man. as in those dayes scrubs mostley cashed in in bed. A verry unrefined way of quitten So Holland if I happen to pass you on the street an you feel a chill like an ice wagon had gon by dont blame me   its the blood of the Nobility Iv got in me   It might pay you to come over an round up this Historical range but as you claime I belive Scotch blood youd have to work the country further north where I dont doubt youd find Hollands onery enough to mix with the King an as near as I can make from history   If a man was a fighter an could count enough notches he was Be Knighted by the King or Be Headed. eather way his pedigree was safe an all those to whome he left his name which was generly all he had to leave were of noble blood . . .

Sir Russells
Departure

from your friend

C M Russell

March 20 1918

Dear Brother Van

I received an invation to your birthday party from Reverend Bunch an am more than sorry that I cant be their but Im on the jury

I think it was about this time of year thirty seven years ago that we first met at Babcocks ranch in Pigeye bason on the upper Judith I was living at that time with a hunter and trapper Jake Hoover who you will remember He and I had come down from the south fork with three pack horses loaded with deer and elk meet which he sold to the ranchers and we had stopped for the night with old Bab, a man as rough as the mountians he loved but who was all hart from his belt up and friends ore strangers were welcom to shove there feet under his table this all welcom way of his made the camp a hangout for many homeless mountian and prairie men and his log walls and dirt roof semed like a palice to those who lived mostly under the sky

the eavning you came there was a mixture of bull whackers hunters and prospecters who welcomed you with hand shaks and rough but friendyl greetings

I was the only stranger to you so after Bab interduced Kid Russell he took me to one side and whispered

boy says he I don't savy maney samsingers but Brother Van deels square

and when we all sat down to our elk meet beens coffee and dryed apples under the rays of a bacon grease light. these men who knew little of law and one among them I knew wore notches on his gun men who had not prayed since they nelt at their mothers knee bowed there heads while you, Brother Van, gave thanks and when you finished some one said Amen I am not sure but I think it was a man who I heard later was ore had been a rode agent . . .

With best wishes from my best half and me   Your Friend

C M Russell

88

My Brother we are both from the
big hills
But our fires have been far apart
We met in a strange land
Lonesumniss makes strong friends
of shy strangers
In this big camp where the
lodges hide the sun and its
people rube sholders but do not
speek
your pipe was mine
It is good our harts are the
same
To Ed. Borein
        From his friend
        C M Russell

1916

We meet again Douglas Fairbanks, alias D'Artagnan tho only on paper.

My hats of to you   I have seen you under many names and you have worn them all well—an actor of action always—And now since you have back tracked the grass grown trails of history and romance I know that D'Artagnan's name will fit you as well as his clothes.

But Doug don't forget our old west. The old time cow man right now is as much history as Richard, The Lion Harted or any of those gents that packed a long blade and had their cloths made by a blacksmith.

You and others have done the west and showed it well, but theres lots of it left, from Mexico north to the Great Slave lakes   The west was a big home for the adventurer—good or bad—he had to be a regular man and in skin and leather men were almost as fancy and picturesque as the steel clad fighters of the old world   The west had some fighters, long haired Wild Bill Hickok with a cap and ball Colts could have made a correll full of King Arthurs men climb a tree.

Your friend

C. M. Russell

90

The trail is long it is good if Seldom writes
makes maney moccasins
an when the grass comes let him travel
to the big hills where the sun sleeps

Three times have the dogs howled at my lodge door
while I ate smoked an slept by the fire of Seldom writes
but never has the grass been bent my way by his moccasins
has Seldom writes grown fast to his shell like the littel
water people that live about him CMR 1909

(A letter written to Will Crawford, an artist friend of his living in New York.
The man on the horse is Charlie Russell and the man painting the robe is Will
Crawford. One represents the Western Indian; the other the Eastern.)

The trail is long   it is good if Seldom Writes makes maney moccasins an when the grass comes let him travel to the big hills where the sun sleeps

Three times have the dogs howled at my lodge door while I ate smoked an slept by the fire of Seldom Writes but never has the grass been bent my way by his moccasins   Has Seldom Writes grown fast to his shell like the littel water people that live about him.

C M R   1909

91

Dec 4, 1922

Charles Furlong
                    My hats to you
Who has traveled on your humped backed mount
a country where mans trails began
You have ridden old trails and blzed new ones
and with word and picture have told the new world
I enjoyed your book Let Her Buck verry much
        With best whishes
                Your friend
                    C M Russell

92

Friend Schatzlein

   since seeing you in those breed garmants its hard to belive youre dutch   it shure dont take much trimings to put you back to the savage

   I have been taken for a white headed breed sevral times myself but youv got me skined

   I dont think theres a drop of Injun blood in you but I wouldent bet on it for the early comers to America were all traders   the first whites in Verginia swaped tobbaco for wives an folks now that clame kin to Pocahontas are mighty chesty over it

   taking history for it the dutch were som traders an it might be that your Great Great Great Grand Dad swaped for a red Wife   from your looks Id advise not looking to far back in your famely tree.

   when are you all coming over with regards

                          your friend
                          CMR

LOS ANGELES
BILTMORE

THE BILTMORE SALON
DEDICATED TO WESTERN ART

March 27
1924

Dear Miss Josephine

Thank you for the birth day card

Old Dad Time trades little that men want   he has traded me wrinkles for teeth
stiff legs for limber ones   but cards, like yours, tell me he has left me my friends and
for that great kindness I forgive him,

Good friends make the roughest trail easy

Mame and I are much better   a fiew days more and I think Il shed the stick
Jack seems to like school.

The above sketch is before Cal. was taken by the Iowans

with best wishes to you and your Mother and Miss Furnald

Your friend

C M Russell

94

Dec 12 1924

Bill Gollings

Friend Bill

Some time ago I received your letter and photos of your self with the long bow Joe tells me you skined your red brothers at thair own game. Bill you aint Injun thats a sinch   maby thair was some Gollingses with Robin Hoods band   Bob and his friends were fast with the long bow

If youd lived where you do now in 1846 Francis Parkman in his book would have told of a white man living with Ogillallahs that packed a long bow and a robe painted by him would bring twenty Poneys   a shield cover was worth five wimen painted by Robe pictures   that was what the Ogillallahs called him   he was rich received no bills and paid no taxes

Aint it hell Bill what we missed by coming late   I supose by this time your meats all jurked and hides all taned   Im back on my feet again and in pritty good shape   Joe is here with me   hes doing lots of painting

with best whishes   Your friend

C M Russell

HETS A LIVE ONE

May 3d 1907

Friend Percy

I am still on dear old brodway among the cliff dwelers every body lives high here but they aint got me skined much   I'm camped above timber line myself

I was down at Madison Square gardon the other day an met Cody   he's lost most of his hair in the London fog but his back locks are still long   the show was good real cow boys an Indians

I learn here that punchers wore red shirts an indians go to ware strung with slay bells but baring these detals the show was all right

this reminds me of central ave but laying all jokes aside Il take our streets bumps an all N Y with cabs under ground an sky sayling car lines is all right for them that like her, but I know a town with two mil of track an a fiew hacks thats swift anough for me   give me the camp where I savy the people

well Percy it wont be long till Il be with you an Il tell you all about it
with best regards to your self and friends

Your friend
C M Russell

96

6816 Odin st
Holley wood Calif
April 14 1926

Ted Abbott
Friend Ted
. . .
Im now camped among the
move cow boys This kind dont ride
Sircle or night gard   their remutha
travels in a truck and their wagon is
a cafeteria   he dont have to know
cows or brands but the move cow boy
must have plenty of guts an no head

It takes sevral kinds to make a
hero on the screen   the beautiful
cow boy that makes love till the
reformers want to burn the picture
houses aint the same man that spures
his horse of a thirty foot rim rock
into the water and swims three miles
to save his sweet hart from a band of
out laws aint the same   they usto
say that camres wouldent lye but
Holleywood has quired that talk

this feller that goes off the rim-
rock is what they call a double
Som actores donte use them. . . .

Most of the moovie men Iv met are good fellers   Maby they aint got much
under thair hats but an Old Injun told me once that real good brave men lived in
thair harts not thair heds and I belive my red brother was right

Well Ted . . . if my good whishes ar aney good to you Im sending them all
that goes for every thing Famely cows horses aney thing waring the three duce iron

Your old friend

C M Russell

PaT RiLy was killed while sleeping
of a dunk at grass range

Pat took a buze joint and
after smoking the place up and
an running every body out till
it looked like it was for rent
fell a sleep the buze boss
gets a gun ancomes back an
catches Pat slumbrin pat
never woke up but quit
snoring

98

Charly Cugar quit punching
and went into the cow business
for him self his start was

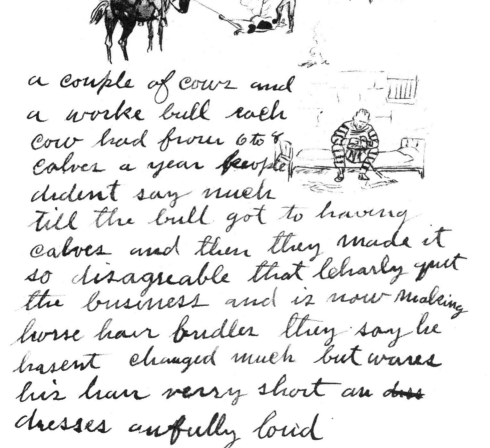

a couple of cows and
a worke bull each
cow had from 6 to 8
calves a year people
didnt say much
till the bull got to having
calves and then they made it
so disagreable that leharly quit
the business and is now making
horse hair bridles they say he
hasent changed much but wares
his hair verry short an dres
dresses aufully loud

Ronan
Flathead
Resirvation
1908

Friend Fred Com on an bring
the bunch the lids off up here
there playing on the first floor
black jack an Monty wide open
be carful an dont tip it off to non
of them Morilests
            with regardst to the bunch
            your friend
            C M Russell

100

Novembr 27
1924

Walter Coburn
Friend Walt

I just received your letter   got the magisines som time ago   liked both the storyes   your cow punchers seemed real to me   they were like those I knew in old days. thair are maney western writers these days but fiew of them knew the range   I red a story the other day   in it the punchers wore bandanas round thair necks   the bandana came and belonged to the sod buster and generly toped bib overalles   I never knew a cow hand to ware aney thing but silk if it wasent the warer thought it was   in late years Iv seen riders that looked like this sketch   this kind are generly found around a soft drink parlor   I don't know whether its CoCo Cola ore mapel nut sunday that works his legs the wrong way but I do know no cow puncher I ever knew if he was going to ride a snake would take aney thing soft as a brave maker   this cococola soke can tell whats the matter with a ford by the nois it makes but he wouldent know that a wet cold horse with a hump in his back is dangerious   Shaps spurs and boots and big hat dont make riders   neather dos bib overalls and caps make pictures ore storyes

This kind I knew they are almost extinct now   a foot he was mighty near harmless but with a horse under him he wase never lame   he is not used much these days but in days before the wires the west needed him

Your modling looked good   stay with it   its a lot easier than drawing

Tell Jim Fisher I have heard Ted Blue talk about him   I am glad he writes well   all old timers who can write should tell what they know of the old west

I will watch for your storys in Adventure   that magazine is my favorite

with best regards
Your friend
C M Russell

101

April 14 1914

Friend Henry

what do you think of it
this is the kind of rider that lives in
this country I see these every day an
I know its on the square cause I havent
drank a drop since I been here
how would you like to start on sircul
with a bunch of these
I wonder what would have happend if old
Peet Jack Anderson or Jim Mcoy would have
jumped one of these on the range
these riders use as many reins on one
horse as a stage driver dos hundeling
four. they tell me these men with these
muly saddels can stay in the middle
of a snakey one. but you know Hank

Friend Henry

What do you think of it   this is the kind of rider that lives in this country I see these every day an I know its on the square caus I havent drank a drop since I been here   How would you like to start on sircul with a bunch of these

I wonder what would have happened if old Peet-Jack Anderson or Jim Mcoy would have jumped one of these on the range   these riders use as many reins on one horse as a stage driver dos handeling fore. they tell me these men with there muly saddels can stay in the middle of a snakey one. but you know Hank Im from that state laying south of Iowa

Well Henry this is shure a old country   I was in the towar of London the other day   It is an old castle built five hundred years before Columbus found America   last Sunday I went out in the country   it looks like one big gar-den   everything is green   I saw small bands of sheep an one place a rider was driving four cows an as he was a boy and driving cows its a sinch he was a cow boy but all joshing aside they shure got good looking horses in this mans land   I havent seen a poor one since I landed

Well High Wood old boy Il close for this time   If you get time betwene feeding the furnace an hearding them hens of yours drop a line   I suppose your still gambling with Hinote for car fare   be carful the reformers dont grab you

with regards to you and yours

Your old friend
C M Russell

address
Dore Gallery
35 New Bond st
London
England

103

Friend Perc

    you are right iv reached another station The road has been long but my friends have made it a pleasant one   And it is goot to know when Im past the half way ranch that my friends still greet me at the stations beond

    Best whishes to you and yours

Your friend

C M Russell

Pasadina Cal

March 27 1920

Friend Perc you are right Iv reached another station The road has been long but my friends have made it a pleasant one And it is goot to know when Im past the half way road ranch that my friends still greet me at the stations beond
Best whishes to you and yours
Your friend C M Russell

Pasadina Cal
March 27 1920

This is the departure of my Great Great Geat Grand dad
some of the Kings men eans to see him off but were a littel late
Grand dad went for his bottls some of his friends told him the
climate in America would lengthen his life an no doubt it did

Friend Trigg

here we are in the land of your birth al so the home of my forfathers but I think mine left early and judging from history I dont blame them America with its red men was some scary but peacful compared with this, scalped men have been known to live but nobody can thrive with out a head

up to a hundred years ago, a man was safer in a skin lodge in the wilds of America than the stone castles of this mans land but this is a quiet country now peacful and law loving maby this gent cleaned out the bad wanes I saw his tools at the old tower an from looks Id say Hed been som busy

Im pritty lame on history but its a sinch bet this gent was the cause of maney a early hom seeker in the new world as an emigration booster he had Jim and Lewie Hill beat to a fair you well

Well Trigg I have seen many strange things all verry interesting but I am shure home sick and hungry for home grub I dont belive theres a biscut or hotcake in the British Iles this is shure a cold bread country its supper time right now an Id lik to be with my feet under your table tell Miss Josephine Id eaven eate some of her salid an I never did yearn for salid . . .

Best regards to You and Yors
Your friend
C M Russell

105

C. M. RUSSELL

GREAT FALLS. MONTANA

Georg Speck

Friend Gorg

    this sketch will show you Im still in Cal   I was at the beach the other day and if truth gose naked like they say it dos folks dont lye much at the sea shore   a man that tyes to a lady down hear after seeing her in bathing aint gambling much   its a good place to pick em but its sometimes Hell to hold em   this is a good country for lawyers and preachers ones tying the others untying an thair both busy

    I met Cut Bank the other day   he looked like hes in the money   hes got a real estate offis   maby hes mixing boot leg with real estate   I hear its a good blend I havent met maney of my friends down here this trip but I havent called on the Jails yet   Saw Sportecus   hes still packing a hide full   he shuck hands with about four of me and said he was glad to see us   I dont understand how he keeps away the snakes maby they dont com with this new moon   aneybody else but Sporticus would of had Crockdiles riding hyenas by this time . . . with best regards to you . . .

Your friend

C M Russell

Hers hoping healths The hoss under you
Ahead a Long easy ride
Good water and grass
To The Top of The pass
Were The Trails cross
The Big Devide

To you and yours
From me and mine

Your Friend
C M Russell
1924

(Card to W. M. Armstrong, Los Angeles, California.)

Hers hoping healths the hoss under you
Ahead a long easy ride
Good water and grass
To the top of the pass
Were the trails cross
    The Big Devide
        To you and yours
        From me and mine
          Your Friend
          C M Russell
            1924

C. M. RUSSELL

GREAT FALLS, MONTANA

July 25 1911

Friend Eaton

It has been a long time since I threw the dimond   I think it was the last trip. My Pardner a farm raised man couldent think of coffe without milk so we blew for som caned cow juce. It was the old kind you know the eagle brand I belive an I think it came from that bird   its a sinch it never flowed from any animal with hornes to make a long story short it got loos on us. an I dont have to tell you what happened when it started wandering through our pack   we had milk in every thing but our coffe

Eaton we would like mighty well to join you but Iv got so much work I cant brake away

Thanking you for the invition
with best whishes from us both

your friend
C M Russell

108

Friend Con   Oct 28 1910

I received your letter an was glad to here from you but am sorry you dont like that appel country   its pritty hard for an old cow puncher lik you to fall to frute rasing   picking appels aint verry exciting   I like appels an so do you but if they will give me the country back the way it was Il agree to eat dryed frute the rest of my life but theres onely a fiew of us that feel that way.

I have been inquiring about a hay ranch but as aney kind of hay sells for $25 a ton they dont seem stuck to sell out but Il keep my eye open   I shure wish you could get a ranch nere here

You spoke of Jonny Lee in your letter   I was one of his pallbearer   he went quick   a cow puncher from Browning that was at the funeral told me he was sick onely a fiew minuts   he had just com home from a dance an his hart quit   I hated to see poor Jonny go but if my friends have to go I want them to go fast

Goodwin an I got home all safe   we had the horses shod at Gelida   they stood like plow horses an since I got hack they have neather one scared at aotoes ore street cares   they act like they were raised on gasilene

I was down town the other day an met Cap Tool Tom Daley   we were standing in front of the Mint an I asked them if they knew the horse in front of the Silver Doller   he was standing with his head down asleep with skunk wagons all around him snorting tooting and blowing   when I told them it was Dave they pritty near called me a lyar an I had to show them the "three E" to proove it

with best whishes from us both to yourself Mrs Price and Leslie

Your friend

C M Russell

109

Here's how to me and my friends
the same to You and Yours

I savvy these folks

Merit Flanigan maried
and got a good job as
stock inspeter at Glasco

THE FIGHTING CHEYENNES

The Red man was the true American
They have almost gon. but will never
be forgotten
The history of how they faught for
their county is written in blood
a stain that time cannot grinde
out
their God was the sun their Church
all out doors their only book
was nature and they knew all
its pages
C M Russell

III

C. M. RUSSELL

GREAT FALLS, MONTANA

W. M. Armstrong

August 14
1922

Friend Armstrong

I guess you think its about time I came across
with som thanks for the cow puncher book
I'm better than a green hand with talk   but with a pen I'm plenty
lame so I'm limping in with my thanks
Since most of the cow folks moovd to Holly Wood and worke for the movies
all the cow punchers I see these dayes are on the screen
Most of the cow now are hornless ware a bell and are punched with a stool
times have changed   the old time cow puncher in the sketch above who sits in
the shade of his hoss   would run off a band of hosses hold up a coach
work a brand over   maby he wore notches on his gun
but he wouldent steal milk
from a calf

The few old raw hids left are found in a blind pig or hide in
the mountians making Moon. they have lived past thair time
they were good cow men they might have braged on thair roping and
riding but the moon shine they make cant be braged on

The cow folks I see on the screen are mighty mussy gun men
and if thair had been as many people killed in real life
as thair is on the screen with blank shells

112

W. M. Armstrong   August 14
Friend Armstrong   1922

I guess you think its about time I came across with som thanks for the cow puncher book   Im better than a green hand with talk but with a pen Im plenty lame so Im limping in with my thanks

Since most of the cow folks moved to Holly Wood and worke for the movies all the cow punchers I see these dayes are on the screen   Most of the cow now are hornless ware a bell and are punched with a stool

Times have changed   the old time cow puncher in the sketch above who sits in the shade of his hoss would run off a band of hosses hold up a coach work a brand over   maby he wore notches on his gun but he wouldent steal milk from a calf

The fiew old raw hids left are found in a blind pig or hide in the mountians making moon   they have lived past thair time   they were good cow men   they might have braged on thair roping and riding but the moon shine they make cant be braged on

The cow folks I see on the screen are mighty mussy gunmen and if thair had been as many people killed in real life as thair is on the screen with blank shells Its a sinch my red brothers would still be eating humped backed cows   it would have been a snap for the Injun to clean up the fiew these gun fighters left

The barbed wire and plow made the cow puncher History and the onley place hes found now is on paper   so I thank you for the book

I just returned from a fishing trip with two friends of yours Church Mehard and Walter Grange   I wish youd been with us   we went on horseback with pack ani-mals and found good fishing   a two year old Lady brown bear called on us

Grange as you know is a ball player   he practiced in and out curves with bold-ers on miss bear till the lady took timber   if the animal had of been a silver tip or grizzly the sport would have gon the other way—a tree climbing contest I think

with best whishes to you and yours

from the Russells

Your friend
C M Russell

113

W. M. Armstrong
Los Angeles Calif
Friend Armstrong

I call you this as I count all those who love the old west friends

The brown hurds and wild men that Parkman knew and told of so well have gon   The long horned spotted cows that walked the same trails their humped backed cousins made have joined them in history and with them went the wether worn cow men   They live now onley in bookes. The cow puncher of Forty years ago is as much history as Parkmans Trapper. The west is still a great country but the picture and story part of it has been plowed under by the farmer   Prohabition maby made the west better But its sinch bet Such Gents as Trappers Traders Prospectors Bull-whackers Mule Skinners Stage drivers and Cowpunchers dident feed up on cocola or mapel nut sundais

To make sketches in Francis Parkman's books has been a pleasure to me
When I read his work I seem to live in his time and travel the trails with him
Whishing you and yours health and happyness

Your friend
C M Russell

114

Feb 24
1909

Friend Sweet

No dought you will be supprised to here from an old night hawk like me but the older I get the more I think of the old days an the times we had before the bench land granger grabed the grass   there was no law aginst smoking sigeretts then an no need of a whipping post for wife beeters   the fiew men that had wives were so scared of loosing them they generley handeled them mighty tender. the scacity of the females give them considerbal edg those days   I never licked no women but Im shure glad I beet these morilests to the country   its hard to guess what they would have don to me. Chances are Id be making hair bridles now for smoking sigeretts or staying up after twelve oclock. but they got here to late to hed of my fun an as I am real good now I aint worring much

but what I started to say is this.

the last time I saw you I think you said you had a photo that was taken at White Sulpher of your self Jim Macoy and I   if so I wish you would send it up to me and I will have a copy made of it and return the origanal or you might have your town photographer make some copyes and send me the bill

with best regards to your self and Wife

Your friend
C M Russell

remember me to all friends

Nolen Armstrong was
bush whacked at Culbertson
while smoking up the town
by the dupty sheriff
I am glad to say th dupty
since got the same medisn

FRANK HARTSEL

Frank was bush whacked
at his ranch on warm
spring creek while pealing
potatoes for supper no one
knowes who did it
he lived longenough to tell
the breed that was with him
to put out the light

Oct 23 1907

Ho Ho Hay-ee
Friend Goodwin

I received your letter some time ago   the lion was heap good   My sketch
shows a Kootnei canoe from a model H. Stanford sent me   it is made of spruce bark,
rough sid in   the modle was verry rough an I could not get much from it   it has
no thorts like other conoes but I think the fellow that made the modle forgot them
it dont look like aney bark boat would hang together with no brace to keep her from
spreding   I wish you were here now   the wether is beautifull   this sounds lik a josh
but its on the square   the sun hasent hid since you left   I fineshed my roping picture
an have done three black and whites two for Bronson and one for Outing.

I went to the stock yards the other day to see a beef heard from the upper sun
river   there was a thousand head   pritty good heard for these days   the punchers
baring a fiew bib overall boys were apritty good bunch   I knew most of the old
timers so I had a good time talking over days of the open range an Im telling you
there was some tolibel snakey ones rode during our talk but as the old ones knew I
don most of my riding bad ones this way . . .

your friend
C M Russell

May 29/1924

Tom Kerwin   Rout 3 Box 223
Friend Tom   Pasadena Cal

Im droping a line to let you know that I'm on my legs again but I dont travel like a colt yet. Gorge Speck wanted to bet hed hold the handels ore buy flowers for me, you tell Speck thair aint a chance, Il be the one that will let him down easy with my hat off.

I called on [an old friend] . . . hes looking fine, is married, and has a fine home, a car, and a man to drive it. . . .

hes on top now and Im glad of it. Hes hit som rough trails since he left Cut Bank where he started in that booze joint called The Mavorick; he played both ways from the middel when the hich rack in frount held lots of horses, he had a big bar trade, when cow punchers left, he used the back door. Fore one doller hed give his red brothers a quart of something that would mak him sing like he did in buffalo days but as thair was always enough sober ones to cash all the guns and knives it was noisy but not dangorus; It was bad booz but it dident kill aney body. I tryed it and I think maby you did Tom

It was rough stuff made for outside men and Inguns and was agin the law to feed it to red men but now since were all inguns that old trade whisky was lemonade compared to what the whites are getting now. . . .

give my regards to Sid and Cal and all friends   best whishes to you and your wife

Your friend

C M Russell

119

Hell o Trigg I'm here
in the big canak
an have visited all the places that
interest me. an am getting lonsum
for home
I was down to the aquarium
the other day they have quite
a number of new fish
I walked back through Bowling
Green which I belive is the oldest
part of the burg
this is where the Dutch uste to
play ten pins

Hello Trigg

Im here in the big camp an have visited all the places that interest me. an am getting lonsum for home

I was down to the aquarium the other day   they have quite a number of new fish   I walked back through Bowling Green which I belive is the oldest part of the burg

this is where the Dutch uste to play ten pins an trade with the Indians. I think it was these limburger eaters that told the red man to plant powder an ball

Mr Ingen put in this crop the sam as corn.

but not beeing a up to date scientific dry lander his crop failed. the dutch like all good boosteres looked sorry an told him he hadent harrowed it under properly that by plowing deep an roling the soil would hold moister that it never had. the same as it did for our farmers last summer. did this stop the red man this plum failure of powder an ball crop   No   he started raising Hair without errigation   this crop was shurer but had its draw backs   imagin a savig who lived in the sweet smeling woods rasing the hair of a dutch man with limburger in every pocket   it must have been tough. right here Trigg I get hazy on history of this Iland but the Injun quit it and the English got it away from the Dutch. I dont know who owns it now but as every other man looks like Mose Kaufmans cousin I think Jerusilam has a large interist here

We took in a Suffereggte meeting the other night an a finer band of Hell raisers I never saw bunched   according to there argumant men would have littel to say in regards to goverment   I will tell you all a bout it when I see you but will close for this time, with regards to all

      Your friend
      C M Russell
      Apral 10
      1911

I suppose this would be an easy throw for aney of them skin string Buckaroos.

Friend Con

a fiew days ago I got your letter and one a long time ago which makes me owe you two   I rote you one since you went down to Cal but you never said you got it

Im glad you like that country and from what you say its a good one. long ago I ust to hear them senter fire long reatia Buckaroos tell about Califonia rodaros but at this late day I dident think thair was a cow in Cal that wasent waring a bell. Poor old Montana is the worst I ever seen an Iv been here forty snows   the Reformers made her dry and the Allmighty throwed in with them and turned the water of an now thair aint enough grass in the hole State to winter a prarie dog, but if the nesters could sell thair tumble weed at a dollar a tun thair all millionairs   its shure a bumper crop

I saw Jonny Rich not long ago   hes running a moovie show in Lewistown and dooing well   he says last winter when the flew hit his town the Doctor advised him to take three mouths full of booze a day to head off the sickniss   to make shure how much hes taking Jonny measurs a mouth full which he says is an eaven pint   he followes the Doctors orders to a hair and the Flew never tuched him said he felt fine all the time but after about a month of this treatment he got to seeing things that aint in the natural history. one day he saw a Poler Bear sitting on a hot stove waring a coonskin coat and felt boots eating hot tommales

I went to the stampeed at Calgary this fall and it was shure good   saw a fiew old timers some old friends of yors

Charlie Furman said a long time ago he had a horse that he was afraid of one day hes riding this animal kinder carful with feet way out and choking the horn when suddenly with out cause this hoss starts playing peek a boo   about the second jump, Charley is unloaded among a crop of bolders an he tells me hes numb all over and feels like every bone hes got is broke in three places but when he starts coming back to life his hart gets big and all of a sudden he remembers he ain't give Con Price no wedding present so next day he saddles a gentle horse and leads peek a boo over and presents him to you

Furaman says he don't see you for quit a while but when he dos meet you you say some things that I cant put in this letter and you said if ever you married again that he needent send no presents

I am sending you a couple of pictures of Jack   Mame sent you som last winter in a Christmas pacage for Leslie but I guess you dident get them   hes shure a fine boy and loves horses   hes got a rocking horse and two stick horses an he rids the tail off the hole string   I still have a cople of old cyuses and some times I take him in the saddle with me and it shure tickles him   we may come to Cal this winter   if we do wel try and look you up. I'v got a long range cousin in that country named Philips that is runing cows down thair somewhere

Well Con I'l close for this time   with best wishes from the three of us to the three Prices

Your friend
C M Russell

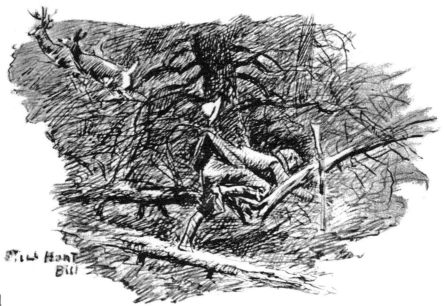

Friend Bill

I guess its about time I said some thing   the portrait was shure skookum an I was plenty supprised when Mame led me to it Christmas morning   you don yourself proud   I think its your best   You certainly spred paint while I was away

we got the spoon an the book of animal and bird beasts   the last will help me in my animal work

well Bill you may not belive it but I miss you   its kind of like missing the ache after the tooth is pulled   I often turn around from my work to cuss you an find nothing but the space where Duck leg sat

Percy an I with our good halves have just returned from Lewis Town where we met maney old timers some I hadent seen for over twenty years   we camped with Johny Ritch   neather He Percy nor I touched the goblet of joy   there was a stag banquet pulled of for us an some of the feeders got pie eyed not maple pied eather   it was a straight case of booze blinde   they couldent eaven see the New Year when it came in   I whish youd been with us   Id herded your hat. . . .

the sketch shows Duck leg hunting white tail in the Mission range   Linderman says your quetest man in the woods hes ever known   if the Kootenais who are great hunters had seen you they would have named you panther foot gost of the woods or som such titel . . . with best whishes from us both to yourself and Julie

Your friend

C M Russell

C. M RUSSELL

GREAT FALLS, MONTANA

April 5
1920

Friend Ed
        I received your
letter the last one but now
at San Diego have met many of
the movie folks here and have had a good
time we expect to leave here the 15ᵗʰ but dont let
our coming hed off aney trips you were going to
make
        With best wishes from us
        your friend
        C M Russell

125

Feb 25 1921

Friend Carey

Last year when I eat at the HC wagon you whisperd to me that thair was som buried treasures on your ranch that wasent no cash of the Old Spanish Bandits But a plant of your own in days when corn and rye juice could be got for one dollor a quart   you were foxy and buried what you couldent swallow but not having the nose of the fox you couldent locate the cash   In these days of drouth there were times when it got on your nurvs. You told me you were going to organize a small band of trusted booze hounds and go prospecting   I hope you raised the cash   we got your note and was glad to here from you

with best whishes to you and yours from me and mine

Your friend

C M Russell

Jan 23 1924
Great Falls Mont

Jim Thornhill
Friend Jim

I got your letter and was glad to here from you   I have been layed up with siatic rumitisum for six months   I been near enough Hell to smell smoke . . .

Jim since you left thairs a lot of old cow punchers friends of yours and mine have cashed in . . . Con Price is among the senter fire men at Gilroy Califonia riding for the Gilroy Cattel Co . . . I saw Tom Daly at Selby in July   he has som oil land and cant talk nothing but oil   Old Horis Brouster is forist ranger in Glacier Park he still loves to talk about cows   he told me hed like to get out and run a wagon I told him if he did it would be a milk wagon   nearly all the cows in Montana these days are waring a bell and most of the old cow punchers that aint in Jail are making moon or boot leging

Dave Clar cam to town the other day   he got married a fiew days ago   when that lady was draging her loop it lookes to me like she dont care what steped in it Since Dave notched his gun a fiew years ago at Cut Bank he dont hang around that country much   the breed he got had friends   Dave was superstitious and Cut Bank dont look like a health resort to Davy . . .

The little picture at the head of this letter is to help you remember what snow looked like   I tryed to make it look like the country and the punchers you usto know before the grangers turned Montana grass side down   shes a has been now but wel remember her for what she was

Your friend
C M Russell

127

St. Louis Mo
No 10th 1903

Friend Trigg

I thought I would write an let you know Im still among the live ones

I have taken in the worlds fair grounds it is verry grand but dont intrest me much   the animal gardens which is near thair is more to my liking   they have a verry good collection among them a cyote who licked my hand like he knew me I guess I brought the smell of the planes with me   I shure felt sorry for him poor deval a life sentence for nothing on earth but looks an general princepales. but you cant do nothing for a feller whos hol famely is out laws as far back as aney body knowes, eaven if he is a nabor of yours   If he could make hair bridles it would bee a hol lot easier but with nothing to do but think of home its Hell thats all

Im stopping with my Folks who live verry neare the place where I was raised and altho the country is much bilt up there is some of the old land marks left an a little patches of woods enough to take me back to boyhood days and I was much suprised the other morning to scare up about 10 quail but as there is no shooting allowed that accounts for it   seeing these birds in this woods reminds me of when I was a youngster of about 9 winters hunting with a party of kids   we had one gun this wepon was the old time muzzel loding musket   there was but one boy in the party long enough to lode her with out the ade of a stump or log so of corse he packed the amuninition an don most of the loding   we were shooting in turns at aney thing in sight   well I kept belly aking saying My turn an the big kid saying Youl get yours an I did. When he loded for me I remember how the rod jumped clear of the barel   he spent five or more minutes tamping the loade then handing the gun to me said thair

a stump or log so of corse he
packed the ammunition in don most
of the loding we were shooting in turns
at every thing in sight
well I kept belly aking saying my turn
an the big kid
saying youl get
yours an I did   when he
                              looked for me
                              I remember
                              how the rod
                              jumped clear
                              of the barel
                              he spent five
                              minutes more tamping
                              the loade

then handing the gun to me said thair
That would kill a tiger an I think it
would if hed been on the same end I was

that would kill a tiger an I think it would if hed been on the same end I was My
game was crows   I climbed to the top of a rail fence to get cleane range. and then
as the Books say for an instant my hawk eye mesured the glistening barrel   then
the death like stillness was broken by the crack of my fathfull wepon an I kept it
broken with howls for quite a while. . . .

Your Friend
C M Russell

129

Al Malison
killed by a falling horse
while cutting out on the beef
round up on the Mirias
range

Hon Paris Gibson
Washington
DC

c/o Cochrane Hotel

6816 Odin st
Hollywood
Califonia

C. M RUSSELL
GREAT FALLS, MONTANA

George Calvert

Friend Georg once more
were down with the jazz and geranums
If its true that the Charlstown is hard on
buildings this country had better slow up
on that dance ore thair wont be a hous in it
that will stand a real shake ay you lenew
they get som down here with out music
to play safe a rubber tent would be the shure
but George you cant bluff a good s port and most of the folks here
that kind win ore loose they dont whine
here in Hollywood most of our nabers are moovie people
like the rest of the world they are good and bad the
ones I lenow are good
The fur baring animal in the sketch below is not
a begm thrower from Russia hes holding down a
job at some of the studioes maby he aint a good
actor but hes got the whiskers and all thats required of him
is to lenow a littel more than the three horses he
drives in a Russian slay before the camra
hers one place where you can hold a job on your
looks if your cook eyed enough you can get a job
Georg the last time I saw you you said maby
youd com to Calif we all wish you would
and go back with us in the car
Mame has a new Lincoln we expect to
start home early in June let us lenow
if you deside to come
with best regards to all your fambly
from us all

Your friend,
C. M. Russell.

131

June 5
1918

Friend Tex

    I got your card asking how my old hoss is   hes standing in my coral right now but neather him nor his owner are aneything like booze   old Dad time aint hung no improventmunts on us   Judging from your card your still in the big camp prooving to them cliff dwelers that a rope will hold things with out clothes pins   If you ever cut Ed Borines range climb to that owls nest of his and kinder jog his memory that he owes me som writeing   tell him I got the tapadaroes and macarthey and thank him for me

    Several months ago I got a card from you saying you was a Dad of a son. youv got nothing on us but ours wasent waring our Iron but his brands vented so hes ours all right and we shure love him   hes a yearling past now and it keeps us both riding heard on him

    with best whishes to your best half yourself and son from the Russell family

Your friend

C M Russell

132

Its pretty scary at
Hollywood
Its wonderful what a man can do
with one gun if hes got blank catrages

Pasadina Califonia
March 30
1920

Friend Joe

I got your letter and paintings   they were wonderfull from an artistick stand-
point not quite bold enough in stroke. Youd have don better with a hay knife   It
would give more teck neque   maby that aint spelt right but you savvy   Thars lots
of moovie cow folks here both male and female   more he ones than thair is cows
the only cows Iv seen is the kind you moove up on with a stool an bucket

Saw Tom Mix and Bill Hart work   both treated me fine   Tom sent his
regards to you and yors   onley saw Neal Hart a fiew minuts   he also sends regards
have seen Bill Rogers work several times   Am going into the mountians with him
Sonday to see them make some real out door pictures   If you ever want to paint
frute roses ore automobiles come to this country   I forgot Bungaloos   they grow
here too   this last groath origanaly came from India where they had to be snake
and tiger proof but judging from the one we got Califonia is like Irland   well Joe
Il tell you all about it when I git home which wont be long

with best whishes to you three from we of the same nomber.

Your friend
C M Russell

133

The Evolution of the Range Beef

Buffalo
1743 to 1832

Long Horn
1832 to 1875

White Face
1875 to 1925

July 9 1926[1]

Friend Charles:

I got your letter and was glad to get it   we could use a lot of Neihart air here right now and I wouldent mind having a chunk of snow from Old Baldy and lay on a bow bed built by Bill Frip an Bill aint such a good bed builder but since I came to Rochester, I love aneything in Montana   if I had a ratler snake here and I knew he was from Arrowcreek I couldent keep my hands off him.

Well Charles tomorrow is Satterday and a week ago tommorrow I climed on the block and maby others dident know but it took every grane of sand I had   I tuck a local anasethic—local means nearby and it was so near by I dident miss much the feeling wasent bad but my eres were tuned up till I could here a bug whisper and the nois of the knife was plane   these Expurts were through in fifteen minutes but thats nothing—give one of these trimmers a good knife and hed skin and quarter Marcus Anderson in ten and wouldent nick his blade

Well Charles these fiew words will tell you that Im still this side of the Big Range—If nothing happens we expect to start home in ten days.

With best regards to you and yours

Your friend
C M Russell

---

[1]Written from the Mayo Brothers' hospital, Rochester, Minnesota, shortly before his death.

Jan 2
1921
Wishing You and Yours
A Happy New Year

Friend Con

I got your letter last summer and so you will know Im still living I am droping you a line   I hope you are still at Gilroy

we leave tommorrow night for New York   expect to be thair about a month   if we gethar aney coin we will go down to Calafonia. . . .

In October I went hunting with a party of seven on the head of the south fork of the flat head   we had 20 head of horses and them that wasent hunting elk was hunting horses   we shure got in a wild country and we had all the meat we wanted and brought back four elk   one of the party said he knew you   Hes an old N - N man   Dude Locket is his name   I dident kill aney thing but I had a good time   we were out three weeks. when we started home the party got split   four of us started with sevon pack horses   the other three stayed back to hunt horses   when we striped the packs that night we found we had all the meat no salt no coffe lots of shuger a tent but no flour and no bedding and the wethe was cold but thair was lots of wood so we made a big fire and eat our meat like a Ingun salt less but non of us eat much

Con I slept under saddle blankets be fore but I never had aney as smelly and hairy as these were   the rest of the party ove took us next day about noon   from that on we lived in comfurt   I will tell you more about it when we meet . . .

best whishes to you all from Jack Chaley and Nancy

Your friend
C M Russell

Aug 28
1915

Friend Berners

I got your letter and am mighty sorry to here about John. but feeling sorry is poor medison for sick friends so Im going to do the next cheep thing write him a Jollyup letter

Old John like the animal above is in a dam dangiros place but the goat dont think so and if I can make my friend feel like the goat I belive hel come across the bad pas

You said in your letter you were lonesum   whats the matter with packing youre war bag and drifting to my camp   a robe is spred and the pipe lit for you always

with best whishes to you and all friends

Your friend
C M Russell

One of Peblos riders

Friend Goodwin

I guess you think its about time I answred your last letter but you know me

if the moos you shot was like your sketch he was a dandy   I was out on a buffalo roundup in October   I wish youd been along   it was on the Flat Head reservation, an open, wild country   we saw lots of wild hosses never getting closer than a mile an dont ever think they wasent wild   it seemeded like they all ways winded us before we sighted them   they were all ways running   our camp was on the Pandrall river surounded by a high roling country   I was camped with the Canadin Officals who bought the buffilo 800 head owned by a Half Breed Peblo by name knowing the resivertion would bee throne open he asked Unkle Sam to leave him a range but Unkle wanted it for farmers   then he asked him to by them and when Unkel shook his head, the Canadians jumped in an grabed them at $2 50 a head since the sale U S has made a buffilo pasture not 30 miles from Peblos range an our country has 4 head two of them presented by Conrad the other two by some man at Salt Lake a large heard for a country like ours   if it had not been for this animal the west woud have been the land of starvation for over a hundred years   he fed an made beds for our frounteer an it shure looks like we could feed an protect a fiew hundred of them but it seemes there aint maney thinks lik us

I am sending you a rough map of the trap that was bilt to cach the Buffilo

Peblos riders wer all breeds an fool bloods making a good looking bunch The first day they got 300 in the whings but they broke back an all the riders on earth couldent hold them   they onely got in with about 1 20

I wish you could have seen them take the river   they hit the water on a ded run   that river was a tapyoker for them an they left her at the same gate   they tuck

138

her catching a phatographer from Butt City on the bank   we all thought he was a goner but whin the dust cleared he showed up shy a camra hat an most of his pants lucky for him there was som seeders on the bank an he wasent slow about using one

we all went to bed that night sadisfide with a 1 20 in the trap but woke up with one cow   the rest had climed the cliff an got away

the next day they onely got 6 an a snow storm struck us an the roundup was called off till next summer   if you come out this sumer we will go over an see it we can take the boat from Kalispell an go down the lake   its onely about 2 5 miles from the foot of Flat head lake to the trap an we could get horses thair an ride over.

I como back by the lake to Kalispell   it is a fine trip   Bob Benn sent his best whishes   he sent us some fine buffilo meet for Christmas

were are having a cold snap out here   last night it was 3 8 below o an it has been snowing for for days

give my regards to Dunten an all who know me

Whishing you and yours a happy New Year

Your friend
C M Russell

139

M. RUSSELL
GREAT FALLS, MONTANA

Pasadena Cal April 14, 1920

Friend Bob the distence bared us from you

Friend Bob

the distence bared us from your Golden Wedding but thair is no trail to rough ore long to stop the travel of the good whishes of our harts to friends so our harts were with you at the scool house. Bob like all your friends we are glad we knew you. Your kind were never plenty. but thair scarce these days. Invention has made it easy for man kind but it has made him no better. Michinary has no branes A lady with manicured fingers can drive an automobile with out maring her polished nailes But to sit behind six range bred horses with both hands full of ribbons   these are God made animals and have branes. To drive these over a mountain rode takes both hands feet and head an its no ladys job   To sit on the nie wheeler with from ten to sixteen on a jirk line ore swing a whip ove twenty bulles strung on a chane an keep them all up in the yoke took a real man   And men who went in small partys or alone in to a wild country that swarmed with painted hair hunters with a horse under tham and a rifel as thair pasporte   These were the kind of men that brought the spotted cattel to the west before the humped backed cows were gon   Most of these people live now only in the pages of history. but they were regular men Bob and you were one of them   Some of them had wives mad of the same stuff as thair husbands true unselfish wimen and mothers who shared equely all hardships of the man of thair choise and desurved realy more prase than thair husbands   Bob you must have looked good to Miss Bickett for her to tie on to a cow trailing drifter like you Girls were scarce them days and Im betting thair were plenty of horses tied to old Doc Bicketts hich rack whos riders clamed to be looking for horses but were realy wife hunting. . . .

your friend

C M Russell

140

Aug 11
1918

Mr and Mrs John Lewis
Dear Friends

    I left with out thanking you for the good time you gave me and my best half

    the above sketch will show that I dident sleep all the time I was at your camp these folks aint so fancy as the old time Injun nor as wild as the cow puncher but for variety of anatomy they got Injuns and cow folks skined to the dew claws.

    I cant back track Howard further than the bufalo range on the Little Missouri but if hes Uncle to all them nephews and neices I met at your camp some of his brothers must have been Bisnops in Utah not buffalo hunters.

    with meny thanks from us both

Your friend
C M Russell

Dont forget you are coming to our camp
and bring the three Bolingers

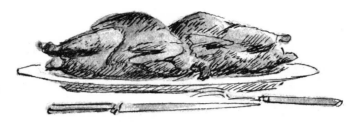

June 29 1916

Mr Paris Gibson,
Dear Friend:

I was asked to write something for your birthday. I have hade several birthdays myself some its a wonder I lived through but they say joy never kills an I Guess this is true caus Iv swollowed enough joy to drowned a cow on sevral occasions.

last year you wrote congratulating me on my success, but spoke as if you were afraid I might get swelled in the head and be near sighted when I passed friends. there is no danger of that, my Friend—talent like birth marks are gifts an no credit nor fault of those who ware them. It is onley men like you can clame credit.

In 1883 I night hearded horses where this town stands. I saw lots of grass plenty of water for the herds a good ford below Sun river. They were old men among us that spoke of it as a good beef county but there was nothing said of a town.

This country was dotted with buffalo skulls which brought to my Imagination many wild pictures but there were no citys among them.

Cow men said the falls were a drawback, they drowned lots of cattle an stoped boat travle.

But there was a man from New England a country where they rais more rock to the acer than aney other land under the sun an thats with out furtelizer ore erigation. This man did not paint pictures ore punch cows but his eyes saw a great city where there was only pararrie and rivers. He showed the people where the town would be: many of them laughed but he called the turn.

You my Friend was the camp finder and have all rights to be proud.

Our trails have not been the same but Iv often seen your tracks but never once have they back tracked ore taken water to fool their followers.

A birthday is onley a place on the trail of life where the travler stops to look back. Like the rest of us, you have rode some lame horses but the trail behind you will never be grass grone ore forggotten.

Your friend
C M Russell

Mr Andrew Pinker
Dear Friend Me an my friendz
wish to thank you for the boost

wishing you luck in 1910 an the same right along till thr
Crash in

GREAT FALLS, MONTANA.

GREAT FALLS, MONT
APR 5
2 30 PM
1905

TAKE THIS TO THE BUTTE
OF MANY SMOKES

Chas Schatzlein
Butte Mont

C. M. Russell

Cʀ 1905

143

September 26
1926

Dr Philip Cole
                    Friend Cole
I just received your gift the books by
Will James
which I like verrey much
when it comes to horses nobody can beat
James
thair is no other horse like our range
horse and James savys every moove they make
we have just returned from our mountian
camp
the big hills look verry beautiful in
thair fall clothing of maney colers
the above sketch is of a small band of
Elk we saw a few days before we left
which I hope will remind you of the
Country you were born and raised in
the camp you live in now can bost
of man made things
but your old home is still the real
out doors

144

and when it coms to making the beautiful
Ma nature has man beat all ways from
the ace
and that old lady still owns a lot of
montana
to show what I mean   man made this
animal   but the old lady Im
takina   about made this one
                        I have made a living painting
                        ofpictures of the horned on and
the life about him   it took regular men
to handle real cows
I would starve to death painting the hornles
deformity
God made cows with horns to defend herself
and when a wolf got meat   it wasent easy
often he was so full of horn holes hewasent
hungry
a weasel could kill the man one with out
getting a serach
but I forgot Iv got no kick coming Iv
been turned my self
but the medicine men at Rochester
onely took from me things I dident need
and was glad to get rid of
I look and feel better but Im still very
weak
if you   see Olaf Seltzer give him my
regards
I suppose by this time hes a real Newyorker
we have been having lots ofsnow but today
it has cleard and I think the storm is over
we all send our best regards to you and
yours
            Your friend
                C M Russell

145

C. M. RUSSELL
GREAT FALLS, MONTANA

Frank Brown

April 4 1922

Friend Frank

I received your letter and was glad to here from you   their is not much to write about down here so Il make my letter mostly picture   The sketch will show you some of the folks that pass my camp   this kind ride the beaches of Calif   Its hard to size up folks in this country but Im betting the he in the lead can get an ace of the bottom   hes probably an oil man from Wyoming or a high class burgelar from New York. The shes are wife and daughter of a well to do Boot leger from Kansas   coming from that state of corse Maws strong for dry baring what she uses around the house and the size drink she takes would make Bill Rance grinde his teeth   both the henna haired daughter and her maw smoke privetly in Kansas but wide open in Cal   Maw aint riding caus she loves horses but her Dock told her it would remove leaf lard. the man in the drag cant be classed among the idle rich he can count his coin with out taking it out of his pocket   Socially he aint got much to say   him nor the hoss under him dont savy much but Spanish. their boath native sons   Pedro maby thats his name dont know his fambly tree but its a safe bet his mother was a pyute and his dad maby a Spanish Gentelman who gathered his coin from the rode in the old stage coach day but compared to the hold up gents here to day Pedros dad was in the kinder garden class   but this party would be out of luck with out Pedro   hes like a packer with a pack trane, puts them on and takes them off   if a pack slips hes their to set it up and see that it stays . . .

Your friend

C M Russell

146

As I imagine San Pedro
in 1820

C. M RUSSELL
GREAT FALLS, MONTANA

Pasadena Cal
April 10
1920

Friend Phil I got your

letter and sketch so long ago I'm almost ashamed to answer it
but I was glad to here from you saven if I am slow about saying so
you will see I'm down among the roses this is a beautiful country all
right but its strictly man made I think in early days it was
a picture country before the boosters made real estate out of it but I'm
about 100 years late the live oak is a native of this country and good
to look at but it didnt looke warm enough so the land boomer stuck
in palm trees and plenty of roses this is bait so when the northern
travler looks out of the steam heated Pulman and sees all these palms
and flowers he thinks hes in the tropicks when the traine stops he
unlodes and prepares to camp if its a warm day he dont hit the ground
till sombodys sells him what he thinks is an oring grove but when it
develps its lemons this is the birth place of Bunko and bungiloos
Phil if I was painting frute flowers automobils are flying mashines this
would be a good country but nature aint lived here for a long time
and thats the old lady I'm looking for
Phil its mighty near time you mad another trip west I think about
the middle of July youd bitter load your war bag and drift to Belton
my shack will be open for you Lake McDonald is not what she ust to
be but thair are still some wild spots near the deer are quite tame and
we see them often if you com we l take another tumb line trip
think this ove Phil
                          with best whishes to you and your Mother
              from us all   your friend
                                    C M Russell

we leave for home
next week

147

Jan 16 1919

Dear Judge

Im a fiew moons late coming across with thanks
for the invitation you sent me to join in the big hunt
an you got plenty of reasons to think I'm a piker so I'm sending in this ink talk to
squar myself   its going to be hard work caus Im mighty lame with a pen. . . .

In the first place long before you and Lewis talked of your hunt I had promised
my friend Frank Linderman a visit at his camp on Flat Head Lake but I had called
that off and was going to throw in with the Bollinger and Lewis bunch   then the
flew broke out and throws a scare in me and this old sickness surtenly trimed this
camp   heres prufe enough I just sold a picture to an undertaker

So as long as old flew rode heard on my camp I dident care to take a long
chance   if I went with you to the south fork Id be out of reach of letter or wire so
I played safe and went to Lindermans   his camp is right on the road   I stayed with
Frank about ten days   done som fishing and had good luck   onley hunted three
days   saw lots of sign   Frank got one white tail   thairs plenty of deer round his
camp but thair shure man wise   I hope you all had good luck   I would like to eat
som elk stake that you cooked . . . My Wife Jack and I whish you all a Happy
New Year

Your friend
C M Russell

A happy New year to you and yourn
George   from Mame and Charley Russell
got your Christmas card and am glade
to know wer not forgoten
in West Port
we may be in the big
camp soon
give our regards
to West Port
your friend
C M Russell

(Card to George Wright, artist.)

Howard. Eaton
Wolf
Wyoming

149

C. M. RUSSELL
GREAT FALLS, MONTANA

April 24 1923

Jim Bollinger

Well Judge I said I'd write
later on I guess this is late enough
were boath a long ways from the South fork   but we
wont forget it   we might forget Citys   but hungary hoss
hoss heven   soup creek   pendigon   spotted Bear   and other
far off places where young men and old boys shake hands
with misery and plesure   we know both these ladys
and wont forget them.   Saw Mr. Mrs Foster than
looking good   both sent regards to you   met a lady
friend of yours   a Miss Preston   She told us S teave was
down at La Hoya   Jim Hobbens is making up a party
to hunt Elk in Jacksons Hole next fall   you are invited
I think its a good country   Frank Linderman and fambly
have been here all winter   left a few days ago   we leave
for home May first   we all send regards to you all

My regards to the Pocohontas Club   Your friend
                                          C M Russell

C. M RUSSELL
GREAT FALLS, MONTANA

Feb 26/1920

Friend Jim

aney time you ore any of your He ore She friends start thinking your loosing the beauty lines that youth gave you come to long beach and youl feel better   nobodys bared   Clothing is mad to hide ore lye but bathing suits are truthfull

for sevral years old dad time has been handing me things I dident want an I aint been thankfull for his favors but since I took a look at Long beach I think the Old Gents been Dam good to me   we are camped now in a bunglow at Pasadena among flowers and palm trees that have been here long enough not to mind the cold ore maby the flowers are like the native sons they wont admit it   A Califonia real estate man can stand mor cold with out humping his back than aney humans I ever knew   its warem enough when the sun shines but when the sky wares scatering clouds and the sun plays peek a boo its like having chills and feaver . . .

your friend

C M Russell

866 Chestor av north Pasadena, Cal

151

Friend Young Boy I
received the shield   and
pictures they wer   all fine
and I thank you   verry
much I will   paint
your picture   as soon
as I can

Your Friend
C M Russell

March 10
1920

Charles F Lummis

  I have eaten and smoked in your camp and as our wild brothers would. I call you Friend Time onley changes the out side of things. it scars the rock and snarles the tree but the heart inside is the same In your youth you loved wild things Time has taken them and given you much you dont want. Your body is here in a highley civilized land but your heart lives on the back trails that are grass grown ore plowed under If the cogs of time would slip back seventy winters you wouldent be long shedding to a brich clout and moccasens and insted of beeing holed up in a man made valley youd be trailing with a band of Navajoes headed for the buffalo range

  I heap savy you caus thaird be another white Injun among the Black feet Hunting hump backed cows

  My brother when you come to my lodge the robe will be spred and the pipe lit for you I have said it

Your friend
C M Russell

153

MERRY ENGLAND

MAY 14 1914

Senitor Paris Gibson

Dear Friend

Here we are in the midle of the Atlantic a bord the Lusitania. Lusitania I think meanes Hold up judging from the easy way the owners take money

The boat I went over in was a hotel   this one is a town about the size of Lewistown an its no slur on that camp eather

we are a littel north of the trail that Columbus broke   our boat aint as safe but wer going faster but Cris wasent in no hurry   he was onley looking for America . . .

I have seen quite a little of old England an its sertenly a pritty country like one great park with an interesting history   I viseted seviral hang outs of Bill the Conquar   saw walls and rodes built before Bill landed by the Romans. saw the ax and block where maney politicans lost there office. an when I looked at that old rustay ax I couldent help thinking that it might be a good thing these days   It sertanly has made a clean quiet country of England a land which for centuries lay seeped in blood   the history of our country has quite a littel read in it but its pale compared to this land   our Injun was a ware lover but blamed no God for the blood he spilt   neather for Cross or King did he war but for his country an well we know it was worth fighting for a Dam good country an a Dam good cause   the Injun was bad all right but Senitor if time were to slip her cogs an drop back some senturies Id prefur scary America to Merry England . . .

With best whishes to you and most of the folks in Montana

Your friend

C M Russell

154

Address R 3 Box 223
Pasadena Calafonia
May 4 1924

Frank B. Brown
Friend Frank

    I got your letter and was glad to here from you but dont think I could build up on that custerd pie diat you advise   I cant forget that littel talk you gave me on custard   Frank the above sketch aint a hold up   its what the hoof and mouth disease has don to the beautiful rodes in Califonia   the quarintene gard has stoped a car   the law says no animal ore vegitable frute ore flower that grows above ground can pass   The dogs out of luck if his friends don't return   fido don't bark no more at the moon   Hes as good as weiners right now

    The lady to the right aint going to be hung ore have a hair cut   Shes been picking popyes and was caught with the goods so thair going to fumigate her and when thair through she couldent stay at a skunk bording house but she could live a month in a leper camp and leave with out a pimple . . . You will notice the ladys in my sketch are scared but dont turn pale   they cant   the wimen to day have got nature cheeted   a lady that can blush ore turn pale through her make up had better see a doctor   shes got blood preshure . . .

    Califonia is all right but I can't see belt ore squar butte from here   Frank give my best whishes to Montana   nobodys bared

Your friend
C M Russell

155

1910

Friend Con

I guess you will be supprised to here from me but I thought I would let you know how we are getting along

I just got back from a visit with John Matheson he sold his teem an bought bench land ranch about 20 miles from here the above sketch showes what it looks like it was cold an plenty of snow the pump froze up we decided to take it out so both o us started liftin thairs a sheet o ice and we cant no moren keep our feet we got her pritty near the top John sliped the pump handel hit me on the head and the spout caut John back of the year when he got to his feet he made a run for the ax an the talk he used wouldent look good in print it was shure strong but it dident get the pump out neather did we. an John gets his water hand over hand it onely takes 3 or 4 ours to water a horse but that all goes with the independent life of the farmer

well Con we had a pritty good Christmas an we thought an talked of you all an we would have liked to have you here. . . . I hope you are all getting along fine Id lik to be up there and help Mrs P bild another calf shed . . .

we both send best whishes to your self Wife and Lesley

Your friend

C M R

Missouri Jim is married and has

a ranch on peoples creek.
his nearest nabor is man
he calls on Jim quite often that sits high
not belong to the working class .
but it can never be said that he
will not ~~helps eth~~ a working man
because he often comes over at
noon time and helps Jim eat

March 24
1926

Dear Miss Josephine

    I want to thank you for the nice birth day card you sent and your Shamrock has brought luck as I feel much better to day   not that Iv been sick but I havent felt real good   That card was shure a Paddys greeting   maby Im not Irish but my fondness for that Race makes me belive Im a breed. . . .

    Miss Josephine Califonia is not the country that Bret Hart knew but the moovie people still make romance   The English woods you see on the screen at the Liberty or aney other show house are realy live Oaks in Cal

    So you see in 1926 when everything is forgoten but right now you are apt to meet armored men of Ritchard the Lion Harteds time

    A fiew years ago, you might of seen Moses and his bunch heading for the Sea somwhere betwine Long beach and Santa Barbra   maby they had harps but if they played it was jass music the same as youl here at the Odan ore Meadow Lark Club.

    Moses is here yet   I saw him the other day   I don't know what he's doing now but its a safe bet he cant write the Ten Commadments. . . .

    With best whishes to yourself and Mother and Miss Furnald from us all

Your friend

C M Russell

This rider didn't quite win!

Jan 28 1916

Friend Guy

I received your letters an am a little slow about coming back with paper talk. But here goes I am glad to here you are going to pull another contest for the folks Those prizes your hanging up shure look good. But judging from horses and steers you delt out at Calgary and Winnipeg the rider or roper that takes a prize shure has something coming I have lived among riders most of my life and late years Iv been taking in contests at different places but yours has got them all skined to the dew claws An Il take my hat off to aney rider who takes or tryes to drag a prize from you An Injun once told me that bravery came from the hart not the head. If my red brother is right Bronk riders and bull dogers are all hart above the wast band but its a good bet theres nothing under there hat but hair

well Guy I hope you git a cross all right and show them Cliff dwelers the real thing they have all seen wild west shows but yours is no show its a contest where horses and ridirs are strangers its easy when a bronk twister knows every jump in a hoss but hes gambling when he steps across one he never saw before you savy

well guy I close with best regards to your self and Wife   Your friend

C M Russell

give my regards to Borine and all friends we will be in New York about the first of March then if you are still in the big camp we talk it over is Ed Borine still in that owels nest on 42